SOFTWARE RELIABILITY AND METRICS

Proceedings of the Centre for Software Reliability Conference entitled

Software Reliability and Metrics
held at the Dorint Sporthotel, Garmisch-Partenkirchen, Germany,
12–14 September 1990

Members of the Centre for Software Reliability

SOFTWARE RELIABILITY AND METRICS

Edited by

N. FENTON

and

B. LITTLEWOOD

Centre for Software Reliability,
City University, London, UK

ELSEVIER APPLIED SCIENCE
LONDON and NEW YORK

ELSEVIER SCIENCE PUBLISHERS LTD
Crown House, Linton Road, Barking, Essex IG11 8JU, England

Sole Distributor in the USA and Canada
ELSEVIER SCIENCE PUBLISHING CO., INC.
655 Avenue of the Americas, New York, NY 10010, USA

WITH 8 TABLES AND 39 ILLUSTRATIONS

British Library Cataloguing in Publication Data

Software reliability and metrics.
I. Title II. Fenton, Norman E. III. Littlewood, Beverley
005.3

ISBN 1-85166-675-3

Library of Congress CIP data applied for

Printed in Great Britain at The Alden Press Ltd, Oxford

Foreword

Information Technology (IT) systems are now all-pervasive. No longer are they found only in the 'professional' environment of centralised data processing installations or in the specialised areas of defence systems, but they have moved into our cars—indeed, our transport systems of all types—our homes and our high streets. Moreover, the majority of the cost and, more importantly, the added value of such systems is now attributable to the software component. For these reasons an ability to deliver software-intensive IT systems that meet the customer's real needs, have predictable patterns of behaviour and are produced within agreed budgets and time-scales, assumes a critical level of importance.

To date, professional developers of such systems have to confess that approaches to achieving these desirable results are still essentially a 'black art'. Moreover, as the basic hardware components become ever more affordable, the complexity and the scale of the software challenge grow. Overall, the issue of how to improve control over the quality of the IT systems that are required to be delivered is a matter that consumes attention on a worldwide basis.

The Centre for Software Reliability has for many years had as its concern the promotion of best practice and the exchange of experience between workers at the leading edge of software development. This collected set of papers from the 1990 CSR Workshop covers approaches that aim to improve both the quality of the development process and the quality of the resulting products. It draws on the experience of leading edge teams from Europe (many of them participants in the ESPRIT programme), the USA and Japan. Its aim is to take a further step in the vital activity of reducing the 'magic' and increasing the 'science' of developing systems that are truly fit for their intended purpose.

DAVID TALBOT
Commission of the European Communities

Preface

The Centre for Software Reliability, CSR, was established in 1982 to provide a focus in the UK for interest in software reliability: its achievement and assessment. CSR is a strictly non-profit-making organisation which is made up of three components:

(1) its Council members—a group of leading UK experts in software engineering drawn from industry and academia who meet regularly, under a formal constitution, to plan and organise CSR activities;
(2) its ordinary members—several hundred interested professionals and academics who regularly attend the CSR seminars which take place four times per year;
(3) the two University research centres, one at the City University, London and one at the University of Newcastle upon Tyne which provide infrastructure to CSR.

CSR first gained a national reputation in 1983 when it contributed to the national 'Alvey' initiative in information technology, defining the software reliability and metrics strategy and acting as the advisory group in that area. Since 1984 it has acted as the Alvey/IED special interest group in reliability and metrics.

Every year since 1984 the CSR has hosted an annual workshop on a different topic and has published the proceedings in book form. The workshop which took place in the beautiful surroundings of the Dorint Sporthotel in Garmisch, Germany, in September 1990 marked an important turning point in the history of CSR. It was the first time that we had extended our formal activities beyond the shores of the UK, although we do now host an annual joint meeting with the Japanese Union of Scientists and Engineers.

As it was our first event outside the UK, we decided that the theme for the workshop should be what was always our primary interest: reliability and metrics. It was gratifying to learn that CSR's reputation internationally ensured that we were able to attract eminent speakers from all around the world. The keynote speakers, Guy Cox from Hewlett Packard, USA and Katsuyuki Yasuda from Hitachi, Japan, provided a fascinating perspective of industrial software measurement activities from Europe's main competitor nations. Set against the numerous talks by European experts from a range of EEC countries, we were given a unique opportunity to compare current practices and research among most of the world's major industrialised countries. The workshop was also unique in that it contained a session in which every major ESPRIT project in the area of reliability and metrics was presented.

To conform to the structure of previous workshops we also had two extended tutorials from internationally renowned experts: Dieter Rombach from the University of Maryland, USA who spoke about goal-oriented software measurement, and Mike Hennell from Liverpool University who spoke about software testing techniques. Both tutorials proved to be extremely popular and useful.

We are indebted to Carol Allen, the CSR manager at City University, without whose efforts neither the workshop nor the production of this book would have been possible. We are of course grateful to all the speakers for attending the workshop and their hard work in preparing their papers. Finally, we acknowledge all the attendees who ensured that the event was such a success. In fact a measure of the success may be gauged from the decision to host all CSR workshops in the foreseeable future in continental Europe.

NORMAN FENTON
BEV LITTLEWOOD
City University, London

Contents

Foreword v

Preface vii

List of Contributors xi

1. Sustaining a Software Metrics Programme in Industry 1
G.M. Cox

2. Software Quality Assurance in Japan 16
K. Yasuda

3. Metrics for Management 39
A. Kuntzmann-Combelles

4. A Rule-Based Approach to Software Quality Engineering 48
H. Hausen

5. Engineering Approaches to Software Development in the 90's . . . 69
S.G. Stockman and M.T. Norris

6. Limits to Evaluation of Software Dependability 81
B. Littlewood

7. Predictably Dependable Computing Systems: An ESPRIT Basic Research Action 111
J.-C. Laprie

8. Software Certification Programme in Europe – SCOPE 132
W. Ehrenberger, C.A. Roan and P. Robert

9. METKIT – Metrics Educational Tool Kit 149
N. Ashley

10. New Approach to Software Cost Estimation 162
P. Kok

11. COSMOS – Cost Management with Metrics of Specification . . . 176
N. Fuchs

12. The Software Productivity Evaluation Model – An ESPRIT Project . 185
P. Comer and L. Mancini

13. Software Certification 192
A.A. Wingrove

14. Practical Benefits of Goal-Oriented Measurement 217
H. Rombach

List of Contributors

N. Ashley
Brameur Ltd, 237 High Street, Aldershot, Hants GU11 1TJ, UK

P. Comer
Advanced Software Technology, Via Benedetto Croce 19, 00142 Rome, Italy

G. Cox
Hewlett Packard, 3155 Porter Drive, Building 28A, Palo Alto, California 94303-0872, USA

J. Dobson
Computing Laboratory, University of Newcastle-upon-Tyne, NE1 7RU, UK

W. Ehrenberger
Gesellschaft für Reaktorsicherheit, Forschungsgelände, D-8046 Garching, Germany

N. Fuchs
Alcatel Austria – ELIN Research Centre, Ruthnergasse 1-7, A-1210 Wien, Austria

H.-L. Hausen
GMD, Schloss Birlinghoven, Postfach 1240, D-5205 St. Augustin 1, Germany

P. Kok
Volmac Nederland BV, Business Information Systems, PO Box 2575, 3500 GN Utrecht, The Netherlands

A. Kuntzmann-Combelles
Corelis Technologie, 31 Av. du Général Leclerc, 92340 Bourg-la-Reine, France

J.C. Laprie
LAAS, 7 Avenue du Colonel Roche, 31077 Toulouse, France

B. Littlewood
Centre for Software Reliability, City University, Northampton Square, London EC1V 0HB, UK

M.T. NORRIS
British Telecom Research Laboratories, Martlesham Heath, Ipswich, Suffolk, UK

B. RANDALL
Computing Laboratory, University of Newcastle-upon-Tyne, NE1 7RU, UK

A. ROAN
Verilog, 150 rue Nicolas Vauquelin, F-31081 Toulouse, France

P. ROBERT
Verilog, 150 rue Nicolas Vauquelin, F-31081 Toulouse, France

H. ROMBACH
Department of Computer Science and Institute of Advanced Computer Studies, University of Maryland, College Park, Maryland 20742, USA

S. STOCKMAN
British Telecom Research Laboratories, Martlesham Heath, Ipswich, Suffolk, UK

D. TALBOT
Commission of the European Communities, Rue de la Loi 200, B-1049 Brussels, Belgium

A. WINGROVE
Centre for Software Reliability, City University, Northampton Square, London EC1V 0HB, UK

K. YASUDA
Information Systems Works, Hitachi Ltd, Hitachi Systems Plaza, 890 Kashimada, Saiwai-ku, Kawasaki-City, Kanagawa 211, Japan

1

SUSTAINING A SOFTWARE METRICS PROGRAMME IN INDUSTRY

GUY M. COX
Corporate Engineering
Hewlett-Packard Company
3155 Porter Drive, Building 28A
Palo Alto, California 94303-0872

ABSTRACT

By creating the "Software Metrics Database" (SMDB) in 1983 Hewlett-Packard Company (HP) became a leader in the area of software measurement. Software and software development continue to be measured at HP throughout the company. Three major factors have contributed to HP's ability to sustain software metrics activities across a large and diverse multi-national company. The first factor is a solid foundation of experience with software metrics. This foundation, developed by working with the SMDB, consists of a set of common terms and measures, a company-wide awareness of software metrics, and a knowledge of what can be accomplished through the use of software metrics. The second factor is an organizational infra-structure to support the software engineering process and software measurement. The third factor is the development of multiple layers of measurement that are responsive to the various needs of the company. From High Level Management to Middle Level Management to Low Level Management the focus of detail becomes increasingly expanded: the lower the management level, the more detail is needed. These three factors have combined to create an environment that encourages the continuation and growth of software metrics at HP.

INTRODUCTION

Hewlett-Packard Company (HP) has been a leader in measurement and measurement instrumentation for many years. The publication in 1987 of Grady and Caswell's book, Software Metrics: Establishing A Company-Wide Program [1], contributed to HP's leadership position and expanded HP's domain into the area of software measurement. Grady and Caswell's book is now frequently used as a basic text on software metrics and HP itself as a model or case study for implementing and using software metrics. The natural question that develops from this situation is, "What has happened regarding software measurement in HP since the establishment of the software measurement program described by Grady and Caswell?"

A simple answer to this question is that, "HP is still measuring software and software development." As with any ongoing program, however, software metrics at HP have changed and developed. This has occurred in response to changes in the industry and in conjunction with our maturing understanding of software measurement.

THE SOFTWARE METRICS DATABASE

In 1983 HP initiated a measurement effort that resulted in the creation of a "Software Metrics Database" (SMDB). This was a company wide effort led by the Software Metrics Council, a collection of managers and software leaders within HP, and the Software Engineering Lab of Corporate Engineering. The metrics collected in the SMDB are mainly concerned with effort and quality. Some of the metrics collected include; engineering effort months and calendar months by life cycle phase, size of product developed in non-commented source statements (NCSS), pre-release defect counts by life cycle phase, pre-release defect density, language, and release date. The creation of the SMDB and successful applications of the information collected in the SMDB provided a basic foundation for the continuing, evolving, software measurement programs in HP.

This foundation consisted of two major aspects. First, the SMDB provided a common ground, a starting point for the whole corporation, including some common terminology, some common measures, and a common understanding of the issues and problems of software measurement. Second, the SMDB raised the level of awareness concerning software measurement among the software developers in HP. Software developers and managers found out what software measurement is, what it can do, and the resources needed to measure.

The SMDB is still used on a voluntary basis within HP and has been ported to a new platform. As the only company-wide software measurement system it has been found to have deficiencies. One of the deficiencies is the lack of information it contains. This lack of data is in the amount of information about a project, not the number of projects the SMDB contains. The SMDB does not contain enough descriptive data about projects to satisfy first and second line manager's needs. They need to adequately understand the "hows and whys" of the quality and productivity results that the database contains. They also need to have confidence in that productivity and quality data, confidence that is derived from knowing about the projects that produced this data. The information in the SMDB on months of engineering effort, non-commented lines of code, number of defects, etc., does not provide this information. The managers also need to know what type of software was being developed, with what methods, how experienced was the development team, what was the development environment. It is this second set of data that would allow a manager to have confidence in the data that is retrieved from the SMDB, understand how and why those data came about, and the applicability of the data to the manager's situation.

The SMDB also did not fully meet the needs of higher level managers at HP. These managers do not estimate and schedule software projects or predict the number of defects that will be found within a module. Higher level managers need to be able to judge the performance and progress of an entire lab, a complete product line, or a complete, complex system [2]. The SMDB was not able to meet all of the needs for information about software development that exist throughout HP. These deficiencies prompted many of the current software metrics activities in HP.

ORGANIZATION OF HP

While the SMDB provided a solid foundation for software measurement in HP, it could not meet all the different requirements for data on software development that exist within the company. It is now necessary to examine the organizational environment in which the SMDB was created to understand how the metrics process has changed and evolved in HP.

HP is a large multi-national company. It is an international manufacturer of measurement and computation products and systems. The company's products and services are used in industry, business, engineering, science, medicine, and education in approximately 100 countries. Of the 93,000 HP employees, approximately 7,000 are engaged in software development. The products produced by these 7,000 people range from the firmware for calculators, other instruments, and computer peripherals to full operating systems and applications. The company is organized into over sixty semi-autonomous divisions that function similarly to small companies. HP divisions, purposely kept small and manageable, either develop, manufacture, or market products. Many divisions are vertically integrated, with their own research and development (R&D), manufacturing, marketing, personnel, accounting, and quality-assurance functions. The divisions are then organized into product groups. Each product group represents a portfolio of related businesses and is responsible for directing and coordinating the activities of its divisions and operations. Examples of product groups include the "Engineering Applications Group" (which develops and manufactures electrical engineering design tools, software engineering tools, etc.) and the "Peripherals Group" (which develops and manufactures printers, plotters, disc drives, etc.). Finally, these groups are combined to make four major business sectors; Measurement Systems, Computer Products, Networked Systems, and Marketing and International.

Separate from the four major business sectors is Business Development. The charter of Business Development is to develop alliances and business partnerships; provide leadership to the functional areas of engineering, manufacturing, and quality; and manage the provision of integrated circuits and printed circuit boards to the entire corporation. Two organizations from Business Development have been very active in supporting software metrics. Corporate Quality coordinates efforts to improve the quality of all HP's products and services as well as the quality and productivity of the company's internal processes. Corporate Engineering helps increase engineering productivity by focusing on engineering management, software engineering processes, training and development programs, and strategic coordination.

Within the structure described above, several organizations are responsible for software engineering processes and software measurement. Corporate Engineering and Corporate Quality are very active in software measurement. There are several organizations at the Product Group level that have a software engineering process focus and conduct software measurement. Finally, most divisions have a Productivity and/or Quality Manager whose responsibilities include software engineering process improvement and the measurement of software and software development processes.

In summary, the **organizational infra-structure** for process engineering in conjunction with a **solid foundation in software measurement**, imparted by the experience of developing the "Software Metrics Database," has created an environment that has encouraged the continuation and growth of software metrics at HP.

Levels of Measurement

Earlier it was noted that the SMDB did not contain enough information to meet all the various needs that exist in HP. This has led to the growth of "levels of measurement." The phrase "levels of measurement" represents the change that has occurred in software measurement in HP in the past four years. At different levels in the company, different measures and/or different amounts of detail are needed. The kind of data and the amount of detail needed by a Group Manager is different from what is needed by a Project Manager.

Let us examine the differences in software measurement that occur across HP, starting with upper management.

High Level Measurement

The "high level measures" are those needed by Group Managers and above. Group Managers have responsibilities spanning anywhere from three to ten divisions (approximately 3,000 to 10,000 employees). The measurements needed by this level of management are similar to what Capers Jones [3] refers to as strategic measures, factors which may influence corporate success. Or, to complete the military analogy, strategic measures are the measures that help a company "win the war."

There are several high level measures in HP. The most well-known are the measures for the "10X goal." In 1986 the company CEO, John Young, set a corporate-wide goal of improving software quality by a factor of ten in five years. Two measures were selected to be used for tracking the 10X goal.

The first of the 10X measures is the total number of defects (reported from any source, during the first twelve months after shipment) divided by the size of the product in non-commented source statements (NCSS). The second is the number of defects reported which are classified as critical or severe that are not closed at the end of each month. The first measure, number of defects versus non-commented source statements, is aimed at the development process. The second measure, number of open critical or severe defects, is directed toward the maintenance process.

In 1987 a second corporate-wide objective was established, to cut product development time in half. This became known as "BET/2" because of the measure adopted for this goal. Break Even Time (BET) is the length of time it takes HP to recover its investment in a new product. It is defined as the length of time from the beginning of a project until the cumulative net profit resulting from the sales of new and affected products equals the cumulative net project investment (Figure 1).

The last of the high level measures used in HP make up the R&D metrics package [4]. This is actually a set of ten measures that includes: deployment of R&D staff across major development functions; the effectiveness of project investigations, measured by the number of discontinued, continuing, and released projects; the effectiveness of development, measured by the number of discontinued, continuing, and released projects; conformance to schedule commitments over time; Pareto charts of reasons for schedule change; and others.

These three sets of measures constitute the high level measures currently used at HP. All three measures are supported by automated internal tools. The 10X measures are supported by the HP defect tracking and reporting system from

FIGURE 1

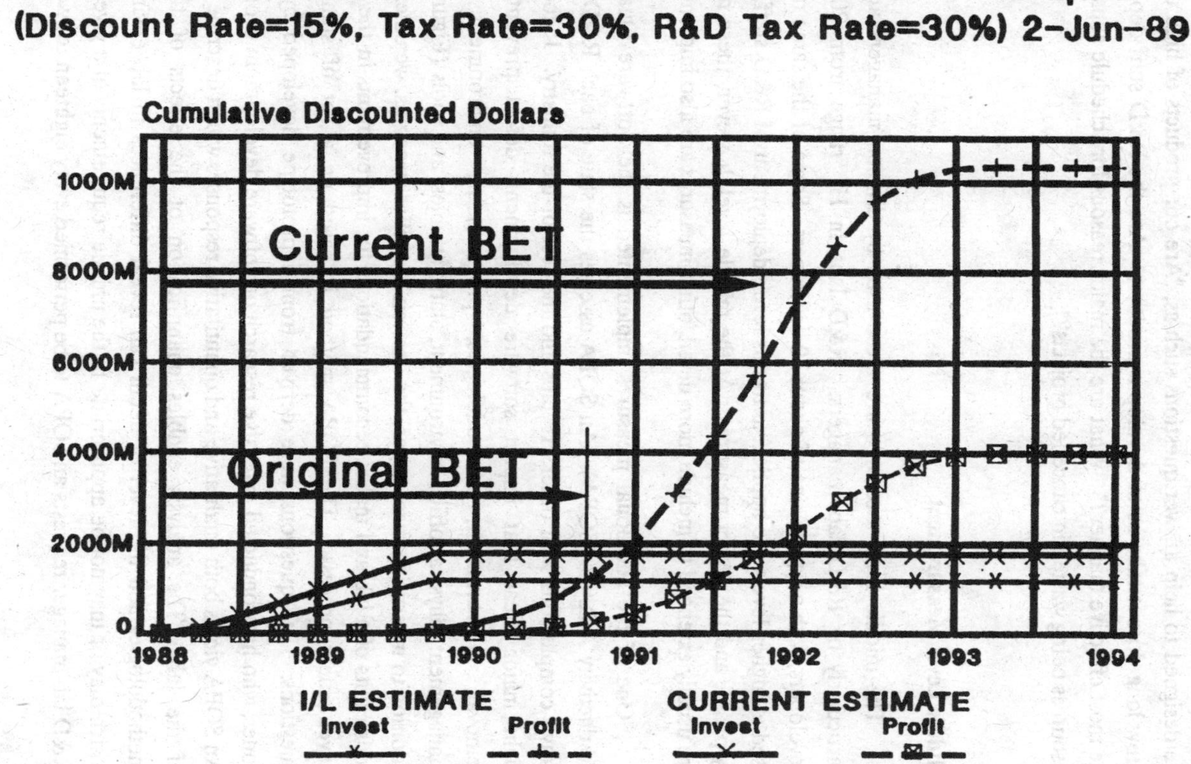
SAMPLE PROJECT - BREAK EVEN TIME = 15 qtrs
(Discount Rate=15%, Tax Rate=30%, R&D Tax Rate=30%) 2-Jun-89
Cumulative Discounted Dollars
1000M
8000M
6000M
4000M
2000M
0
Current BET
Original BET
1988
1989
1990
1991
1992
1993
1994
I/L ESTIMATE
Invest
Profit
CURRENT ESTIMATE
Invest
Profit

Corporate Quality. BET and the R&D metrics package measures are supported by PC tools from Corporate Engineering.

In review, these measures are appropriate to the strategic business level. They are designed to help answer questions such as, "Are our products of high quality?" "How long does it take us to develop a product?" Are the R&D staff deployed in the most effective manner?" "What are the major reasons for schedule slips?" "Are resources being wasted in cancelled projects?"

Middle Level Measurement

The middle level measures are those used by division managers and more particularly by R&D lab managers. R&D labs in HP range from 20 to 150 developers, with a typical size of about 50 developers. Some of the same measures used at higher levels are applicable to this level; deployment of R&D staff, staffing by phase, and the defect measures. At the middle level, however, these measures are usually extended to include more detail, other measures are also implemented.

One of the additional measures implemented is the Software Quality and Productivity Analysis (SQPA). An SQPA assesses the state of each R&D lab and draws comparisons with other HP labs and the rest of the industry. It focuses on eight major areas that impact software development; defect prevention and removal, measurement, methodologies, programming environment, project management, physical office environment, staff variables, and tools (Figure 2). In addition to measuring these areas, the analysis identifies strengths, weaknesses, and constraints of a lab and makes recommendations for improvements in the software development process. The SQPA method is based on a set of standardized questions. The questions were derived from a prototype developed by Capers Jones, who has conducted extensive research on software development productivity. An SQPA yields both qualitative and quantitative responses which describe the state of the lab. The analysis enables quantification of the effects of tools and methodologies and the level of detail can reveal differences in lab environments which may or may not be appropriate to the unique requirements of a given lab. A R&D lab manager requests an SQPA to be performed every eighteen to twenty-four

FIGURE 2

SOFTWARE DEVELOPMENT PROFILE

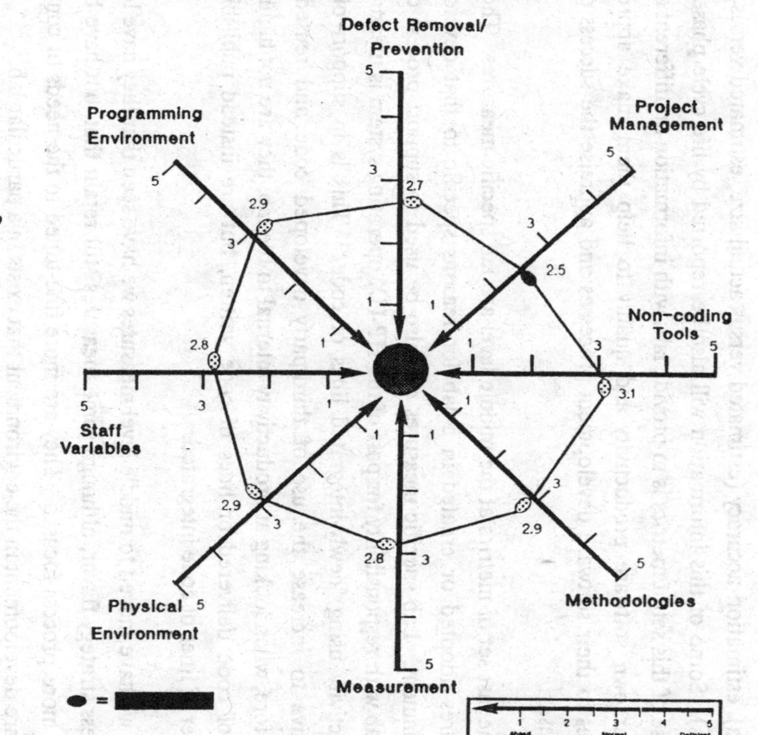

CORPORATE ENGINEERING
EXT34 6/90

HEWLETT PACKARD

months. Then a team from Corporate Engineering is scheduled to visit the lab and conduct an SQPA.

A second set of middle level measures is currently being developed in Corporate Engineering. These measures perform the function of providing the R&D management team with an "annual productivity and quality report." It will provide each lab with some standard software measures with both HP and industry comparisons. Examples from this set of measures include, size (NCSS) versus effort in engineering months (Figure 3), size (NCSS) versus product (NCSS) per engineering month, defect density (NCSS versus number of defects found pre-release), estimation accuracy (estimated versus actual size, estimated versus actual defects). Some of this information will also be reported by life cycle phase. The purpose of this set of metrics is to provide labs with information on different aspects of their own software productivity and quality to help them make appropriate changes to their software development processes and appraise the success of such changes.

The last set of metrics at the middle level are lab specific measures. These are measures adopted or created in a lab for reasons specific to that development environment. Lab specific measures can also be used to support process change. One lab with responsibility for part of the HP-UX operating system is measuring its productivity using "newly-integrated lines of code." This is in support of a lab objective to increase the use of third-party developed code and reused code. Therefore, when looking at productivity internal to the lab, they are not highlighting lines of code delivered or lines of code written, but are instead publishing the number of lines of code integrated.

As we have moved to middle level measures we have seen that they have less of a business strategy flavor, although some measures still retain that, but have become much more process focused. They are more fine-tuned to the needs of controlling software development in the environment that exists in a particular lab.

Low Level Measures

Low level measures are those used by project managers during a software development project. A software project in HP may range from approximately

FIGURE 3

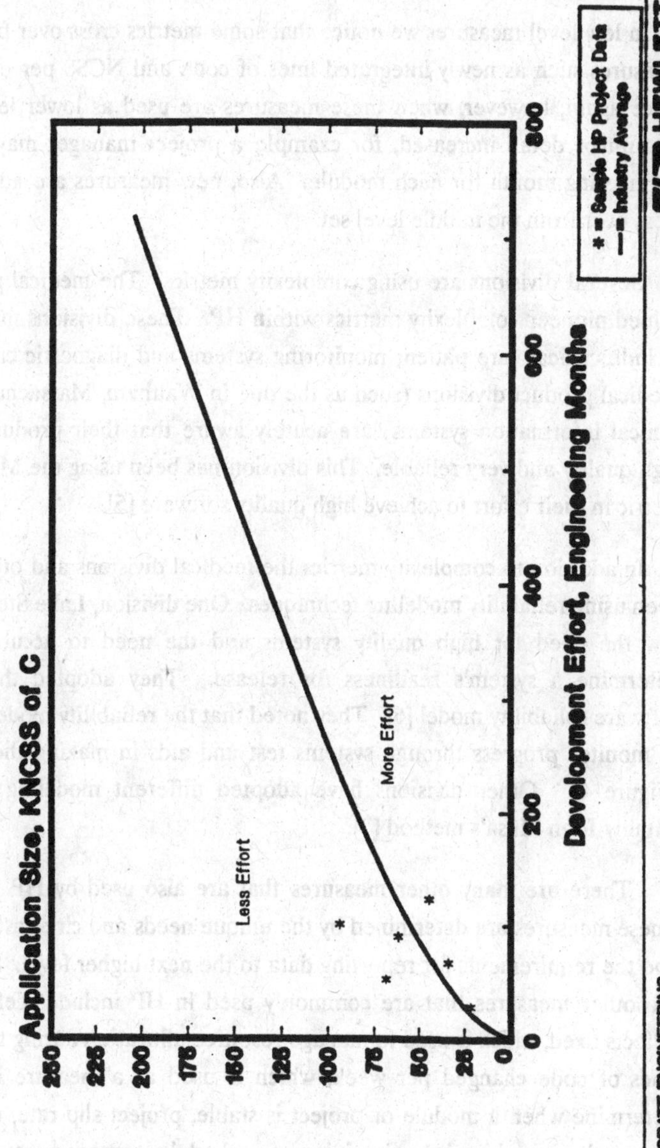
DEVELOPMENT EFFORT BY APPLICATION SIZE
INDUSTRY AVERAGE SOURCE: SOFTWARE PRODUCTIVITY RESEARCH, INC 1990
Application Size, KNCSS of C
250
225
200
175
150
125
100
75
50
25
0
Less Effort
More Effort
0
200
400
600
800
Development Effort, Engineering Months
* = Sample HP Project Data
— = Industry Average
HEWLETT PACKARD
CORPORATE ENGINEERING
GC14 8/90

three developers to twelve developers. Large applications or products will frequently be composed of several projects that may be dispersed across several divisions and even in different geographical locations.

In low level measures we notice that some metrics cross over from middle level: measures such as newly-integrated lines of code and NCSS per engineering effort. Once again, however, when these measures are used as lower level measures the amount of detail increased, for example a project manager may have NCSS per engineering month for each module. Also, new measures are added to those that cross over from the middle level set.

Several divisions are using complexity metrics. The medical products divisions helped pioneer complexity metrics within HP. These divisions make products that include critical care patient monitoring systems and diagnostic cardiology systems. Medical product divisions (such as the one in Waltham, Massachusetts, which does clinical information systems) are acutely aware that their products need to be of high quality and very reliable. This division has been using the McCabe complexity metric in their effort to achieve high quality software [5].

In addition to complexity metrics the medical divisions and other divisions have been using reliability modeling techniques. One division, Lake Stevens Instruments, saw the need for high quality systems and the need to accurately predict and determine a system's readiness for release. They adopted the Goel-Okumoto software reliability model [6]. They noted that the reliability modeling process helps to monitor progress through systems test and aids in making the release decision (Figure 4). Other divisions have adopted different modeling techniques, most notably John Musa's method [7].

There are many other measures that are also used by HP project managers. These measures are determined by the unique needs and circumstances of a project and the requirements for reporting data to the next higher level. Some examples of the other measures that are commonly used in HP include: defects found versus defects fixed, which is used to manage resource allocation during testing; per cent of lines of code changed per week, which is used as a measure of turmoil and to determine when a module or project is stable, project slip rate, used to determine how well a project is maintaining its schedule commitment; and branch flow analysis, as a measure of test coverage.

FIGURE 4

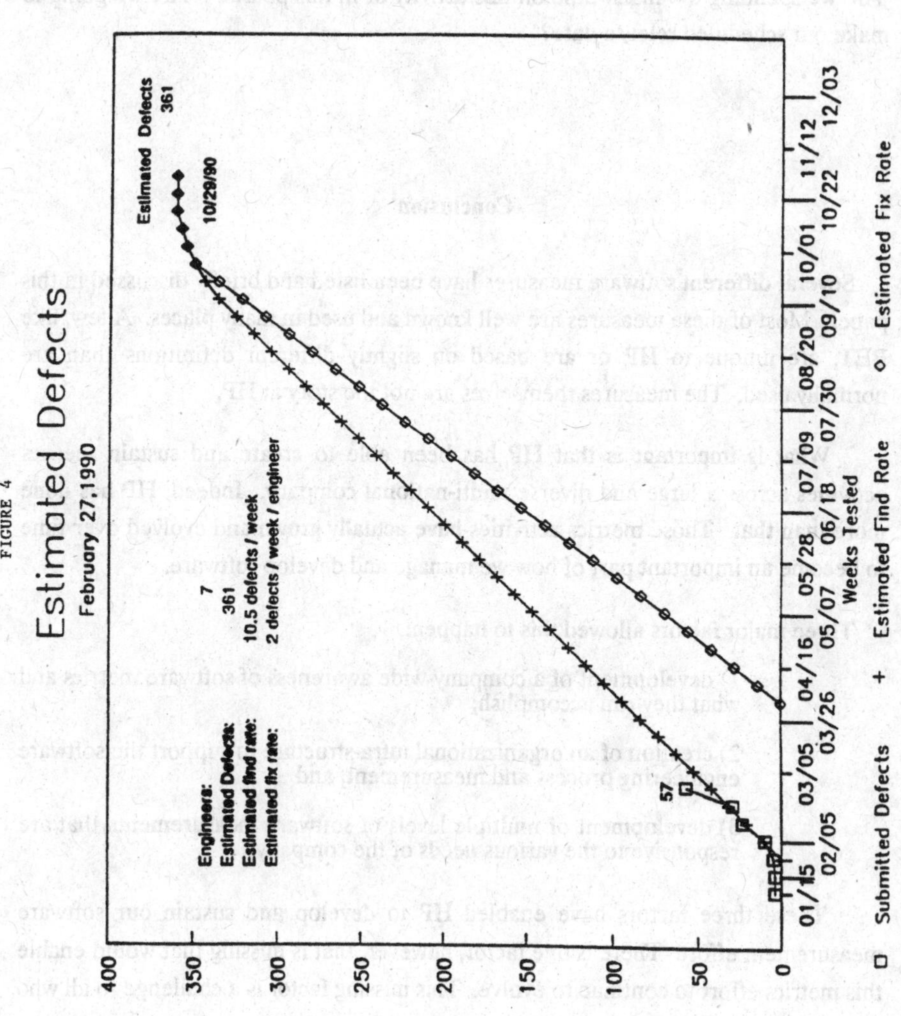
Estimated Defects
February 27,1990
Engineers: 7
Estimated Defects: 361
Estimated find rate: 10.5 defects / week
Estimated fix rate: 2 defects / week / engineer
Estimated Defects 361
10/29/90
57
defects
400
350
300
250
200
150
100
50
0
01/15 02/05 03/05 03/26 04/16 05/07 05/28 06/18 07/09 07/30 08/20 09/10 10/01 10/22 11/12 12/03
Weeks Tested
Submitted Defects
Estimated Find Rate
Estimated Fix Rate

These measures represent the day-to-day reality of developing software. They provide information to project managers to help them decide, "Who should work on what today?" "Are we ready to integrate this module into the rest of the product?" "Are we spending too much time on this activity or in this phase?" "Are we going to make our scheduled release date?"

Conclusion

Several different software measures have been listed and briefly discussed in this paper. Most of these measures are well known and used in many places. A few, like BET, are unique to HP or are based on slightly different definitions than are normally used. The measures themselves are not the story at HP.

What is important is that HP has been able to create and sustain metrics activities across a large and diverse multi-national company. Indeed, HP has done more than that. Those metrics activities have actually grown and evolved over time to become an important part of how we manage and develop software.

Three major factors allowed this to happen:

1) development of a company-wide awareness of software metrics and what they can accomplish;

2) creation of an organizational infra-structure to support the software engineering process and measurement; and

3) development of multiple levels of software measurements that are responsive to the various needs of the company.

These three factors have enabled HP to develop and sustain our software measurement effort. There is one factor, however, that is missing that would enable this metrics effort to continue to evolve. This missing factor is a challenge to all who are concerned with software metrics: a challenge to create new software metrics.

Software development is a very complex technical activity. The development of software requires many interfaces: between the developer (or developers) and their creation, between the software created and the users, between the developer and the users, between developers, between the software and the hardware, and between all the different software components. Additionally, the complexity of the software development process increases as the scope of the project increases.

The software measures discussed above have been a great help in managing software development efforts. They have also provided, at times, useful insights into the development process. The measures, however, are mainly concerned with the control of software development. These measures are necessary, nevertheless, we also need new measures; measures that will help us understand the software development process; measures that will help us learn about software, and about how software is developed; measures that will not only allow us to control software development, but allow us to **research** how software is developed.

If this challenge is met, then we will not only be measuring what has already happened, we will also be able to help lead the software development community as it responds to new challenges and adapts to new technology.

REFERENCES

1. Grady, R. B. and Caswell, D. L., Software Metrics: Establishing A Company-Wide Program, Prentice-Hall, New Jersey, 1987.

2. Patterson, M., Managing R&D Productivity. Sixth IEEE-USA Careers Conference,

3. Jones, C., Software Measurement: The Key To Improving Quality and Productivity. Software Productivity Research, Inc., March 1990.

4. Patterson, M., Managing R&D Productivity. Sixth IEEE-USA Careers Conference,

5. Ward, W. T., Software Defect Prevention Using McCabe's Complexity Metric. Hewlett-Packard Journal, 1989, **40**, 2, 64-69.

6. Kruger, G. A., Project Management Using Software Reliability Growth Models. Hewlett-Packard Journal, 1988, **39**, 3, 30-35.

7. Musa, J.D., Iannino, I., and Okumoto, K., Software Reliability, McGraw-Hill, New York, 1987.

2

SOFTWARE QUALITY ASSURANCE IN JAPAN

Katsuyuki Yasuda

Information Systems Works, Hitachi, Ltd.

ABSTRACT

Software quality assurance in Japan is the unique result of a combination of Western software engineering expertise and Japanese style quality control, which has proven to be so successful in other industries. We believe that the principle of "quality first" can be applied to the software industry. This paper introduces software quality assurance for a software factory which features an independent inspection department such as is used for hardware.

The inspection department does not concentrate only on final product inspection, but also performs quality control for earlier processes. Overall quality assurance performed from design until shipment involves the following phases:

- o Design review and documentation inspection, in the design stage.
- o Intermediate quality audit, in the testing stage.
- o Product inspection.

Preventive measures against defects remain important even after shipment.

1. Introduction

The quality of products made in Japan has increased greatly in recent years, mainly due to Japanese style Quality Management. Quality improvements in the field of software have resulted from the introduction of similar developmental organization and Japanese Quality Management to that used for hardware products.

This paper discusses software quality assurance for manufacturers of main frame systems in Japan, focusing on "critical software", which has a significant influence on society. Quality assurance examples provided in this paper are based on Hitachi computer systems.

2. Problems with Current Software Development in Japan

A typical example of software development would be for an online banking system. Third generation online systems placed into service recently show vast improvements over second generation online systems of 10 years ago, tying into a worldwide network, with around the clock operations and integrating a comprehensive set of applications. Modern systems have 20 times the capacity of these older systems, requiring two to three times the capital investment, about US$500 million per bank. The size of software developed for these systems has also increased by three or four times, reaching 7-10 million lines of code.

We have been very successful with programs being of such great size, but it can be difficult just to complete a project on time, let alone to satisfy the levels of reliability required by society. Increasingly large and complex software systems appear to be the trend in general. In addition, the ramifications of defects in such software have increased greatly, as has news of damage to public operation occurring due to software defects.

In a recently published investigation [6] on the reliability of computer systems, the No. 1 cause of system malfunction is defects in the software, causing 27% of all system malfunctions.

3. Japanese Quality Management

3.1 Definition of Quality

The ISO 8402 defines "Quality" as "the totality of features and characteristics of a product or service that bear on its ability to satisfy stated or implied needs".

In Japanese Quality Management, "Quality" is defined as "the degree of user satisfaction".

In the past, good quality meant satisfying national and in-house standards. Although these are necessary conditions for quality, they are not complete. Meeting the needs of the user is the ultimate determinant of quality.

The following two conditions must be satisfied for software to satisfy the determinants of quality:

1) Design specifications must conform to the needs of the user.

2) Software must operate according to the design specifications.

In order to establish design specifications that are in line with the needs of the user, it is important to determine what are the quality characteristics. The ISO/IEC JTC1/SC7 is attempting to standardize these characteristics, [7] and have recognized six quality characteristics: Functionality, reliability, efficiency, usability, maintainability, and portability. These are all further expanded into a total of 21 sub-characteristics.

3.2 Quality Management

The ISO 8402 defines "Quality Management" as "that aspect of the overall management function that determines and implements the quality policy".

3.3 Characteristics of Japanese Style Quality Management [5]

1) Total employee involvement

o Not only Quality Management, but all departments and all employees, from top management down to the programmers, are involved.

o The QC circle activities promote voluntary improvements.

2) Quality first

o Short term profit cannot take precedence over quality.

o Elimination of defects leads to improved productivity.

3) Attention to user needs

o Products should meet the requirements of the customer.

4) Speak with data

o Quality of data is more important than quantity.

5) The next process is the customer

o Quality at every step in the process should be done as if the next step were the customer.

3.4 Successful Quality Management

1) "Management" is defined as "continuous and efficient activities performed to achieve goals".

The Deming PDCA circle (Plan-Do-Check-Action) is necessary for successful management. The feedback provided in the Check-Action part of the circle is of particular importance.

2) Functional standards

If standards are not revised within six months of being issued, that can be taken as evidence that they are not really being applied.

3) Corrective measures and prevention of recurrence

Corrective measures are important, but even more important is the prevention of problem recurrence. This is achieved by pinpointing and removing the basic causes of problems, and generally accompanies improvements in the process involved.

4) Process management

Quality must be built-in at every step in the process.

4. Software Quality Assurance

4.1 Definition of Quality Assurance

The ISO 8402 defines "Quality Assurance" as "all those planned and systematic actions necessary to provide adequate confidence that a product or service will satisfy given requirements for quality".

This definition can be applied without modification to software products. Quality assurance activities for software products are the same as for other products, covering every step from product planning to design, programming, testing, inspection, and post-installment support. In addition to the so-called 'development' stage, from design through to inspection, it is important with software products to meet the specifications and quality characteristics of the diverse needs of the user and, for post-installment support, to adapt the software to changes in the user environment.

4.2 Characteristics of Software Quality Assurance in Japan

Quality assurance in Japan differs from that for typical software development in Europe and the United States in three main areas.

Development organization. While in the West the project manager usually has complete control over the project team, in Japan software manufacturers use the same production system as for hardware products. In other words, an independent inspection department performs checks on products, shipping only those which pass all tests. The progress of the project is also followed by an independent department.

The enforcement of quality management. Whereas in the West a specialized quality management staff generally performs this function, in Japan the line department responsible for the development performs quality management activities.

Total staff involvement in quality management. Quality management is performed not only by top management down to the programmers themselves, but by all staff involved, including the subcontractors. Thus, all encountered problems are reported and, within the QC circle, related and similar problems are pinpointed and corrected. The important point here is not individualism but a system of team-play.

4.3 Software Characteristics and Quality Assurance

Although quality assurance for software is very similar to that for hardware, the uniqueness of the requirements for software quality assurance must be fully recognized and considered. The following points should be considered for the assurance of quality software.

Software characteristics	Points to consider
Aggregation of logic	
o Difficulty in accurate design of logic	o Structured design method and design review
o Difficulty in reliable	o Systematic testing method

testing of logic	
Invisibility	
o Invisibility of software	o Design and notation methods
o Invisibility of the development process	o Visualization of quality and progress status.
Meeting the needs of the user	
o Difficulty in understanding the needs of the user	o Requirement analysis, definition technique
o Difficulty in understanding the conditions for use	o Testing under user conditions
Great dependence on individuals	
o Reduction in dependence on individuals	o Standardization and automation of development methods
	o Re-use and technology transfer
o Educating individuals	o Education, training

4.4 Software Inspection

The concept of inspection that applies to hardware products also applies to software products.

1) Definition of inspection

The ISO 8402 defines "Inspection" as "activities such as measuring, examining, testing, gauging one or more characteristics of a product or service and comparing these with specified requirements to determine conformity".

The JIS (Japan Industrial Standards) definition of "Inspection" is "judging each product's acceptability by comparing the product test results with quality acceptance criteria".

2) Inspections stipulated by JIS

An independent inspection department should be established in order to impartially determine product acceptability.

Inspection takes on two forms:

Inspection from the point of view of the customer, which entails rejecting those products which fail to satisfy the quality criteria.

Continued customer oriented quality assurance after delivery of a product.

The range of the activity of the inspection department is not limited to product inspection in the final stages, but encompasses the entire production process. This includes ensuring quality to satisfy the user even after the product has been accepted.

4.5 Software Quality Assurance System

Software quality assurance is achieved by clearly defining the responsibilities of each department in the development process. An inspection department independent from the design and production departments performs a quality audit at every stage, prior to the product inspection. The inspection department thus verifies quality for the output of each development process.

1) Quality audit of each process

The quality audit consists of audit of the development plan, documentation inspection to ensure design quality, and audit during the testing process.

2) Product inspection

The inspection department operates from the standpoint of the user, and tests software by running it on a computer system. Any unacceptable products are returned to the design department.

5. Software Quality Assurance Activities

5.1 Development Plan Audit

The major causes of failure for development projects in the past have been insufficiently trained staff, organization, underestimation of the requirements, delay in setting specifications, and frequent changes in the specifications. These problems quite often surface as defects or delays in development in the latter half of the development process. Of these causes, the first two must be considered during the development planning stage.

The necessary characteristics and target values for quality must be determined, and procedures must be enforced to ensure compliance.

5.2 Management of Design Quality

5.2.1 Design Review

1) Preparation of documentation for use in design review.

For example, for the performance design review, data is prepared to evaluate critical performance.

2) Preparation of a checklist for use in design review.

3) Maintenance of data related to past problems.

4) Participation of appropriate personnel, including people not on the project team.

For software requiring high reliability and high performance, it is necessary to review whether or not the reliability requirements (such as the down-time tolerance) and the performance requirements in the design are feasible. With critical software, it is particularly important that design reviews be conducted focusing on the fault tolerance.

5.2.2 Documentation Inspection

There are two types of documentation, internal documentation (design specifications) and external documentation (manuals).

Inspection of internal documentation has two main goals, preliminary management of software quality and to improve precision in process management by verification of intermediate products.

Inspection of manuals is necessary because manuals are an integral part of the product. The goal is to produce a manual easily understandable from the standpoint of the user.

5.3 Quality Management in the Testing Stage

5.3.1 Testing

1) Setting appropriate targets for the number of defects to be detected

It is important to set targets for the testing stage which will ensure early detection of defects. (See discussion of SQE in Section 6.3.)

2) Emphasis on desktop testing (code review)

The target should be to detect 70% of defects during desktop testing. Until this is successful, machine testing should not be performed.

3) Systematic testing

a) Use both black box and white box testing.

b) Apply a systematic test item generation method.

In black box testing, test items are selected based on notation from the logical space model and the finite state model (e.g., cause and effect graph, decision table, state transition diagram).

In white box testing, the control structure model and the data structure model are used.

c) Evaluate test status based on the degree of test coverage.

d) Improve test efficiency and avoid reductions in quality by repeating the test procedures.

5.3.2 Forecasting Defects and Management of Target Values

Start by setting a target for the number of defects. Next, set the growth curve parameters, to determine the upper and lower management limits. This is done before testing is started, and satisfies the P (Plan) stage of the Deming circle. [5] While testing, plot the cumulative number of defects on a graph. This is the D (Do) stage. Check if any test values exceed the limits set for acceptance. This is the C (Check) stage. If any results exceed the limits, analyze the results of a quality probe and the defect. A quality probe is a sampling test performed by the Inspection Div. prior to product inspection to evaluate product quality. Perform what is necessary to improve reliability. This is the A (Action) stage. Perform follow-up on any defects detected after installation, as this provides valuable feedback to the development process.

5.4 Product Inspection

The purpose of product inspection is to pass or reject a software product prior to delivery, validating that the product satisfies the requirements of the customer.

Prior to product inspection, it is important to ensure that the quality exceeds a minimum level. If inspection starts out at a low level of quality, quality generally stays at a low level.

Inspection is performed by an independent inspection department, which prepares data based on predetermined items and uses the actual machine for testing.

If defects are detected during product inspection, the software must be returned to the design department. The design department then examines not only the discovered defect, but searches for related defects. Often a single defect is accompanied by related defects.

5.5 System Testing

Hitachi developed a system test 10 years ago called the SST (System Simulation Test).

The SST ensures system quality by performing in-house system testing while simulating an environment as near as possible to that of the user. The SST uses actual application programs, actual data, and appropriate tools and know-how.

The purposes of SST are to simulate the system environment at the plant, in order to better ensure quality. This significantly reduces the number of defects found on site.

Difficult to test items can be tested in a simulated environment, such as overload and performance testing for future expansion under the user environment and error testing which can simulate various types of errors.

A large computer center (the SST Center) has been established exclusively in order to achieve the above using a hardware configuration similar to that of the user. Multi-terminal systems can be simulated, as can all types of errors. While executing under a user simulated environment, the application programs and files of the user can be used, increasing the quality of the simulation.

5.6 Product and Process Improvement Through Operational Results

The evaluation of product quality is reflected through operational results. What we should aim for are measures to be taken to truly avoid similar fault recurrence. This involves improvement in the development process. Removal of faults requires improvement both in the process wherein faults are introduced and in the process of fault removal. This is a fault avoidance approach. For critical software, a fault tolerant approach is also important. Availability can be improved by using fault localization and an instantaneous restart function.

Feedback is vitally important in Japanese quality management as a means of improving the processes which encompass this problem. This is promoted from both a top-down approach, as with the Committee to Study the Avoidance of Recurring Faults, promoted by management, and a bottom-up approach, such as the QC circle activities.

6. Software Quality Assurance Technology and Management

This can be divided into production technology and production management.

6.1 Software Production Technology

HIPACE is a good example of Hitachi's system development methodology. The system development methodology of HIPACE covers all processes of system development in the lifecycle of the application system, from analysis to design, production, and operations. It was first put into service 10 years ago, and has since been expanded and improved.

HIPACE comprises system development standard procedures (SPDS), their development technology, and the EAGLE development support software.

The system development standard procedures break the processes down into detailed steps, each of which is provided with an outline of work and a worksheet. Project management and system management also follow standard procedures.

The main development techniques are structured analysis, structured design, structured programming, and systematic testing.

EAGLE is system development support software, aiding in the abovementioned system development standard procedures.

The main points are as follows:

1. Development environment to provide a set of tools to support development of all processes.

The tools connect closely to form a seamless system.

2. Visualized software development style.

Diagrammed expression of designs and programming at the workstation.

3. Centralized management of software resources.

All specifications and source programs are managed in a data dictionary.

4. Reuse of software parts.

Software programs are created from program patterns (skeletons) and parts (standard subroutines).

The reuse of parts improves development efficiency, and is very important from the standpoint of quality assurance. Approximately 50% of source code for application software can be automatically generated in this manner.

6.2 Software Production Management

Production management can be divided into quality control and process control, which is mainly progress control. These controls are intimately related to the development support system.

Production management requires establishment of production plans and evaluation of results. First, standardized estimations must be set for the number of work hours and the amount of computer time. From the computed number of work hours and the number of days, a production plan can be established. This is used as a base for process control and results evaluation.

The production management system (CAPS) is a total production management database system which manages process control data from the design process to the inspection process and which has a process control data structure corresponding to the software structure, based on the structured design method. This system has as its target visualization of the entire software production process, enabling quick understanding of the current status of any part of the software, as well as what can be anticipated for the future.

6.3 Example: The Software Quality Estimation System - SQE [4]

The Software Quality Estimation System (SQE) is a quality estimation program which supports quality management, as described in Section 5.

The SQE system focuses on reliability in software quality, and is composed of the following subsystems:

1) Design quality estimation subsystem
2) Test quality estimation subsystem
3) Total quality estimation subsystem

Figure 1 shows an outline of the SQE system.

7. Conclusion

This publication discusses quality assurance of critical software products, whose main concern is reliability.

This includes the stages through which the software quality assurance approach has developed.

Although there was a time when there was little management, inspection has now been introduced to reduce customer problems. This stage places an emphasis on shipment quality. This results in delays in delivery time and cost problems. The next stage is thus emphasis on testing quality, wherein defects are detected and

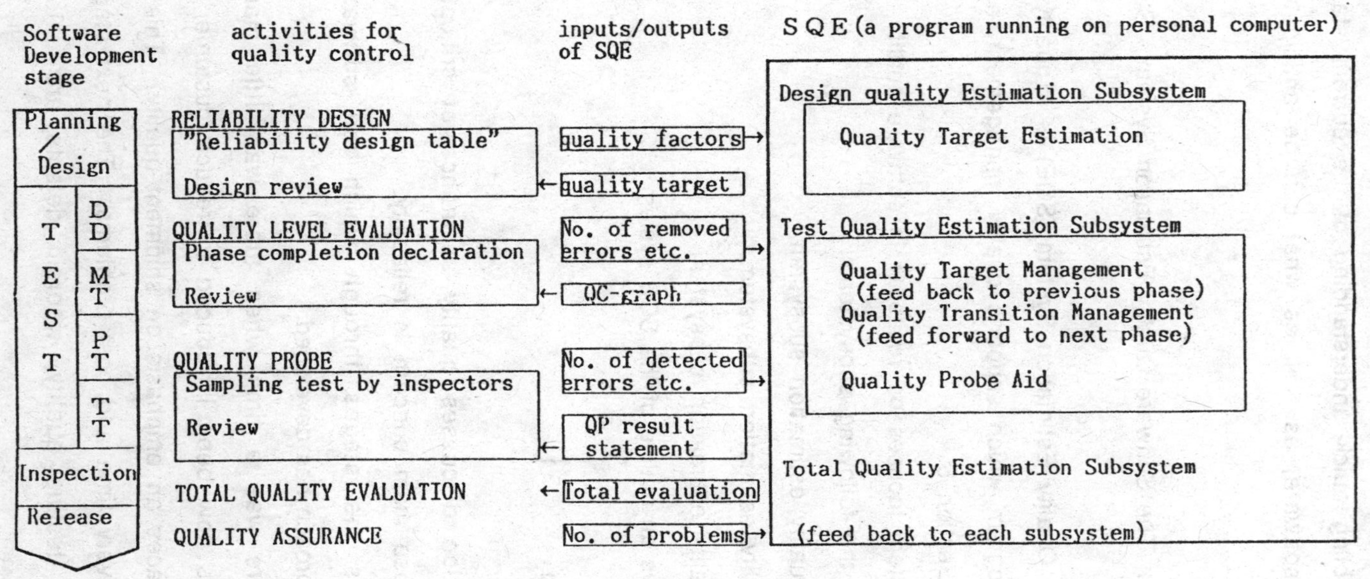

Figure 1 Outline of SQE [4]

corrected as much as possible during the development process, prior to inspection. Now, delivery time and quality have stabilized, but that does not mean that the number of generated defects is reduced. We are now ready to challenge the next step of emphasis on design quality. The goal of problem-free steps is not an easy one. The final stage will see products with attractive qualities which will meet the user's needs more exactly and will increase the manufacturer's competitive edge in the market.

There is no royal road to quality assurance. Every day there are improvements, and we must keep moving forward.

References

[1] K. Yasuda: Software Quality Assurance Activities in Japan, Japanese Perspectives in Software Engineering, Addison-Wesley, 187-205 (Apr. 1989)

[2] T. Chusho: Functional Testing and Structural Testing, Japanese Perspectives in Software Engineering, Addison-Wesley, 155-185 (Apr. 1989)

[3] H. Mimura, H. Maezawa: SEWB: Distributed Software Development Environment on Workstations, proc. of COMPSAC89, 428-432

[4] K. Koga, M. Ikoma: Software Quality Estimation System "SQE", proc. of 6th International Conference on Reliability and Maintainability, 194-198 (Oct. 1988)

[5] K. Ishikawa: What Is Total Quality Control? The Japanese Way (Lu D.J., transl.), Englewood Cliffs NJ, Prentice-Hall (1985)

[6] Y. Tohma: Technical Report for Computer Reliability Technology, Japanese Standards Association (1990)

[7] ISO/IEC JTC1: Software Product Evaluation - Quality Characteristics and Guidelines for Their Use, DIS 9126 (1990)

3

METRICS FOR MANAGEMENT

Annie KUNTZMANN-COMBELLES
***CORELIS* TECHNOLOGIE, France**

1. Introduction

The role of software within systems development is rapidly increasing. Different types of application domains can be analysed :

- Technical and scientific applications where the functional complexity is increasingly growing, i.e. 10 years ago, embedded systems were focusing on technology transfer from analog circuits into computers. Nowadays, functions are achieved that have never been installed previoulsy.

- Expert systems and decision-making system : a completely new discipline that technical or scientific systems must integrate as added value. Final user demands are becoming more and more precise in terms of reasoning techniques and scenarii simulation in front of complex context evolution.

- Software engineering tools : CASE tools have emerged in the last few years to support software development. They must take into account :

  - automatization of methods and concepts
  - integration of diverse tools through a common data base
  - distributed environment configuration from micros to mainframe

- Information systems where complexity of data structures is also growing. These applications now have to be executed on heterogeneous distributed networks and are becoming huge economic investments.

Through this rapid overview of software systems evolution and needs, we will keep in mind three primary characteristics :

- the increase of software costs in companies budget (either buying or developing),

- the need for conformity checking to demonstrate operational behavior of systems that represent a large part of the companies investment,

- the need for control and prediction to ensure reasonable progress of development.

I would like to make an additional remark in this description of software economics concerning the decision process in buying software components or tools. The percentage of budget dedicated to software compared to hardware equipment generally remains very low. Managers (especially project managers) have difficulty in deciding to invest in a CASE tools environment where the price is equivalent to 4 or 5 man months charges compared to the 10 people who will work during 2 years on the project (this situation is very frequent).

The problems of software management can be organised into three main topics:

- budget and planning prediction, and as a consequence organization,
- regular control and adjustment,
- conformity certification in terms of both functionalities and performances,

taking into account the evolving context of applications we pointed out previously.

It is obvious that software metrics are particularly relevant to there topics.

2. The state of metrics practice

Within these three main topics in software management, we will focus on metrics that help activities identified as the main concerns of project managers :

- costs and delays (effort and duration) discussed in 3.1,
- development process characterization not explicitly discussed in sect. 3, covered implicitly in 3.1 with working a separate sub-section.
- product measurement : reliability, completeness discussed in 3.2, performances in general.

CORELIS **TECHNOLOGIE** is involved in several promotional programmes launched by French companies to put software metrics into practice, and has consequently a good insight into the software community.

A very brief historical summary:

- beginning of 80's : development of QA policy and achievement of company's QA plan to be adapted to projects development. This implicitly supposed that development methods were selected and practiced.
- mid of 80's : analysis of the existing tools to support development methods : starting to use tool-boxes on pilot projects under UNIX environment. Overview of new language concepts.
- beginning of 90's : starting the use of CASE tools, Object Oriented strategy is emerging.

Through the decade, software measurement has not really taken off and project management techniques have not evolved in depth. Software Engineering Economics from B. Boehm (published in 1981) remains a very good book to get started in software engineering even if new concepts have emerged in the more advanced communities. In January 1985, the EEC was encouraging metrics with the first ESPRIT project dealing with quality and reliability for software : REQUEST. Between 1985 and 1990 about 8 ESPRIT projects started with software metrication objectives (MUSE, COSMOS, METKIT, TRUST, MERMAID, ...) and we can suppose that industrial bodies involved in these projects were convinced of the strategic interest of such activity. In fact, only a few researchers were making effort in the field and did not represent a deep involvement of the company itself relating to its usual practice. Other wide programmes must be cited such as UK Alvey programme or US TAME project. From my own knowledge, only AT & T and H.P. have really devoted significative effort to practice and use of metrics for management.

The question is why is this the situation ? I personally have two answers but certainly there are a lot of other good reasons :

1. the empirical characteristics of metrication,

2. the lack of confidence in metrics support,

the second point being partly a consequence of the first one. Another reason should also be the cost of data collection and data analysis as it is perceived by the management.

As the final point of this state of practice section, I will outline the fact that software metrics have been recognized by the EEC as one of the main topics to be put in the ESPRIT framework for year 2000. The illustration of this effort is the two new 2 year projects AMI and PYRAMID, that will start in October 1990, with EEC 50 % financial support in order to promote metrication throughout European Industry.

3. The industrial needs

If practice is low, needs are huge. Some figures extracted from on-going French software projects can illustrate diverse types of needs :

Project 1 : Forecast

Software budget	2.5 MF
System budget	15 MF
Duration	18 months
Type	real time embedded
Size	20 000 lines of C language

Reality

Software budget	more than 2.5 time initial budget
Duration	+ 12 months
Technical status	uncomplete (30 % of functionality implemented) uncertainty on the capability of the software architecture to evolve to support 100 % of functionalities

Project 2 : Forecast

Software budget	30 000 hours
Duration	13 months
Type	real time on ground and embedded
Size	80 000 lines of C language

Reality

Software budget	more than 50 000 hours
Duration	+ 7months

Project 3 : Forecast

Software budget	200 MF
Duration	4 Years
Type	Information system
Size	11 millions of lines COBOL

Reality

Duration	+ 6 months at least
Technical status	acceptance test correct but no validation by final users.

DOD/AJPO has collected some statistics on Ada programs last year, with the following results :

Project	Type	Real effort	Model 1 (Softcost Ada)	Model 2 (Cocomo)
1	C3I	302 MM	+ 14%	- 37%
2	C3I	684 MM	+129%	- 25%
3	Tool	134 MM	+ 11%	-
4	Tool	144 MM	+ 9%	+147%
5	Embedded	190 MM	+ 86%	- 51%

From these different experiences, we confirm that one prior need is to be able to predict and control development effort versus final product performance. In order to improve software manager confidence in metrics, I will recommend simple methods to control effort (numbers of people and duration) and reliability of the product. This is naturally not independent of putting the emphasis on development methods and using CASE tools that make development homogeneous between engineers and improve visibility and development phase framework definition. This topic will not be further developed in this paper.

This suggestion for metrics to be collected warrants a new section rather than following on from industrial needs.

3.1 Effort evaluation and control

There are generally two different ways to estimate the software budget :

- the use of cost models,
- the use of analogous reasoning, comparing each elementary component to existing data base items.

From my experience, I recommend the use of both of them concurrently, with comparison of results obtained to explain discrepancies and find a satisfactory evaluation.

Both techniques need historical data that unfortunately is not always collected. A few years ago, trying to calibrate the COCOMO model for a company, I had a lot of trouble in gathering global figures on projects, the way of counting hours of development varying from project manager, to technical director and to accounting department !

In the first stage, only simple data has to be collected, refinement coming later on. The minimum set is :

For each component analysed :

- type : (data acquisition, algorithm, real time, ...),
- size : lines of code are the most usual unit (providing that the definition has been set up) number of objects might be another unit,
- complexity : qualitative scale with 3 levels is sufficient,
- critical : of the component in the whole architecture - same remark as above,
- language : type of language used,
- reusability : % of code reused from another project (if any) or need to develop a reusable component,

- effort : number of man months that have been necessary to develop it from the specification of final users needs to the software acceptance test per development phase.

Remarks : A software life cycle is usually selected by a company : consequently, development phases have the same definition from project to project.

Software technology may evolve and raw historical data might be difficult to use in that case. In consequence, Expert people will need to adapt the old data by use of an adaptive coefficient.

Of course human factors may influence several of these characteristics : I would plan to consider these refinements later on, when the other parameters are well controlled.

The process of software cost estimation should be based on the following schema :

• Imagine a technical solution to the problem (which is usually described in the proposition to the customer),

• Decompose the solution into elementary components (the granularity may differ from one project to the other : the finest granularity is recommanded) and identify completely new or unknown components as a percentage of the whole system,

• Evaluate each component with the two approaches if possible : by cost model selected and calibrated to the company profile and by analogy to previous projects,

• Compare evaluations and take decisions,

• Make the sum of elementary estimations and add "unknown" components,

• Add a percentage for global acceptance test and installation (between 5 to 10 %),

• Add training effort,

• Add a percentage for quality assurance (between 3 and 8 %),

• Add project management (about 10 %),

• Split the whole budget across development phases, identifying development, project management and quality.

During the project progress (monthly or twice a month) the summary of efforts will be collected through the team and compared to estimations. It might be very useful to indicate to the project manager, month by month, and phase by phase, the evolution of the figures. We suggest the following table.

Project : XXX

Component	**Phase 1 Effort spent**	**Estimation**	**Remaining To produce**	**Phase 2.....**
A	5 MM	10 MM	6 MM	
B	3 MM	5 MM	1,5 MM	
C	2 MM	10 MM	8 MM	

Remark : the column called "Remaining to produce" is not the difference between budget and reality ; it is the actual estimation of the people in charge of the work. Each phase is estimated separately : the project manager must take the right decisions to fulfill the overall planning. He has also all the data necessary to re-estimate phase 2 as a function of :

- time really spent on phase 1,
- personal context appreciation,
- external constraints he knows,
- development environment.

This method can be used for any project, regardless of its size. A "little" project might look less dangerous economically but relative figures (% of loss) could be very similar to the ones of a big project.

As a conclusion to this cost section, I want to point out that research for cost modelling is absolutely necessary to refine the estimation methods and especially the size estimation. The concept of function point developed by IBM is an example of what can be used to analyse a project when functions are new.

The TAME project at University of Maryland is looking at a classification technique to help resource allocation on software project development.

3.2 Reliability evaluation and control

Similar considerations and advantages can be seen for reliability evaluation and control to ensure :

- product operational behavior,
- effort control to reach adequate acceptance level,
- maintenance cost limits.

Reliability evaluation is usually based on historical data collected on the product. Basic information is:

- number of failures which have occured,

- time (which may be CPU time or calendar time) of the failure occurence,

I will not redevelop here reliability theory and modelling but simply point out that adequate environments now exist to help non-statistician project managers to practice reliability evaluation and prediction. The presentation of results might help them to make correct decisions such as :

- change the testing strategy because the one in use does not improve the component reliability sufficiently,

- appreciate the role of specific components in the global system reliability and define the corresponding testing effort as a consequence,

- calibrate testing effort compared to specification constraints,

- evaluate and plan maintenance effort according to the analysed reliability.

In this discipline too, research is still needed and refinements possible : the hypotheses on which the various models are based might be seen as drawbacks but again according to my own experience, even if predictions and reality are not completely consistent, the project manager has a better visibility and control of the product when using these models.

4. Conclusion

The lack of maturity in the software metrics field we have pointed out perhaps arises from the fact that things are measurable only when they are understood. The software development process seems to remain empirical for too many software teams and project managers.

The reasons for such situation are certainly complex and introduce psychological characteristics that are difficult to analyze completely : instead of looking for clarification and explanation about delays, bad quality of product and budget discrepancies, engineers might be afraid of consequences to their career within a department or a company.

We do believe that promotion of very simple metrics should be possible based on three main actions :

- action 1 : give assistance in setting up data collection, validation and analysis supported by tools and a huge set of examples,

- action 2 : develop standardization and recommendations from well known organizations (i.e CEC, ESA, MODs ...),

- action 3 : research focus on improved models and formalization of software development process.

5. Bibliography

H.D. Drake, D.E. Wolting : Reliability Theory Applied to Software Testing, HP Journal April 1987

V.R. Basili, H.D. Rombach : TAME, Integrating Measurement into Software Environments, TR-1764 June 1987, University of Maryland

G.C. Low, D.R. Jeffrey : Function Points in the Estimation and Evaluation of The Software Process, IEEE TSE Vol 16 N° 1, January 1990

IEEE Software : Special Issue March 1990

Manager's Handbook for Software Development, NASA Goddard Space Flight Center, SEL 84-001, April 1984

B.A. Kitchenham, B. Littlewood : Measurement for Software Control and Assurance, Elsevier Applied science, 1988

R.B. Grady, D.L. Caswell : Software metrics, establishing a Company Wide Program, Prentice Hall, 1987

J.D. Musa, M.L. Shooman : Development of current Practice Guidelines for Using Software Reliability Technology in Software Development. Plan of the AIAA Working Group, December 1989

4

A RULE-BASED APPROACH TO SOFTWARE QUALITY ENGINEERING

Hans-Ludwig Hausen
GMD, Schloss Birlinghoven, D-5205 St.Augustin 1

Abstract

Effective software quality engineering requires well organized methods and tools for evaluation, measurement and assessment. Also required are a standardized, minimal set of product and process descriptions. A software system has to be defined at least by three layers: application concept or requirements specification, data processing concept or system specification, and realization or programs. In order to be able to appraise a complete software system one has to examine and assess all its components and layers.

Quality is defined by evaluation factors and quality factors, each connected to quality objectives and goals. Methods and tools for evaluation, measurement and assessment are also connected to the factors and to goals. The particular problem domains are represented by set of rules; their interrelations are also defined by rule sets. In order to assist the implementation of quality engineering the approach provides a generic framework for both learner defined and teacher directed instruction.

1 Introduction

As a preface we will briefly describe software development and assessment. The terms and definitions introduced will be used in later sections for the definition of software quality. In order to introduce assessment terminology this section surveys also selected concepts for software quality assurance.

1.1 Software Layers and Views

From the collection of requirements and tasks the activities (to be) performed in the application department and the corresponding objects are identified, analysed or defined. The definitions of the application concept activities must identify those parts which can be combined to functions of a data processing operation. Simultaneously, the objects have to be investigated for its suitable data-processing-oriented representation. Thus, we obtain a function model and a data model of the software system to be developed. For the precise definition of the data processing facilities to be provided by a software system we require the definition of the states to be assumed by the system at the application of functions. This state definition specifies the relations between the data and the functions using the data.

The computer programs can then be designed on the basis of this data-processing-oriented specification. In this phase the control and data structures are designed in accordance with the desired object machine defined by the programming language it requires. This forms again the basis for developing the executable code or that part of program development which is automatically carried out by compilers, linkage editors and loaders.

The documentation is produced in parallel to this development of formal descriptions (application specification, data processing specification, programs). Apart from the formal descriptions, it comprises the natural-language description of tasks, requirements, conditions, approaches to solution, etc., i.e. a prose definition of all aspects of the implemented system. The development should suitably consider the fact that both the formal and the informal development documents are produced in parallel. This is the only way to secure that system definitions that cannot be represented by formal descriptions are documented and that alternative solutions are selected on the basis of reconstructible, namely documented decisions.

```
..................................................................
:LAYERS                    : TASKS        STATES        ITEMS    :
:..........................:.....................................:
:                          :model of  _ _ _ _ _ _ _ _  model of:
:APPLICATION CONCEPT       :activities                 object    :
: or                       :   | \                      / |      :
:REQUIREMENTS SPECIFICATION:   |  application states      |      :
:..........................:...|...........|..............|......:
:                          :model of  _ _ _|_ _ _      model of:
:DATA PROCESSING CONCEPT   :functions      |            data     :
: or                       :   | \         |            / |      :
:SYSTEM SPECIFICATION      :   |data processing states|          :
:..........................:...|...........|..............|......:
:                          :model of  _ _ _|_ _ _      model of:
:REALIZATION               :procedures     |          variables:
: or                       :     \         |          /          :
:PROGRAM CODE              :        programs states              :
:..........................:.....................................:
```

Figure 1: Layers in the Software Development Process

This is to conclude the description of the relevant representation forms of software and the steps producing them. Since most of the tasks in a software development project are performed in parallel and since it is possible to group tasks according to the individuals performing the work one can define views in a life-cycle. A view describes all the actions and items handled in a specific way with respect to a selected set of objectives. In general one might define a construction view, a validation view, and a management view in order to separate the different responsibilities. A layer model might be developed for each view in order to be able to define for each view actions and items in a coherent, low-complex manner.

1.2 Quality Assurance

To avoid the well-known problems of undesirable developments recognised too late, an assessment of all intermediate and final result is required. This should be done in parallel to the respective development activities, i.e. a continuous validation and not only a final validation is the most effective one.

The following introduces the most effective techniques. The following presents some personal opinions about the state of software quality assurance in the following fields: inspection, walkthrough (a.o.), statistical analysis, static analysis, metrics, dynamic analysis, testing, test quality, symbolic execution, symbolic evaluation, formal verification, quality modeling, productivity modeling, security analysis, reliability, project and product management. Inspection (including walkthrough, etc.) is the oldest, most widespread, most effective, but also most expensive assessment technique. Its instrumentation is insufficient. Automation by means of information systems and conferencing systems is suitable. In addition to that, the interactive, incremental analysis of software texts by means of grammar-controlled tools should be rationalized.

Static analysis includes everything to be tested with compiler techniques (e.g. scanning, parsing and semantics analysis). The necessary knowledge is supplied with the (compiler-oriented) language definition, otherwise the use of a language has to be refused from quality engineering viewpoint. The tools should be generated with compiler generators. The procedures of static analysis of documentations are still insufficient; solutions might be imported from machine translation.

Evaluation of structural complexity is defined for flow of control, data flow, state transitions as well as for texts. Its instrumentation is mostly done via specific tools, a generic one should however be possible by means of compiler-compiler. The metrics are still defined insufficiently from the viewpoints of mathematics and computer science, i.e. correct ones should be defined first. The practical tools fall far behind theory (at least in the Federal Republic of Germany). A consistent theory for sequential, non-sequential, functional and relational or logical programs as well documentations (i.e. natural-language texts) is missing. Logical complexity (computation complexity) test is developed in the theory of algorithms and is unfortunately of no importance to quality engineering. Even some computer scientists do not know it obviously.

Black box testing examines the input-output behavior of a program with respect to its specified functions. Today, black box test cases (i.e. test data) are based on experience or are derived from specifications by means of statistics. Test quality can be defined as coverage of the input area or as coverage of the tested functionality. Despite of many publications on black box testing, the definition of sufficient test cases and suitable test criteria still seems to be a problem. White box testing tests the internal behavior of a program. A program is "decomposed" into data flow, flow of control and state. Test strategies and test data are defined by means of language-construct-specific quality criteria for flow of control testing (x% path coverage, y% instruction coverage, z% module coverage, ..., and hybrids), data flow testing (r% data relations of type r_t, s% value definitions, t% value referencings, ..., and hybrids) or state testing (m% expression values, n% predicate values, ..., and hybrids). This works (to a certain extent), though not efficiently enough, for (well-structured) sequential programs. Test quality is defined as coverage for individual or several criteria. The effective computation of test data for a specific strategy should be automated. Effectiveness and efficiency should be increased. In addition, the importance of an obtained test quality (test coverage) to correctness should be discussed.

Formal verification is important to the testing of security-relevant, imperative software. Each proving method has already been tried once, but so far, nobody has been able to specify constructively methods for constructing proofs, i.e. how to find a proof for a given program. It is still open: how to show the equivalence of program proof and specification? Inverse program verification is given if programs are generated from a correctness proof or subproofs. This is then an approach for program synthesis.

Quality analysis is based on the investigation of product factors and measured quantities which are often defined insufficiently. There is a great number of so-called quality models. Unlike others we say that quality is relative, it should be expressed as a distance between target and actual state. Since there cannot be the one and only quality model in our opinion, I suggest a generic model which can be tailored to project and product characteristics. A number of software metrics are used for quantifying software attributes. Many of them have been and are being developed, but most of them are not sensible from the viewpoint of mathematics or computer science. Productivity analysis is like quality analysis, but only for projects. Productivity is the quality of a project. Our generic procedure is applicable to this case too. A well-defined project model should be the prerequisite.

2 Software Measurement and Assessment

Both from the historical and methodological point of view, measuring is one of the fundamentals of science; without a well-founded theory of measuring, the further development of empirical sciences would not be possible. It is therefore also important in the field of software engineering to establish a comparable basic theory of measuring.

By measuring we understand the determination of the value of the factor of an object. In measuring theory, this is done by assigning numbers to objects that are carriers the rule whereby specific relations between the numbers (numerical relative) reflect analog relations between the objects (empirical relative). Such a mapping of observations onto real numbers is also called a scale; of importance in the software sector are the quality measures which perform this assignment.

It is necessary to derive from the world of observation those operational characteristics of software that are easily measureable, i.e. that can be mapped onto elements from the world of numbers in such a way that the specific relations are maintained. However, the problem is how to obtain the suitable characteristics and how to relate them to the factors to be described. A quality model is therefore required as a basic. This quality model defines and decomposes the relevant factors and determines their interrelations.

Evaluation is a special form of measurement; it is to be understood as the subjective determination of factor values if these are not measurable. Evaluation regarded as mental measuring is performed analog to the mathematical measuring described above though it is not based on a mathematical function, but on a relation. Values once determined cannot be reproduced, they are nut unambiguous. Evaluations can be performed, for example, by means of check lists or given scales.

Another problem encountered with regard to the correct use of quality measures is their validity and measurability. According to definition, a quality measure is valid if it does actually measure the factor that it is supposed to measure or claims to measure. The validity of quality measures can be examined by means of specific methods, such as correlation analysis, factor analysis or expert rating. Measures for which no statements are available as to their validity should be used with extreme care for quality measurement.

Assessment is understood as determining whether one or more agreed, required or expected conditions have been fulfiled for an object. The assessment process is performed by comparing given factor values (target) with factor values which are actually available (actual state obtained by examination and measurement) for an object (or several objects). Therefore, assessment always involves a decision being made; its results are ranking statements, such as program X is more efficient than program Y or the actual state of an application concept is more complex than its target state.

Quality assessment always requires both specification of requirements (target quality graph) and object measurement (actual quality graph). The results of quality examinations or measurements do not yet produce any statements on whether and to what extent the actual software quality ascertained meets the requirements or expectations of the software user. While the factor values for the software are obtained by means of examinations and measurements, it is in nature of assessment to map and compare the results of examinations and measurements and to associate them with subjective value perceptions.

An assessment determines the degree of accordance or deviation of the target graph with or from the actual graph; we also speak of distances (differences) between target state and actual state. There are several ways how to perform an assessment process. On the one hand, the assessment of each factor regarded as relevant can be carried out by assigning evaluation values to the measurement or examination results or by using metrics to determine the 'distances' between the target factor values and those tested or measured. On the other hand, quality assessment can be performed by means of a synthesis of the various assessment, measurement and examination values or a combination of these.

In general, we distinguish between one-dimensional and multi-dimensional assessment methods. One-dimensional methods consider only one single factor. A possible approach is the successive paired comparison of alternative software products or of comparing an ideal product with the product to be assessed. In the simplest case, the 'distances' between the measurement or examination values of the products in question are determined by means of suitable metrics. The great disadvantage of one-dimensional assessment methods is the fact that more complex relations cannot be considered. It does not seem useful to assess software quality by means of these methods.

Multi-dimensional methods, however, allow several factors to be considered. Many multi-dimensional methods used in practice can be reduced to one basic method, i.e. the cost-benefit analysis.

Assessment requires quantification and operations on values of quantification expressions. A measure is the homomorph mapping of a quantification expression on to a nominal, ordinal, interval or rational scale. Quantification expressions are formulated in terms of the language of the observed world, in to a quantitative expression, formulated in terms of the language of the model world. The latter expression can be formalized much easier than a qualitative one. In formalized quantitative expression operators have to be defined which define relations between the formalized quantitative expressions. Those operations must be homomorph to operations on the non-formalized, verbal qualitative expression.

The most typical characteristics are complexity and dependence. Complexity of an software product can measured by counting of sub-elements (e.g. subroutines), nested elements, defined elements, refered elements, predicate variables or other variables. For dependence one might be interested in module or programs. The module dependence can be measured by the counting of: modules, module invocations or passed data items. Program dependence is determined by the counting of functions or data used in more than one program, file accesses, data base accesses, operating system accesses or user interface invocations.

For a specification we might want to measure specification text (i.e. the string of specification) or the static structure of the specification expression (i.e. the structure of the specification functions).

For a program we want to measure Program text, Control flow graph, Data flow graph, Storage space usage or Execution time consumption. In case of program text we measure number of chars, number of chars, number of words, number of sentences, number of chapters, number of variables and types, number of operators and control structures, frequency variables and types or frequency operators and control structures. If we have to measure a graph we count edges, nodes, subgraphs, connected subgraphs, strong connected subgraphs, maximal connected subgraphs or nesting of subgraphs.

Based upon these principles we are able to measure quality or productivity (which is considered as quality of a project). N-ary vectors are used to represent both the actual and the required values for the particular factors. In formula we get the following assessment procedure:

Actual evaluation factors $aefv = \langle aef_1, aef_2, aef_3, ..., aef_{n_2} \rangle$

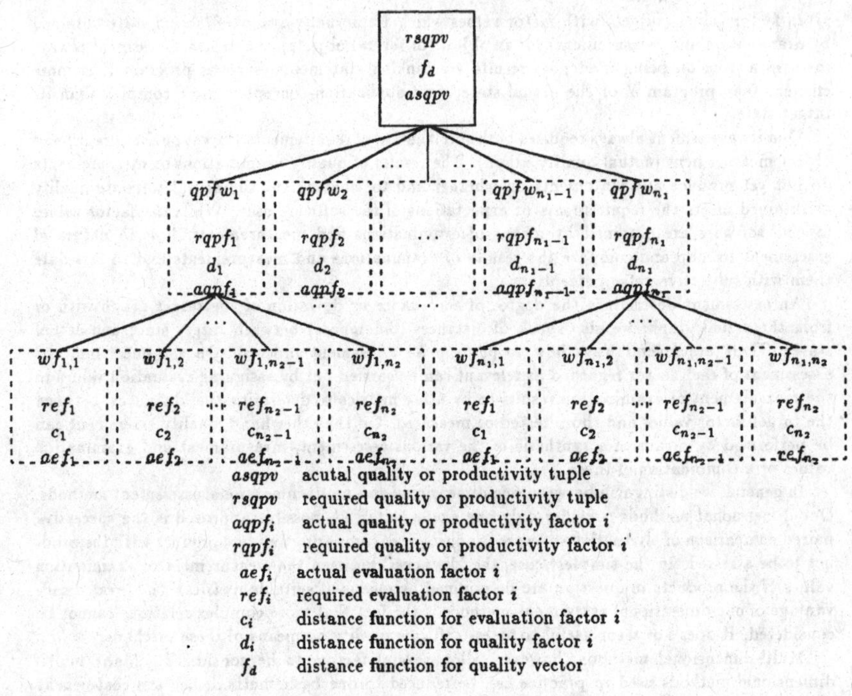

Figure 2: Required versus Actual Quality

Actual quality or productivity factors $aqpfv = \langle aqpf_1, aqpf_2, aqpf_3, ..., aqpf_{n_2}\rangle$

where $aqpf_i := (a_{i,1} \otimes aef_1, a_{i,2} \otimes aef_2, ..., a_{i,n_2} \otimes aef_{n_2})$

and $0.0 \leq a_{i,j} \leq 1.0$ or $a_{i,j} \in \{0, 1\}$

Required evaluation factors $refv = \langle ref_1, ref_2, ref_3, ..., ref_{n_2}\rangle$

Required quality or productivity factors $rqpfv = \langle rqpf_1, rqpf_2, rqpf_3, ..., rqpf_{n_1}\rangle$

Now we can compute a **Level-0-System-Value** by an **actual system value vector**

$asvv0 = \langle asv0_1, asv0_2, ..., asv0_{n_2}\rangle$ where $asv0_i = c_i(aef_i, ref_i)$ and c_i is a correlation funciton

and the **required system value vector**

$rsvv0 = \langle rsv0_1, rsv0_2, ..., rsv0_{n_2}\rangle$ where $rsv0_i$ ideal or required value for $sv0_i$

or $rsv0_i = c_i(ef_i^{max}, ref_i)$ and c_i is a correlation funciton

We obtain the **level-0 system value**: $sv0 = c_0(asvv0, rsvv0)$

where c_0 is a correlation function.

On the next step we compute the **Level-1-System-Value** by an **actual system value vector**

$asvv1 = \langle asv1_1, asv1_2, ..., asv1_{n_1}\rangle$ where $asv1_i = c_i(aqpf_i, rqpf_i)$ and c_i is a correlation (distance) function, and the **required system value vector**, which is defined to

$rsvvl = \langle rsvl_1, rsvl_2, ..., rsvl_{n_i} \rangle$

where $rsvl_i$ is an ideal or required value for svl_i

or $rsvl_i = c_i(qpf_i^{max}, rqpf_i)$ and c_i is a correlation (distance) function.

An asvv and a rsvv can be computed for each decomposition level. Finally we get an *level-s system value*:

$sv.s = c_s(asvvl, rsvvl; asvv2, rsvv2; ...; asvvs, rsvvs)$ where c_s is a distance function.

3 Handling of Quality Methods and Tools

In order to build-up a knowledge-based quality assurance system knowledge about methods and tools has to be represented. Knowledge can be acquired from literature, from expert interviews and from one's own experiments. Knowledge might be represented by rules. Generally, a rule consists of a condition-part and an action-part:

IF	condition part predicates
THEN	action part predicate

For the representation of method knowledge we get rules of the following scheme:

IF	(sub-) method(s)
THEN	method

Selecting appropriate tools requires availability of knowledge about their structure and applicability. This knowledge is represented by rules of the form:

IF	(sub-) tool predicates
THEN	tool predicate

In general there are a lot method tasks which are too complex to be instrumented immediately. These tasks have to be decomposed into those subtasks which might be instrumentable. Often it might be required to have a number of decomposition if one arrives at implementable tasks. These decompositions are not part of a method and therefore a separate rule set is required to define these decompositions. We have the a set of interrelation rules of the form:

IF	interrelate predicate
THEN	method predicate

IF	tool predicate interrelate predicate
or	method predicate interrelate predicate
THEN	interrelate predicate

And finally we get:

IF	tool predicate
THEN	method predicate

If we would use this forms it might happen that we will end up with a large set of independent rule sets, each of which applicable within particular conditions. Using weights to rank the alternatives within the condition part and parameters for the complete rule we will reduce the amount of rules to be developed. Introducing the weights and parameters we get:

IF	condition part	**WEIGHT**	weight part
THEN	action part	**ENVIRONMENT**	parameter part

An example might illustrate how this extension is to be used:

IF	WALK THROUGH	**WEIGHT**	$x \in \{0 \ldots 1\}$
	CODE INSPECTION		$x \in \{0 \ldots 1\}$
	DESIGN INSPECTION		$x \in \{0 \ldots 1\}$
	REQ. INSPECTION		$x \in \{0 \ldots 1\}$
THEN	INSPECTION	**ENVIRONMENT**	VM or RM

By this rules the quality assurance techniques inspection, testing, verification are ranked for a validation to be applied in the environments SM, LM, VM or RM, which indicate software process models. Rule two and three define inspection for the respective environments as indicated.

For tools we might want to define their application area as follows:

IF	tool decomposition part	**WEIGHT**	weight part
THEN	tool part	**PARAMETER**	parameter part

An example of which is:

IF	LINE EDITOR	**WEIGHT**	$x \in \{0 \ldots 1\}$
	SCREEN EDITOR		$x \in \{0 \ldots 1\}$
	GRAPH EDITOR		$x \in \{0 \ldots 1\}$
	...		$x \in \{0 \ldots 1\}$
THEN	EDITOR	**ENVIRONMENT**	OS1 or OS2 or OS3

By this rule the tool EDITOR is defined as applicable within the environments OS1, OS2 or OS3, which might indicate operating systems. Tool weightening define the order in which they might by applied to accomplish an editing tasks.

The rule schema for the interrelation rules now is as follows:

IF	interrelate predicate 1	**WEIGHT**	weight
OR	interrelate predicate 2	**WEIGHT**	weight
THEN	method predicate 1	**PARAMETER**	parameter
OR	interrelate predicate 3	**PARAMETER**	parameter

The general form now is:

IF	if conjunction 1	**WEIGHT**	weight
OR	if conjunction 2	**WEIGHT**	weight
...	...	...	...
OR	if conjunction n	**WEIGHT**	weight
THEN	then conjunction 1	**PARAMETER**	parameter
OR	then conjunction 2	**PARAMETER**	parameter
...	...	...	...
OR	then conjunction m	**PARAMETER**	parameter

This rule form allows a very compact definition of the rules. The disjunctions in the then part of the rules make it possible to have one rule whereas otherwise a rule for each disjunction would be required. THe disjunction in the if part provides freedom to express a number of possible decompositions of a method or a tool or an interrelation.

4 Metrication and Assessment

In order to avoid complexity we have to search for a generic framework, which we can use to define models of quality or productivity, to document objectives and selection decisions, and thirdly to the describe applications. Because we do not have a theory for each problem area a rule-based approach should be appropriate.

4.1 Rule-based Representation of Models

As shown quality or productivity factors are too complex to be mapped directly onto evaluation factors. High level factors have to be decomposed into subfactors and subfactors, if to complex, have to be decomposed a further level down. Finally factors, subfactors, and subsub...factors are mapped onto evaluation factors. This leads to acyclic graphs for quality or productivity. Those acyclic graphs can be easily represented by basic *if ... then ..* rules of the form:

IF	predicate over items on decomposition level n+1
and	predicate over items on decomposition level n+2
	...
and	predicate over items on decomposition level n+k
THEN	predicate over an item on decomposition level n

In general some factors are constructed from subfactors, and subfactors are constructed from subsubfactors or from evaluation factors. Some other factors might be defined directly in terms of evaluation factors. The schema of the definition rule then has be of the form:

IF	evaluation factor prédicate
and	subsub quality or productivity factor predicate
and	sub quality or productivity factor predicate
THEN	quality or productivity factor predicate

Using the formulas given in the previous section we now can write:

IF	$\langle f_{h,1}(a_{h,1}, ef_1), \ldots, f_{h,n_1}(a_{h,n_1}, ef_{h,n_2})\rangle$
and	$\langle f_{i,1}(a_{i,1}, qpf_i), \ldots, f_{i,n_2}(a_{i,n_2}, qpf_{n_2})\rangle$
and	$\langle f_{r,1}(a_{r,1}, sqpf_r), \ldots, f_{r,n_r}(a_{r,n_r}, sqpf_{n_r})\rangle$
THEN	qpf_k

Each rule defines a quality or productivity factor, whereas the set of all quality or productivity rules describes the quality or productivity factor matrix. But, if we have a two-level quality or productivity graph the rule schema is reduced to:

IF	evaluation factor predicate
THEN	quality or productivity factor predicate

In terms of formulas we get:

IF	$\langle f_{h,1}(a_{h,1}, ef_1), f_{h,2}(a_{h,2}, ef_2), \ldots, f_{h,n_1}(a_{h,n_1}, ef_{h,n_2})\rangle$
THEN	qpf_k

On top of the factors we define the overall quality or productivity by a rule of the form:

IF	evaluation factor predicate
and	sub quality or productivity factor predicate
and	quality or productivity factor predicate
THEN	quality or productivity predicate

For the formulas given above we now obtain:

IF	$\langle f_{h,1}(a_{h,1}, ef_1), f_{h,2}(a_{h,2}, ef_2), \ldots, f_{h,n_1}(a_{h,n_1}, ef_{h,n_2})\rangle$
and	$\langle f_{i,1}(a_{i,1}, qpf_i), \ldots, f_{i,n_2}(a_{i,n_2}, qpf_{n_2})\rangle$
and	$\langle g_1(b_1, f_{1,1}(a_{1,1}, ef_1)), \ldots, g_1(b_1, f_{1,n_2}(a_{1,n_2}, ef_{n_2}))\rangle$
THEN	Q

From the rule schema for the general case, we construct a reduced version for the two-level quality or productivity graph:

IF	$\langle g_1(b_1, f_{1,1}(a_{1,1}, ef_1)), \ldots, g_1(b_1, f_{1,n_2}(a_{1,n_2}, ef_{n_2}))\rangle$
THEN	Q

The factor rules and the overall quality or productivity rule are not different in structure. The latter is special case of the former, it does not define other quality or productivity factors but is described the same way as they are. A quality or productivity rule defines the root of the quality or productivity graph, quality or productivity factor rules describe the intermediate nodes.

4.2 Rule-based Representation of Objectives

From the beginning of modeling software quality and productivity on one will find schematic representations of quality and productivity objectives (motivations, concerns, criteria, etc.) in one way or another. Definitions of objectives have to be as precise and clear as possible, and, as any other reliable definition, they must not be circular at least. An acyclic graph might be an appropriate instrument to explain the structural decomposition of objectives. And, as we have shown, *if ... then ...* rules are suitable to describe acyclic structured information. The schema we get is of the form:

IF	assessment objective predicate
and	subsub quality or productivity objective predicate
and	sub quality or productivity objective predicate
THEN	quality or productivity objective predicate

For the top level of McCall's model we obtain:

IF	usability objective predicate
and	integrity objective predicate
and	efficiency objective predicate
and	correctness objective predicate
and	reliability objective predicate
THEN	operation objective predicate

IF	maintainability objective predicate
and	testability objective predicate
and	flexibility objective predicate
THEN	revision objective predicate

IF	reusability objective predicate
and	portability objective predicate
and	interoperability objective predicate
THEN	transition objective predicate

As demonstrated for McCall's model we are now able to describe objectives by a set of production rules, the same type of rules we used for the factor description. The description and documentation of objectives in terms of rules makes it possible to create specific sets of objectives, each of which suitable for a particular application.

4.3 Rule-based Representation of Applications

Volume and effort has been defined by a number of functions and attributes. The generation of an 'application' then is a configuration task, where the appropriate functions and constants have to be compiled into a set of proper formulas. The process is guided by the set of objectives selected as being essential for that particular application. Following the definitions given in the previous section we are able to describe volume by rules as follows:

IF	f_{vol} predicate
and	volume$_{ap-concept}$ predicate
and	volume$_{dp-concept}$ predicate
and	volume$_{imp}$ predicate
THEN	volume predicate

IF	$f_{apc-vol}$ predicate
and	volume$_{activities}$ predicate
and	volume$_{objects}$ predicate
THEN	volume$_{ap-concept}$ predicate

IF	$f_{dpc-vol}$ predicate
and	volume$_{functions}$ predicate
and	volume$_{data}$ predicate
THEN	volume$_{dp-concept}$ predicate

IF	$f_{imp-vol}$ predicate
and	volume$_{procedures}$ predicate
and	volume$_{variables}$ predicate
THEN	volume$_{imp}$ predicate

IF <some arithmetic operator>	**THEN** f_{vol} predicate
IF <some arithmetic operator>	**THEN** $f_{apc-vol}$ predicate
IF <some arithmetic operator>	**THEN** $f_{dpc-vol}$ predicate
IF <some arithmetic operator>	**THEN** $f_{imp-vol}$ predicate

For the estimation and prediction of volume we get the following rules:

IF	*predicate*$_{\alpha_a}$*predicate*$_{\beta_a}$*predicate*$_{\gamma_a}$ activity estimation$_{expert}$ predicate
THEN	volume$_{activities}$ predicate

IF	*predicate*$_{\alpha_o}$*predicate*$_{\beta_o}$*predicate*$_{\gamma_o}$ object estimation$_{expert}$ predicate
THEN	volume$_{objects}$ predicate

IF	*predicate*$_{\alpha_f}$*predicate*$_{\beta_f}$*predicate*$_{\gamma_f}$ volume$_{activities}$ predicate
THEN	volume$_{functions}$ predicate

IF	*predicate*$_{\alpha_d}$*predicate*$_{\beta_d}$*predicate*$_{\gamma_d}$ volume$_{objects}$ predicate
THEN	volume$_{data}$ predicate

IF	*predicate*$_{\alpha_p}$*predicate*$_{\beta_p}$*predicate*$_{\gamma_p}$ volume$_{functions}$ predicate
THEN	volume$_{procedures}$ predicate

IF	*predicate*$_{\alpha_v}$*predicate*$_{\beta_v}$*predicate*$_{\gamma_v}$ volume$_{data}$ predicate
THEN	volume$_{variables}$ predicate

For a rule-based description we need the following predicates:

IF <some selected α_i>	**THEN** predicateα_i	**IF** <some selected ρ_i>	**THEN** predicateρ_i
IF <some selected β_j>	**THEN** predicateβ_j	**IF** <some selected σ_j>	**THEN** predicateσ_j
IF <some selected γ_k>	**THEN** predicateγ_k	**IF** <some selected τ_k>	**THEN** predicateτ_k
IF <some selected $f_{c,a}$>	**THEN** predicate$f_{c,a}$	**IF** <some selected q_a>	**THEN** predicateq_a
IF <some selected $f_{c,o}$>	**THEN** predicate$f_{c,o}$	**IF** <some selected q_o>	**THEN** predicateq_o
IF <some selected $f_{c,f}$>	**THEN** predicate$f_{c,f}$	**IF** <some selected q_f>	**THEN** predicateq_f
IF <some selected $f_{c,d}$>	**THEN** predicate$f_{c,d}$	**IF** <some selected q_d>	**THEN** predicateq_d
IF <some selected $f_{c,p}$>	**THEN** predicate$f_{c,p}$	**IF** <some selected q_p>	**THEN** predicateq_p
IF <some selected $f_{c,v}$>	**THEN** predicate$f_{c,v}$	**IF** <some selected q_v>	**THEN** predicateq_v

And finally we get the general rules for the quality dependent layer and element specific cost estimation:

IF	predicateρ_{ap-c} predicateσ_{ap-c} predicateτ_{ap-c}
and	predicate$f_{c,a}$,predicateq_a,volume$_{activities}$predicate
and	predicate$f_{c,o}$,predicateq_o,volume$_{objects}$predicate
THEN	effort$_{ap-concept}$ predicate
IF	predicateρ_{dp-c} predicateσ_{dp-c} predicateτ_{dp-c}
and	predicate$f_{c,f}$,predicateq_f,volume$_{functions}$predicate
and	predicate$f_{c,d}$,predicateq_d,volume$_{data}$predicate
THEN	effort$_{dp-concept}$ predicate
IF	predicateρ_{imp} predicateσ_{imp} predicateτ_{imp}
and	predicate$f_{c,p}$,predicateq_p,volume$_{procedures}$predicate
and	predicate$f_{c,v}$,predicateq_v,volume$_{variable}$predicate
THEN	effort$_{implementation}$ predicate

In order to describe the models proposed by the different author we have to instantiate the predicates with the proper functions and values. Because of space restrictions this is avoided here. Nevertheless it must be noted that some estimation and prediction models can not be described by our approach, not because of the inappropriateness of rules, but because of the lack of calculation functions in those models.

4.4 Considering Views and Environments

Handling quality and productivity has some constraints and conditions. First, most models of software quality or productivity are applied within specific environments (i.e. life-cycle models) and for particular purposes (e.g. for management, construction, validation). Second, every software project is unique therefore a model of quality and productivity has to be tailored to the particular needs of that project. And thirdly, a number of models have been proposed and more might be developed in future. As a result we might get a very large set of rules. In order to avoid an explosion of the rule system we have to have a very condensed rule representation mechanism. We therefore enriched the form the plain rules by a parameter part and a weight component. Enriched rules are of the form:

IF	condition part	**RANK**	weight part
or	condition part	**RANK**	weight part
THEN	action part	**ENVIRONMENT**	parameter part

Both the weight part and the environment component are used to reflect needs and interests. Weights are appropriate to define an ordering amongst rules to be used to decompose a quality factor or an objective. A parameter in the environment part indicates for which life cycle models, types of products and projects, and models of quality or productivity a rule is applicable. The general rule schema then is:

IF	condition part	**RANK**	weight part
or	condition part	**RANK**	weight part
...	...	...	
or	condition part	**RANK**	weight part
THEN	action part	**ENVIRONMENT**	parameter part
and		**LIFE-CYCLE**	parameter part
and		**PRODUCT TYPE**	parameter part
and		**PROJECT TYPE**	parameter part

An example is given by the following rule, defining software correctness:

IF	verification coverage	**RANK**	1.0
or	test coverage	**RANK**	0.75
or	inspection coverage	**RANK**	0.50
or	symbolic execution	**RANK**	0.25
or	reader test	**RANK**	0.25
THEN	correctness	**ENVIRONMENT**	$ENV_{something}$
and		**LIFE-CYCLE**	$LCM_{waterfall}$
and		**PRODUCT TYPE**	$PDT_{realtime}$
and		**PROJECT TYPE**	$PJT_{consort}$

According to this rule verification is of highest interest, then testing. It follows inspection and finally symbolic execution and reader test, both equally ranked.

Obviously, the rules are evaluated stepwise. First we extract all those rules for which all the environments predicates are valid. The resulting subset of the total set of rules defines the model we have to work with. For each remaining rule we try to satisfy the condition parts starting with the one bearing the highest rank. As soon as a condition part is fulfiled a rule evaluation stops.

4.5 Explication by Author

A rule describes a decomposition of goals and objectives or refinement of a quality or productivity factors. Each decomposition as well as each refinement needs to be justified in order to end-up with a well-defined YAQUAPMO model. On the other hand a definition in natural language text is associated to each item (regradless whether it is a leaf node or an intermediate node) in the model. This text is either the text as provided by the author of an quality or productivity factor or by constructor of the particular model. Thirdly an example is given for each item in order to provide some pragmatic information ad each level of decomposition and on each refinement layer. As result we have to extend the rule scheme and we get the following rule form:

IF	condition part	**RANK**	weight part
or	condition part	**RANK**	weight part
...	...	...	...
or	condition part	**RANK**	weight part
THEN	action part	**ENVIRONMENT**	parameter part
and		**LIFE-CYCLE**	parameter part
and		**PRODUCT TYPE**	parameter part
and		**PROJECT TYPE**	parameter part
EXPLICATION BY	author		
justification	justification	OF	DECOMPOSITION
definition	natural language description	OF	ITEM
example	set of examples		

The rule defining software validation is to be extended into:

IF	verification coverage	**RANK**	1.0
or	test coverage	**RANK**	0.75
or	inspection coverage	**RANK**	0.50
or	symbolic execution	**RANK**	0.25
or	reader test	**RANK**	0.25
THEN	correctness	**ENVIRONMENT**	$ENV_{something}$
and		**LIFE-CYCLE**	$LCM_{waterfall}$
and		**PRODUCT TYPE**	$PDT_{realtime}$
and		**PROJECT TYPE**	$PJT_{consort}$
EXPLICATION BY	author		
justification	it's because ...	and	...
definition	ref to a text		
	or text itself		
example	ref to a project		
	or text of an example		

Using that rule scheme we are able to describe the construction of an YAQUAPMO model. Secondly, we can get an explication for each item in the model. Such an explication will be created form the author's definition text, the justification for the particular decomposition, one or more selected examples or from other parts of the rule. The is a potential for rule validation in the proposed scheme. Since the range of the rule is defined by the parameters environment, project type and product type and the definition is given by the authors text an inspection of the rules would detect missmatch as well as missing declarations.

4.6 Explanations for Reader

Explications, i.e. justifications, definitions and examples, are given from the authors point of view. For a particular application it might be difficult to make effective use of such descriptions, because the author has used a particular vocabulary. Therefore it is worthwhile to upgrade the information given by the author by an additional explanation, which can by used to (self-) instruct a designer of a quality or productivity model. An explanation might be dedicated to particular audiences, such as novices, occasional users, frequent users or experts. If we consider an explanation as a reader-specific ü̈pdateöf the explication, i.e. the justification, definition and examples, an explanation is to be represented by an explanation part, which might have the same structure as the explication part, but different contents.

IF	condition part	**RANK**	weight part
or	condition part	**RANK**	weight part
...	...	...	...
or	condition part	**RANK**	weight part
THEN	action part	**ENVIRONMENT**	parameter part
and		**LIFE-CYCLE**	parameter part
and		**PRODUCT TYPE**	parameter part
and		**PROJECT TYPE**	parameter part
EXPLICATION BY	author		
justification	justification	OF	DECOMPOSITION
definition	natural language description	OF	ITEM
example	set of examples		
EXPLANATION FOR	reader	type	
justification	justification	(upgraded by	instructor)
definition	natural language description	(upgraded by	instructor)
example	set of examples	(upgraded by	instructor)

If we have to provide explanations for different readers we have to add an explanation part for each type of reader. On the basis of these explanations we are able to define an explanation tour throughout the set of quality or productivity rules.

4.7 Rule Set Interrelations

Adopting the roman principle of *divede et impera* we have separated the decomposition of objectives, the definition of the quality or productivity factors and the description of the application. For each of which we have a specific set of rule. In order to make the approach coherent we have to describe the relations between these complementary sets, i.e. we have to define the interaction of the three rule classes. If we consider the objectives as the most important of the three set of rules a mapping of the objectives rules onto the factor rules and onto the the application rules brings the solution. This mapping is now defined in terms of a third category of rules, namely interrelation rules. Interrelation rules are of the general form:

IF	interrelate predicate 1	**RANK**	weight
or	interrelate predicate 2	**RANK**	weight
...	...	...	...
or	interrelate predicate n	**RANK**	weight
THEN	objective predicate	**ENVIRONMENT**	parameter
EXPLICATION	author **justification ...**	**definition ...**	**example ...**
EXPLANATION	reader **justification ...**	**definition ...**	**example ...**

IF	factor predicate	**and**	application predicate
THEN	interrelate predicate		

Since objectives are defined by the objective rules there is no need to have objective predicates in the condition part of this rule. As an examination of quality or productivity models shows there are no obvious relations between the objectives and the factors. Therefore both weights and parameters are independent in each rule set.

4.8 Objectives Factors Methods Tools Interrelations

If a project manager has to instrument a project he has to identify factors of quality or productivity, methods and tools to be used in the project in order to achieve the goals and objectives. Each problem domain (goals, factors, methods, tools) is defined and structured by appropriate rules.

Interrelations between these four sets of rules might be defined alternatively by one set of interrelation rules which define (or instrument) objectives in one step in terms of factors, methods and tools or by three independent set of rules. The second approach leads to a three step process. In the first step appropriate factors are selected for each particular goal. Methods are associated to each factor in the second step. And finally, methods are instrumented by tools.

The lead to the following structures for interrelations between goals, factors, methods and tools:

One Step Interrelations

First a basic version of an one step rule:

IF	(factor **and** method **and** tool) 1	**RANK**	weight
or	(factor **and** method **and** tool) 2	**RANK**	weight
or	...		
IF	(factor **and** method **and** tool) z	**RANK**	weight
THEN	objective predicate	**ENVIRONMENT**	parameter
EXPLICATION	author **justification ...**	**definition ...**	**example ...**
EXPLANATION	reader **justification ...**	**definition ...**	**example ...**

Three Step Interrelations

IF	of-interrelate predicate 1	**RANK**	weight
or	of-interrelate predicate 2	**RANK**	weight
...	...	...	...
or	of-interrelate predicate r	**RANK**	weight
THEN	objective predicate	**ENVIRONMENT**	parameter
EXPLICATION	author **justification ...**	**definition ...**	**example ...**
EXPLANATION	reader **justification ...**	**definition ...**	**example ...**

IF	fm-interrelate predicate 1	**RANK**	weight
or	fm-interrelate predicate 2	**RANK**	weight
...	...	...	...
or	fm-interrelate predicate s	**RANK**	weight
THEN	factor predicate	**ENVIRONMENT**	parameter
EXPLICATION	author **justification ...**	**definition ...**	**example ...**
EXPLANATION	reader **justification ...**	**definition ...**	**example ...**

IF	mt-interrelate predicate 1	**RANK**	weight
or	mt-interrelate predicate 2	**RANK**	weight
...	...	...	...
or	mt-interrelate predicate t	**RANK**	weight
THEN	method predicate	**ENVIRONMENT**	parameter
EXPLICATION	author **justification ...**	**definition ...**	**example ...**
EXPLANATION	reader **justification ...**	**definition ...**	**example ...**

IF (	factor predicate 1	**RANK**	weight
or	factor predicate 2	**RANK**	weight
...	...	...	...
or	factor predicate m	**RANK**	weight)
THEN	of-interrelate predicate	**ENVIRONMENT**	parameter
EXPLICATION	author **justification ...**	**definition ...**	**example ...**
EXPLANATION	reader **justification ...**	**definition ...**	**example ...**

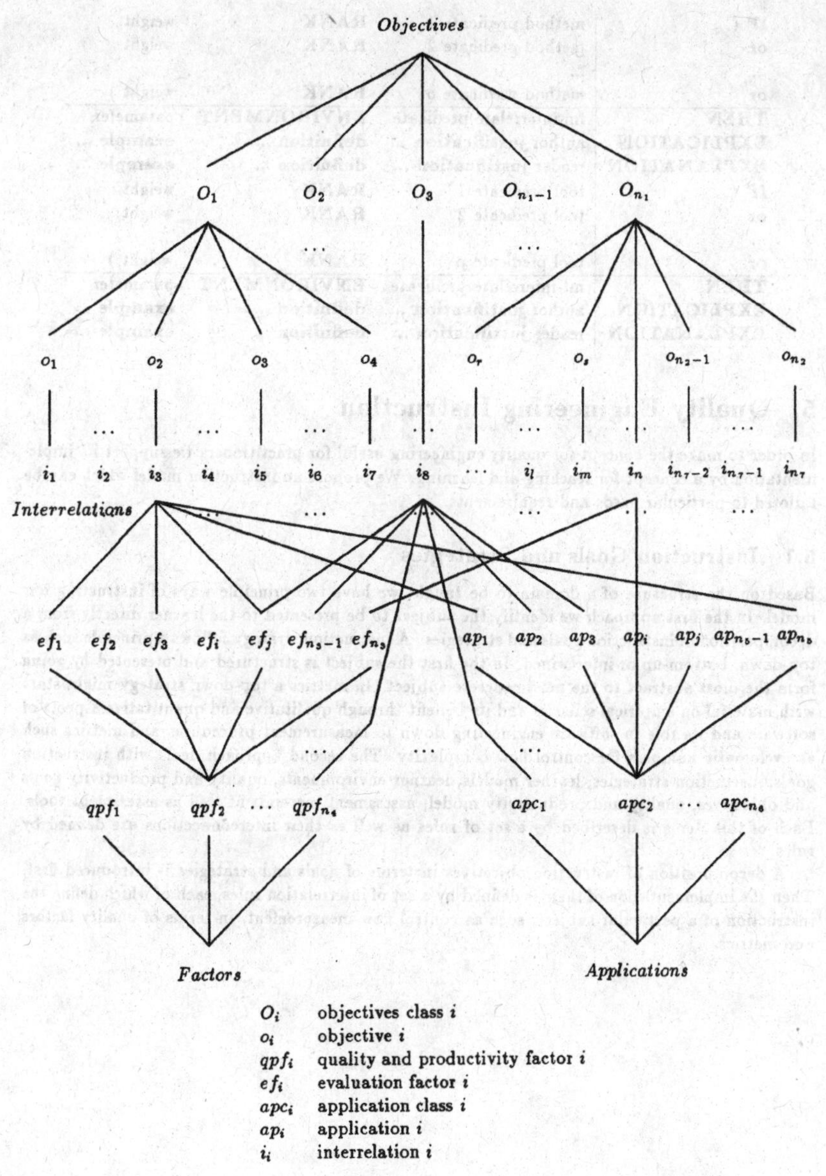

Figure 3: The Set of Rules

IF (	method predicate 1	**RANK**	weight
or	method predicate 2	**RANK**	weight
...	...	...	...
or	method predicate o	**RANK**	weight)
THEN	fm-interrelate predicate	**ENVIRONMENT**	parameter
EXPLICATION	author **justification ...**	**definition ...**	**example ...**
EXPLANATION	reader **justification ...**	**definition ...**	**example ...**
IF (	tool predicate 1	**RANK**	weight
or	tool predicate 2	**RANK**	weight
...	...	...	...
or	tool predicate p	**RANK**	weight)
THEN	mt-interrelate predicate	**ENVIRONMENT**	parameter
EXPLICATION	author **justification ...**	**definition ...**	**example ...**
EXPLANATION	reader **justification ...**	**definition ...**	**example ...**

5 Quality Engineering Instruction

In order to make the concept for quality engineering useful for practitioners we support its implementation by a concept for teaching and learning. We propose an instruction model which can be tailored to particular needs and requirements.

5.1 Instruction Goals and Strategies

Based on the structure of a domain to be taught we have two principle ways of instructing our model. In the first approach we identify the subject to be presented to the learner directly from a decomposition of instruction goals and strategies. A instruction strategy follows a principle such as top-down, bottom-up or intertwined. In the first the subject is structured and presented by going form the most abstract to the most concrete subject. In metrics a top-down strategy might start with material on empirical sciences and its benefit through qualitative and quantitative aspects of software and its role in software engineering down to measurement procedures and metrics such as cyclomatic numbers for control flow complexity. The second approach deals with instruction goals, instruction strategies, learner models, learner environments, quality and productivity goals and objectives, quality and productivity model, assessment methods as well as assessment tools. Each of this items is described by a set of rules as well as their interconnections are defined by rules.

A decomposition of instruction objectives in terms of goals and strategies is introduced first. Then the implementation of them is defined by a set of interrelation rules, each of which define the instruction of a particular subject, such as control flow measurement, in terms of quality factors and metrics.

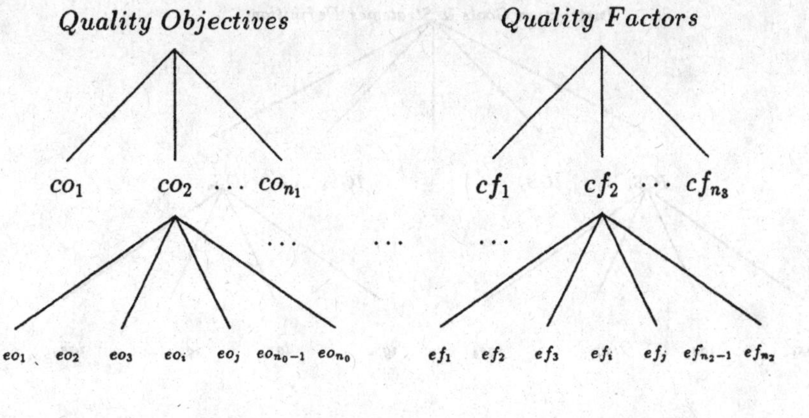

i_1 i_2 i_3 i_4 i_5 i_6 i_7 i_8 … i_l i_m i_n … i_{n_8-1} i_{n_8} *Interr.*

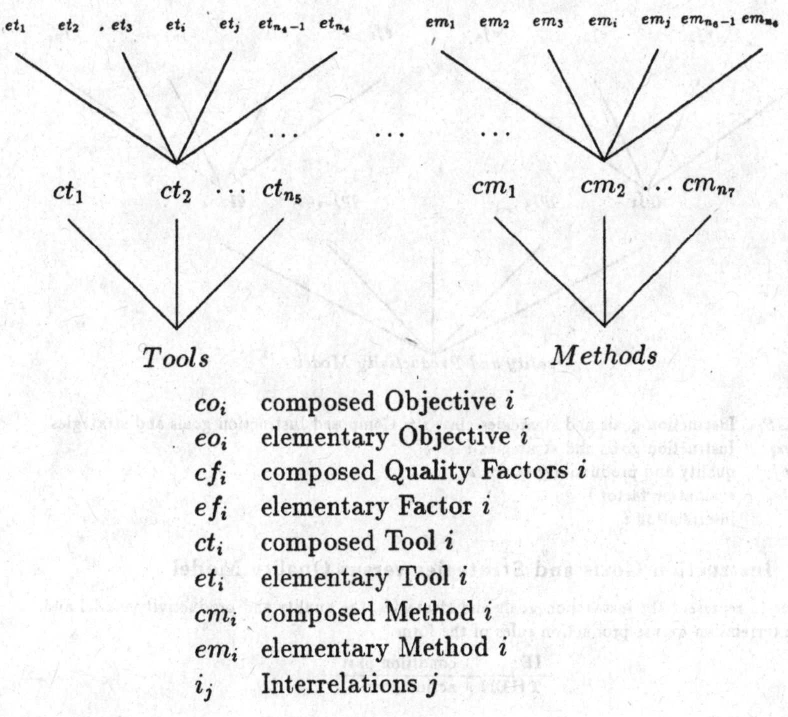

Figure 4: The Rules

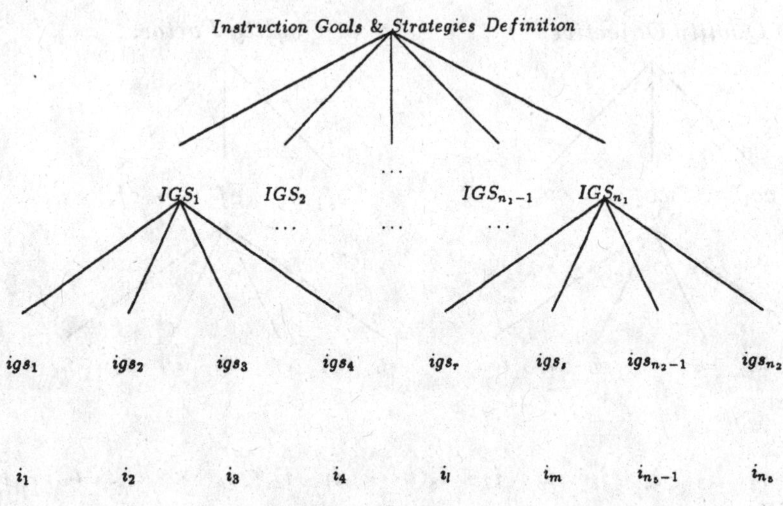

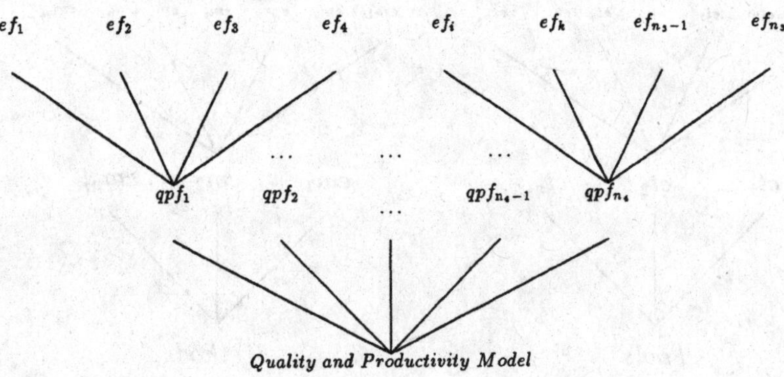

IGS_i	Instruction goals and strategies class i = Composed Instruction goals and strategies
igs_i	Instruction goals and strategies i
qpf_i	quality and productivity factor i
ef_i	evaluation factor i
i_i	interrelation i

5.2 Instruction Goals and Strategies versus Quality Model

In order to represent the instruction goals and strategies, the quality and productivity model and their interrelation we use production rules of the form

IF	condition part
THEN	action part

For instruction goals and strategies we get the following rule scheme:

IF	sub-instruction goals and strategies predicate
THEN	instruction goals and strategies predicate

Quality and productivity are defined by

IF	sub-quality predicate
THEN	quality predicate

INTERRELATION RULES

And finally we define the relation between instruction goals and strategies one one side and quality and productivity on the other side by interconnection rules of the form:

IF	interrelate predicate
	and quality predicate
THEN	instruction goals and strategies predicate

5.3 Representation of Instruction Goals and Strategies

IF	instruction goals and strategies predicate
and	subsub quality or productivity instruction goals and strategies predicate
and	sub quality or productivity instruction goals and strategies predicate
THEN	quality or productivity instruction goals and strategies predicate

In the context of McCall's model we obtain rules like:

IF	usability instruction goals and strategies predicate
and	integrity instruction goals and strategies predicate
and	efficiency instruction goals and strategies predicate
and	correctness instruction goals and strategies predicate
and	reliability instruction goals and strategies predicate
THEN	operation instruction goals and strategies predicate

5.4 Model Based Instruction

In order to achieve more flexibility and general acceptability we now draw an instruction concept which comprises a

- instruction model,
- learner model,
- quality and productivity goals and objectives model,
- quality and productivity factors and metrics model,
- assessment methods model,
- assessment tools model and
- interrelations between them.

The first two models define the instruction technology whereas the later four models define the domain of the instruction, i.e. the structured subject of software examination, measurement and assessment.

Instruction technology and subject domain are interconnected by association rules. They are defining the implementation of instruction goals and instruction strategies for selected learner types which are working in specific learner environments. There are two ways in defining an implementation. In an one step approach the instruction objectives and strategies as well as the learner type and the learning environment are interconnected to the subject domain, i.e. to the quality and productivity goals and objectives, the quality and productivity factors, the assessment methods and assessment tools. A second approach implements instruction in two steps. Connecting the instruction model, which comprises instruction objectives and instruction strategies, to the learner model, which includes the learner type and the learner environment, constitutes step one. In second step the learner model is connected to the subject domain. Since we are not interested to restrict the design of instruction systems we provide the basic mechanisms to define the two approaches.

We obtain the following set of rules:

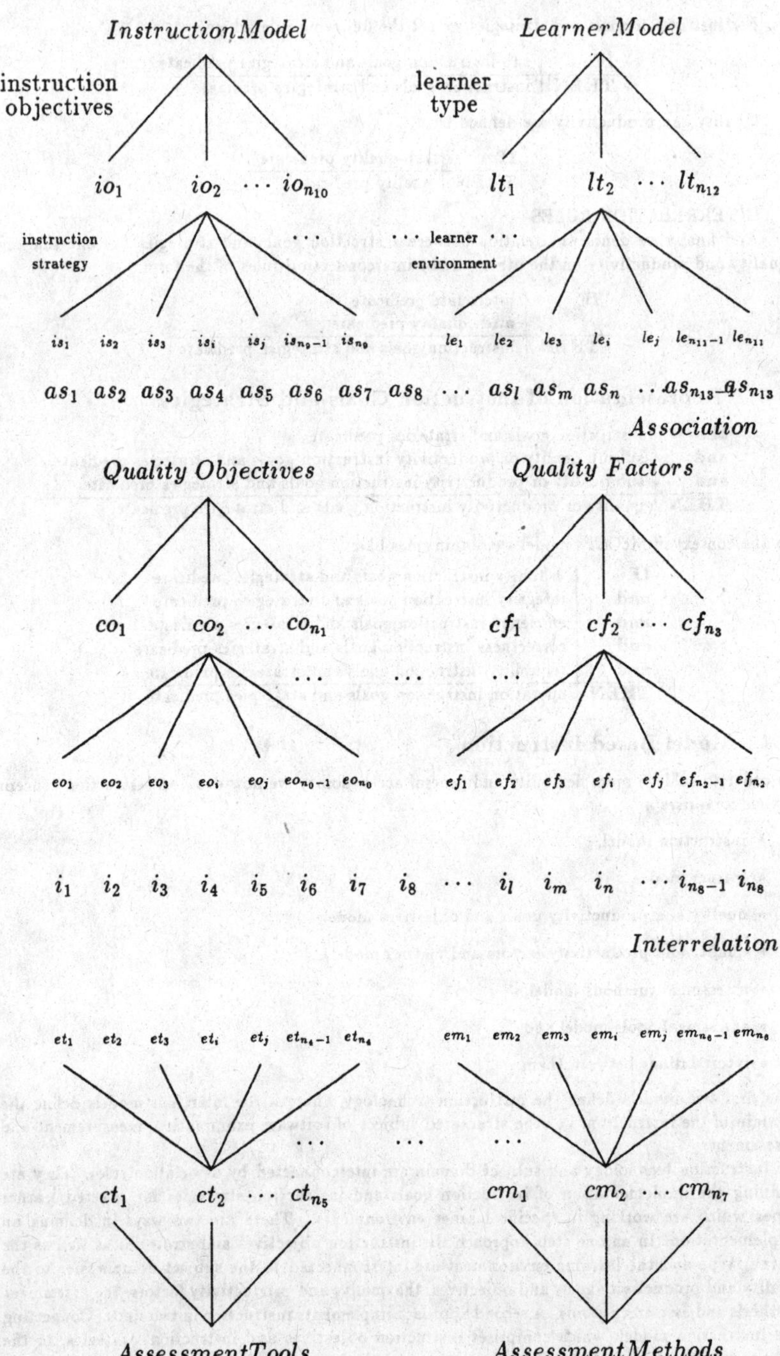

Figure 5: Instruction Learners Objectives Factors Methods Tools

io_i	instruction objective i
is_i	instruction strategy i
lt_i	learner type i
le_i	learner environment i
co_i	composed objective i
eo_i	elementary objective i
cf_i	composed quality factors i
ef_i	elementary factor i
ct_i	composed assessment tool i
et_i	elementary assessment tool i
cm_i	composed assessment method i
em_i	elementary assessment method i
i_j	interrelation j between objectives, factors methods and tools
as_i	association i of learner model and instruction model to tools objectives, factors, methods, tools, and to theit interrelations

Given the rules of model-based instruction a learner has the possibility to adopt and customize an instruction procedure defined by a particular instructor to his particular needs and requirements. Leaving the instructor defined rules as the backbone he can change or enhance the rules in all six models thus developing his individual instruction objectives and strategy as well as their implementation.

Using the model-based approach both an instructor and a learner are able to define guided tours through the subject domain, i.e. guided instruction, as well as direct access and ad-hoc touring of the subject domain, i.e. free traversal instruction. Moreover following the model-based approach it is easily possible to switch between guided instruction and free traversal or direct access learning.

6 Summary

We discussed the various software quality engineering techniques, including inspection, testing, verification, symbolic execution, measurement and assessment. Since these are heterogeneous areas of knowledge we had to search for a common representation scheme in order to be able to define interdependencies and interrelations. We selected production rules as the common representation scheme and introduced ranking weights and environment parameters as a means to keep the rule sets small. Quality objectives and goals are also represented by rules. Finally we defined a scheme by which the quality model can be presented to learners and users.

References

[Chri84] M.-L. Christ; W.D. Itzfeldt; M. Schmidt; M. Timm; R. Watts (Hrsg.) *Measuring Software Quality* Final Report of Project MQ, Vol. II, Software Quality Measurement and Evaluation St. Augustin, Manchester: GMD, NCC, 1984

[McCa76] McCabe, T. *A Complexity Measure* IEEE Transactions on Software Engineering, Vol. SE-2, No. 4, December 1976, S.308-320

[McCa77] McCall, J.A.; Richards, P.K.; Walters, G.F. *Concepts and Definitions of Software Quality* Factors in Software Quality, Vol. 1, Springfield, Va.: NTIS, Nov. 1977

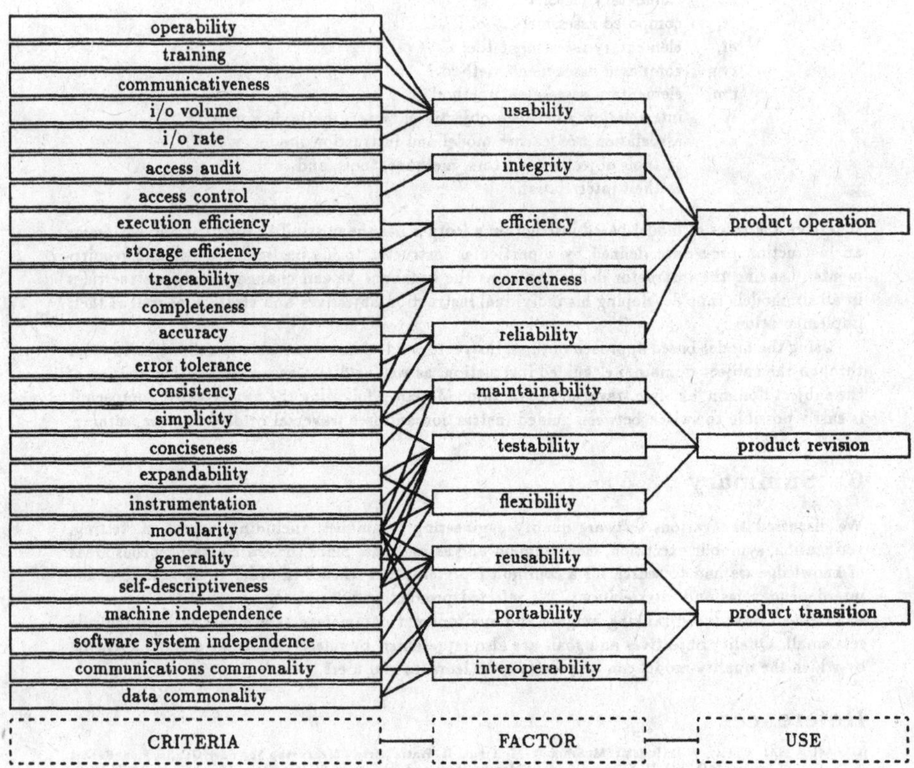

Figure 6: The Quality Model of McCall

5

ENGINEERING APPROACHES TO SOFTWARE DEVELOPMENT THE 90S

S G Stockman & M T Norris
British Telecom Research Laboratories,
Martlesham Heath, Ipswich, Suffolk, UK

ABSTRACT

This paper discusses how current R&D work in software engineering can be exploited to improve quality of software produced in the 1990's.

The paper starts with a very short review of current approaches to improving software quality. It then moves on to discuss how work in the areas of rigorous specification and design notation, development process frameworks, design reuse and measurement promise to improve the quality of the software development process by addressing some of the major causes of quality failure.

Underlying the thesis of this paper is the view that the reliability of the systems developed during the 90s will have to increase significantly, and indeed the ability to produce software of high reliability will be a major differentiating factor in the marketplace during the 90s. The European software industry must rise to this challenge if it is not to become increasingly vulnerable during the 90s.

INTRODUCTION

The central importance of software to all companies involved in information technology can readily be illustrated with a few telling figures (1).

• Software currently accounts for about 5% of the UK gross national product

• The proportion of IT costs due to software rose from 40% in 1980 to 80% in 1990. Further growth is expected over the next ten years.

• The European software market, currently at 40BEcu is set to rise to 60BEcu by 1993

In addition to these gross size figures, a number of strategic reports (2,3) have identified some key problems facing the industry, the main ones being:

• On average, software systems are delivered a year behind schedule

• Only 1% of software project finish on time, to budget

• 25% of all software intensive projects never finish at all

The effects of the above factors has been estimated, in cost terms, to be of the order of two billion pounds a year in the UK alone. The overall picture is of a costly area of technology, growing rapidly in which failures are rife. It would seem that there is more than sufficient cause for concern over the quality of software. The question is what can be done to achieve 'quality'.

The following list represents some of the current approaches to improving the quality of software development processes.

- Management discipline
- Defined methods
- Tool support
- Work station platforms
- More productive implementation languages
- Significant reliance on testing
- Quality assurance by review and audit
- Descriptive measurement
- Configuration management and product control

The impact and relevance of each of these is considered, briefly, below. The key point being highlighted is that there are many contributions - both technical and organizational - that affect software quality. Although all important, it is clear that no one approach provides a complete answer and the quality of significant software systems will become increasingly reliant on many diverse factors. Taking each item in the list in turn:

• Management Discipline

The introduction of a more disciplined approach to the management of the software product lifecycle has more than any of the other 'advances', probably been responsible for the bulk of improvements in software quality over the last decade. (4)

• Defined Methods

Increasingly, developers are making use of defined recognizable methods, and in many cases procurers are mandating the use of these methods in their software contracts. This in turn is leading to the development of audit requirements for the users of such methods. (5)

• Tool Support

Improved tool support, based largely on the availability of low cost, high resolution development workstations has greatly facilitated the use of diagram based design techniques. During the past few years the ergonomics of software engineering design tools has made considerable progress, so that the 80s has really been the decade when the dream of the electronic whiteboard has come to life. (6)

• Languages

Implementation languages have progressed considerably. 4GLs, object oriented programming languages and AI orientated languages are now available in robust implementations, although they are still not always viable as implementation vehicles for large developments, thence the continuing dominance of Cobol for large data processing applications.

• Testing

Software production, at present, is highly testing intensive. On the positive side, a more professional approach is being adopted to testing. (7) Measurement is being used extensively to determine the coverage of test scripts, management of the testing activity is being more systematically addressed and test tools are available which facilitate interactive testing. On the negative side, testing is a retrospective technique, which at best can facilitate quality control, but does not design the necessary quality into a system. As ever, a test can only positively determine the existence of a fault and not the correctness of a design or programme. This is a serous issue when working with complex systems and those which require high levels of reliability.

• Quality Assurance

Quality Assurance techniques are increasingly accepted as 'part of the furniture' of software development. This in itself is exceedingly encouraging, as long as the furniture is not allowed to gather too much dust (8). Most techniques depend on the informal application of the appropriate types of expertise, and are therefore very reliant upon individuals.

• Metrics
Measurement is increasing used by the major developers and producers of software systems (9). Management based cost and schedule measures are the most commonly used, with defect analysis being applied with increased rigor. The application of other quality measures, both as part of the specification process and final acceptance of the product is still not widely used.

• Quality Control
Ultimately, the current approach to software development is control orientated. We are becoming better at identifying when something is going wrong early in the lifecycle and thereby putting on the brakes and trying to put it right. The next decade must progress, however, towards the goals of quality improvement and quality by design.

THE CHALLENGES OF THE 90's

Whilst the techniques discussed above have undoubtedly led to significant improvement in the quality of the software development process, the sheer volume of software we are producing in our progress towards an information society, where we are increasingly reliant upon software controlled systems for the information upon which we make our decisions, should they be personal, commercial or administrative, clearly indicates that we cannot afford to stand still with respect to the quality of our software development processes.

Factors driving the need to improve include:

- Increased complexity of the systems we are developing
- Rapidly changing requirements
- Increased functionality of requirements
- More stringent non-functional requirements
- Higher reliability requirements
- Commercial survival

This list provides high level goals for what needs to be done in terms of improving software quality. These overall goals need to be linked through to the technical and procedural development that can enable them. There are a number of approaches to such prediction (all, to some extent, tentative) but there is reasonable consensus on areas that will play a major part in improvement. (10)

In the remainder of this paper we will discuss some of the R&D work currently under way which has the potential of addressing some of the main causes of quality failure in the software development process, and which therefore may contribute significantly to quality improvement during the 90's.

SOFTWARE TECHNOLOGIES FOR THE 90's

The following software technology areas are addressed in this paper:

- Design notations
- Development process frameworks
- Design reuse
- Front end measures

This is not meant to be an exhaustive list, and there are several notable areas, such as requirements capture, which this paper will not address, but which will undoubtedly have a major influence over our approach to software development in the 90s. The list will, however, serve to illustrate how current R&D work can be brought to bear on the very concrete problem of improving the quality of the systems we develop.

The product lifecycle, and we emphasize the word product here, for it is the product which is ultimately our main interest inasmuch as it satisfies the needs of our respective customers and thereby leads to our improved commercial well-being, has four main stages these are:

- Definition
- Design
- Delivery
- Operation

It is probably in the first two of these, the definition and design stages, that we have the greatest scope for the introduction errors, which subsequently manifest themselves, mainly in the operation phase, often an great cost.

The work we will concentrate on is concerned mainly with how we can improve the design phase of the process. Design is the main technical/innovative activity during the product lifecycle (though there are those who would argue that the operation phase often calls for even greater innovation either on the part of the user or the support staff). It seems likely that the greatest strides forward in the 90s will be in the design area (10).

A second theme covering the next four sections of the paper is the importance of transferring technological advances into the operational areas that will benefit most from them (11). This latter should not be underestimated, especially in a large company, as new ideas only show true benefit if they can be widely applied.

DESIGN NOTATIONS

The first approach involves the reduction of errors due to 'ambiguity', by using notations which are more precise. In Europe certainly, formal notations or methods have been portrayed in some quarters as the ultimate answer to the problems of software engineering as long as a decade ago (12). It is only now that the practical usefulness of these notations is becoming better understood. Whilst they are far from the ultimate answer, they do offer significant benefits in reducing the ambiguity in specifications and designs of the systems we are trying to develop. Hefty textural specifications are not an appropriate medium for the specification or design presentation of systems of relatively high complexity. Diagrammatic representations, where the syntax and semantics of the diagrams are ill defined are equally inappropriate. We are finding that as the complexity of systems increases, so we must turn towards more mathematically based notations for use in specification and design. Whilst these notations are already being used commercially in 'safety critical' applications, (13) there is increasing evidence that they are not also appropriate for non-safety critical applications and that there is not a significant, if any, cost premium involved in their use. Typically, it has been the case that extra time spent in specification is balanced by reduced time (and increased accuracy) in the testing phase. Specifications written in a mathematical notation provide a much sounder basis for the creation of system test scripts, and indeed there is now evidence that the process of test case generation may be able to be automated.

The use of these more mathematical notations has interesting implications for the review process. When one is reviewing a formal design or specification, it is possible to pose what-if questions to the presenter and from the specification or design, they will be able to demonstrate unambiguously what will happen under the circumstances you have postulated. This is a far cry from the less provocative review mechanisms currently in use. Again, experience of applying the techniques in 'typical' software projects has proved that a large number of errors can be trapped, even after a specification has passed the rough rigorous informal review.

Another major course of error during development is the transformation from one stage of design to the next. Currently this process is largely left to the individual designer with post checks being applied to ensure that they have performed the transformation correctly. The current approach is doubly suspect because often the initial representation is itself ambiguous and a very poor basis upon which to perform checks. The use of more rigorous notations at least removes much of the initial and final ambiguity, but it remains no small task to demonstrate that the two representations are in fact equivalent. In practice, formal refinement has yet to prove viable. Even so the use of more formal notations gives us a means, in theory, of overcoming some of the problem (14). One of the more pragmatic areas of experimental work being undertaken in this area is how to transform from Z specifications to functional languages in a correctness preserving manner and subsequently refining this functional language representation into a system meeting all of the non-functional requirements of the system (15). Whilst this work is still at an early stage, its success would ultimate lead to a much higher level of automation of the software development process, with associated improvements in productivity as well as reliability.

A more pragmatic approach to the introduction of rigorous into the development lifecycle involves making use of the current structured methods approach as a framework within which to fit rigorous notations, where this is considered advantageous.

An important advantage of using structured techniques as the basis for the introduction of formal notations, is that the user, who in this case is the design engineer, is familiar with the structured methods lifecycle, and is therefore less likely to be put off by the use of an unfamiliar notation.

DEVELOPMENT PROCESS

The principle of looking at the use of more formal lifecycles has wide implications when looking at quality management systems for software development. To date, most quality management systems in software development have been based on the waterfall model or some close derivative of it. Whilst this model has served us very will in the introduction of greater management discipline in the software industry, we are rapidly getting to the stage where there are a variety of lifecyles in use, which are not easily related to the waterfall model, and which therefore do not fit easily into quality management systems based on the waterfall lifecycle model. (16)

Examples of these include risk based lifecycle models, evolutionary lifecycles, object orientated lifecycles, refinement based lifecycles and reuse based lifecycles.

If we are to remain competitive, it is vital that our engineers are working with the most appropriate lifecycle for the problem they are tackling. It is equally vital that they are working within some form of common lifecycle framework. Current work in these areas is focusing on trying to establish a top level framework which will provide engineers with access to the range of design notations and lifecycle processes in a controlled fashion, whereby the most appropriate notation and approach can be selected at different stages of development across a range of systems.

This framework approach has significant implications for the approach to quality assurance in software development. Firstly, quality management systems will have to be evolved which are based upon the top level framework rather than a detailed instantiation of the framework, such as the waterfall model.

Secondly, this framework will provide a powerful platform for the development of a set of quality measures and tools which can be applied consistently across a range of software developments.

DESIGN REUSE

Possibly one of the key steps forward in the 90s will be the realization of higher levels of reuse within the software development process. As systems become more complex in terms of functionality, size, distribution and non-functional requirements, so we will no longer be able to take the 'start from scratch' approach to development (17).

A major barrier which will have to be overcome if reuse is to become a reality is that the focus of management performance, in terms of quality, cost and schedule, will have to be shifted from the individual project level, to the product level. At present, it would be a very brave project manager in most organizations who would expend effort in increasing the reusability of their design or code, as this often will lead to increased costs for the current development, even though it may in the long run lead to significantly reduced overall product line costs. In the same way that it has become accepted that many of the benefits of quality assurance and control costs are realized in the post development phase, the same mindset must be created when considering the benefits of reuse.

To support this process, we will have to develop measures of 'reuse', based upon those attributes of a design which we believe, contribute to reuse. Whilst the 'organizational' factor is an important one, there are several technical factors which have to be addressed. Perhaps the key one will be the realization that to achieve a high level of reuse, developments must be based upon stable architectures. This has already been demonstrated with examples such as the OSI stacks. It is unreasonable to expect components to be developed which can be readily be used across a range of architectures.

The issues of classification and retrieval have plagued software reuse. It was often said, that the main characteristic of a software reuse library was that they were the only libraries where everyone want to put things in, but no one wanted to take things out. But there are some shining examples of reuse libraries which have worked, notably in the scientific field. We believe one of the keys to success in overcoming the classification and retrieval problem will be the use of more formal notations to describe designs and components at appropriate levels of abstraction, coupled with formally defined architectures within which to use these components.

Of course, to realize reuse, it will be necessary to work within development process frameworks which are reuse based. In this sense, object orientated approaches hold out significant promise. In terms of the impact on quality, there are several implications:

Firstly, if significant proportions of systems are comprised of previously developed parts, the quality of those parts is likely to be higher than if they had been developed from scratch. This of course presupposes that the risks of incorrect selection or errors, when previously unrelated components are put together, is smaller than the risks of errors from developing from scratch. It is in this area that the use of more rigorous notations and formally defined architectures is of great importance.

Secondly, the component validation cycle time should be significantly reduced. This will become increasingly the case as firm interface standards emerge.

Thirdly, we will have to develop attribute definitions and measures for those attributes which either enhance or reduce the reusability of a design or a component.

Fourthly, we will want to develop meaningful measures of reuse.

There are obviously a lot of problems left unstated. For example, when a design is comprised of a significant proportion of reused components and an error is found, the developers will not have a high level of familiarity with many parts of the design, yet it is this very familiarity which often is the major element in allowing us to develop systems successfully at present. There are both technical and organizational factors that militate against the introduction of wide spread reuse. Nonetheless, the potential benefits are great and there is growing evidence that commitment to reuse is rewarded (18).

FRONT END MEASURES

Most measurement is currently focused on the back end of the lifecycle (e.g. an assessment of what has already been done). Yet, it is widely agreed that the main quality problems are introduced at the front end of the lifecycle (9). If measurement is meant to be a tool to support quality control, assurance and improvement, why the discrepancy.

The honest answer is that we find it easier to measure at the back end. The reason we find it easier is that we are dealing with more concrete objects. Code has relatively well-defined syntax and semantics. Counting measures are easy - there usually isn't much disagreement over what constitutes a code loop for example, even though there may be lots of disagreement over what use it is to measure them. So, whilst there remains the problem of interpretation at the back end of the lifecycle, we are at least happy in the knowledge that there are lots of things we can measure (19)

At the front end, the story is very different. Not only are we faced with the problem of interpretation: for example, what are the characteristics of a good design, but the notations which are used to describe specifications and designs are often ill-defined.

It is in this area that the use of more rigorous notation can be of significant benefit. When using a notation such as Z or LOTOS, then there are certain basic entities and constructs which can be meaningfully counted. In the case of LOTOS, it is possible to develop a graphical model of the state structure of the specification (20). In the case of a language such as Prolog, which has some potential as a specification language, it is possible to develop a graphical model of the clausal structure of the specification. The structural model in the case of a Z specification is not as obvious, though we have undertaken some interesting work in trying to model the scheme relations in a Z specification.

At this stage, it is not the detail of these measures which is of major interest, as the notations themselves have not been extensively enough used for an understanding of what constitutes a desirable attribute or an undesirable attribute to have been developed. The significant observation is that it is possible to derive well-defined measures of attributes as a direct consequence of the formal nature of the notation we are using.

CONCLUSIONS

This paper has described several lines of work in software engineering R&D which have the potential to improve the quality of the software development process in the 90s. The next decade is likely to be one of significant changes in the area of software engineering. As we move towards a more engineering based approach to software development in the 90s, so there will be an increased skill requirement for our development staff. The focus of software development activity will move away from implementation to design, coupled with an increase in the level of automation of the development process.

All of these trends are characteristic of a move from quality control approach to software development, to a quality improvement and quality by design approach. Whilst this holds out many opportunities for the European software industry, it also holds out many threats which must be faced if we are to survive and prosper into the year 2000.

REFERENCES

1) Hobday, J. Opening address Software Engineering 90 Conference (Brighton July, 1990)

2)"Software - A vital key to UK competitiveness UK Cabinet Office report ISBN 011 630829 X

3) Future impact of information technology BCS trends in IT series, ISBN 0901865478

4) Brook F The mythical man month

5) Norris, M. & Jackson, L., An engineering approach to system design Proceedings of Globecom 87, Tokyo (November 1987)

6) Tinker, R. & Norris, M. , Tools to support the design of systems, BT Technical Journal 4.3 (1986)

7) Graham, D. Software Verification and Testing Tools Proc Software Engineering '90 Conference (Brighton July, 1990)

8) Rigby, P., Stoddart, A. & Norris, M. , Assuring quality in software - practical experience of attaining ISO 9001 BT Engineering Journal **8.4**

9) Stockman, S., Todd, A. & Robinson, G. , A framework for software quality measurement IEEE Journal on selected areas of Communication, **3.2** Feb '90

10) Higham, R. et al, Technology prediction in software engineering Proc Software Engineering '90 Conference (Brighton July, 1990)

11) Raghaven, S. & Chand, D. , Diffusing software engineering methods IEEE Software **6.4** July 1989

12) Norris, M., The role of formal methods in system design BT Technical Journal **3.4** (1985)

13) Norris, M. & Stockman, S. Industrialising formal methods for telecommunications 2nd European Software Engineering Conf (Warwick, Sept 1989)

14) Martin, G., Norris, M. & Shields, M., The Interface Equation Mathematics Bulletin **25.4** (June 1989)

15) Sanders, P. et al, From Z specifications to functional implementations BT Technical Journal 7.4 (1990)

16) Kerola, P. & Freeman, P. , A Comparison of Life Cycle Models Proc 5th Int Conf on Software Engineering (San Diego, 1981)

17) Goguen, J. , Reusing and interconnecting software components IEEE Software February 1984

18) Tracz, W. Software Reuse : Motivators and Inhibitors Proc COMPCON S'87 (1987)

19) Todd, A. , Experiences in collecting and analysing quality metrics to appear in BT Engineering Journal, Summer 1991

20) Pengelley, A. , Software structure and cost management to appear in BT Technical Journal, June 1991

6

Limits to evaluation of software dependability

Bev Littlewood
Centre for Software Reliability, City University
Northampton Square, London EC1V 0HB, UK

Abstract

There is now a considerable body of work on the evaluation of software reliability, and it is often possible to obtain accurate estimates and predictions of reliability *and know that they are accurate*. Unfortunately, these techniques only work for relatively modest reliability levels. In the case of certain safety-critical systems, there is a demand for extremely high reliability to be assured against design faults, particularly those arising in software. In this paper we question whether it is possible to obtain such assurance, and examine various ways in which supporting evidence might be obtained. We show that none of the candidate approaches seems likely to be close to being able to provide assurance of dependability at the highest levels that are now being proposed for real systems.

> *As far as I can tell, "engineering judgment" means they're just going to make up numbers!*
>
> **Richard Feynman** [Feynman, 1988]

1 Introduction

This paper is about the *evaluation* of design dependability. More particularly, I want to investigate the limits to what can currently be measured. This work is prompted by a feeling that we are now building systems whose dependability requirements are so high that it is beyond the capability of present methods to validate them, and may be beyond the capability of all foreseeable methods.

Of course, the most dramatic examples involve computers systems in which *software* is required to have a very high dependability. But it would be a mistake, as we have seen, to view the problem as merely involving the distinction between hardware and software. Rather the issues centre upon the differences between failures due to design faults and those due to other, primarily physical causes

Conventional hardware reliability theory has been very successful in addressing the second of these [Barlow *et al*, 1975; Mann *et al*, 1974], so that we now have a good understanding of, for example, the life-time characteristics of physical components, and of the effect their unreliability has on overall system reliability. In particular, it is often claimed that we have ways of combining relatively unreliable components in ways which give very high overall system reliability. However, these methods essentially ignore the effects of design faults. Thus the 'solution' we sometimes hear to the software problem - 'build it in hardware instead' - is in fact no solution at all. If the 'it' is the same in each case, i.e. the same functionality is required, the problem of design dependability remains the same and we would have the same difficulty validating the 'purely hardware' system version. The difficulty arises in each case because the *complexity* of the systems is so great that we cannot simply assume that they are free of design faults, which would allow us to concentrate solely on the conventional hardware reliability evaluation.

It could be argued here, in favour of the 'hardware solution', that the discipline of building a system purely in hardware might serve as a constraint upon complexity and thus contribute to greater design dependability. The price paid, of course, would be a reduction in functionality. In fact, however, the tendency seems to be to move in the opposite direction: to implement as much as possible of the functionality in software in an expectation that this will minimise the 'hardware' unreliability. Ideally such trade-offs would be made quantitatively, but this is rare. Even in those circumstances where it is reasonable to use software to overcome a difficult problem with the unreliability of hardware, it is often accompanied by a decision to take advantage of the use of software to build a *more* complex product, providing more desirable functionality but at the risk of lower design dependability. This tendency to exploit the versatility of software-based systems, at the expense of greater complexity, is understandable in many routine applications where the benefits are demonstrable and the risks minimal, but it is more questionable in the safety-critical area.

It could be argued that there is nothing new in building systems upon which human lives depend, *and yet not evaluating their design dependability*. Indeed, many examples of serious system failure in which computer software is not a culprit appear nevertheless to be caused by design faults [Perrow, 1984], and these would not have been revealed in conventional 'hardware' reliability or safety evaluation. It seems likely that in such cases there was an unwarranted, and perhaps unconscious, assumption that the design was sufficiently simple that it could be assumed to be completely free of design faults. That this eventually turned out not to be the case, even for a simple design, emphasises the danger of assuming it to be true in the presence of high complexity. If we cannot assume that design faults will contribute *nothing* to the unreliability of the system, there seems no alternative to estimating the actual contribution they do make.

'Dependability' in this paper will be taken to mean, in the spirit of Laprie [Laprie, 1988], all those aspects of a system which allow someone justifiably to place dependence upon its use. These include, in an informal terminology, such things as reliability, availability, and security. For a safety-critical system, the most important aspect of evaluation concerns the dependability of the product in operational use. We are not, for example, likely to be satisfied with more general measures of 'quality', such as an estimate of the number of design faults in the product, or the number of faults per 1000 lines of code. Whilst such measures may have some bearing on the operational dependability, they are not sufficient in themselves to enable a user to arrive at a *measure* of operational dependability.

The precise way in which it is appropriate to express dependability requirements will vary from one application to another. In the case of reliability, with which we shall be primarily concerned here, the following are some examples:

- *Rate of occurrence of failures* (ROCOF). This would be appropriate in a system which actively controls some potentially dangerous process, such as chemical plant. It has been used as the means of expressing the reliability goal for the certification of flight-critical civil avionics, and in particular the manufacturers of the A320 fly-by-wire system are on record as stating that the reliability requirement for this system was a ROCOF no greater than 10^{-9} failures per hour [Rouquet *et al*, 1986].

- *Probability of failure on demand.* This might be suitable for a system which is only called upon to act when *another* system gets into a potentially unsafe condition. An example is an emergency shut-down system for a nuclear reactor. In the UK, the power industry rule of thumb is that such a probability of failure on demand can never be expected to better 10^{-5} for a system susceptible to failures resulting from design faults, particularly software faults. Such a figure would only be accepted in very special circumstances and a more usual limit would be 10^{-4} [CEGB, 1982a and 1982b].

- *Probability of failure-free survival of mission.* In circumstances where there is a 'natural' mission time, such as in certain military applications, it makes sense to ask for the probability of the system surviving the mission without failure.

- *Availability.* This could be used in circumstances where the amount of loss incurred as a result of system failure depends on the length of time the system is unavailable. Rather surprisingly, it seems to be the sole dependability requirement for the AAS (Advanced Automation System), the proposed new US air traffic control system [Avizienis *et al*, 1987].

These are meant to be examples only, and are by no means exhaustive: for example, the *mean time to failure* (or *between failures*) is still widely used.

More importantly, it should be clear from these few examples that selection of an appropriate way of expressing a dependability requirement is a non-trivial task. The measures above are obviously interdependent, and the selection of a particular one, or more, is a matter of judgment. For example, in the case of the air traffic control system, it would be dangerous to rely solely upon availability of the critical functions, without also being concerned about the precise way in which unavailability might show itself: a very infrequent occurrence of a fairly large down time is probably less serious than a frequent occurrence of very short down times, or simply of certain kinds of incorrect output. It might be better to be also concerned, therefore, with the *rate* of incidents rather than merely their contribution to total down time. In the case of the A320, the probability of safety-related failure during a flight is unlikely to be very strongly dependent upon the length of the flight, partly because the greatest chance of failure will be during landing and take-off (since more complex functionality is being called upon then), and partly because the consequences of failure during level flight are likely to be less serious. It may be more sensible here to express the requirement in terms of a probability of a failure-free flight: i.e. as a rate per flight rather than a rate per hour.

In what follows I shall not be concerned with these niceties about the way in which dependability requirements should be expressed. My concern is rather with the actual numerical levels, and whether we can reasonably expect to be able to say that a certain level has been achieved in a particular case.

2 The law of diminishing returns for fault removal

We shall consider here the direct evaluation of the reliability of a software product from observation of its actual failure process during operation. This is the problem of *reliability growth*: in its simplest form it is assumed that when a failure occurs there is an attempt to identify and remove the design fault which caused the failure, whereupon the software is set running again to, eventually, fail once again. The successive times of failure-free working are the input to reliability growth models, which aim to use this data to estimate the current reliability of the program under study, and to predict how the reliability will change in the future.

In the area of software dependability evaluation, this reliability growth problem is the most studied. There is an extensive literature, with many detailed models purporting to represent the stochastic failure process [Abdel-Ghaly *et al*, 1986; Musa, 1975; Jelinski *et al*, 1972; Littlewood, 1981; Brocklehurst, 1990]. Unfortunately, there is no single model that can be trusted to give accurate results in all circumstances, nor is there any way in which the most suitable model can be chosen *a priori* for a particular situation. Recent work, however, has largely resolved this difficulty, by providing methods of analysing the predictive accuracy of different models on a particular source of failure data [Abdel-Ghaly, 1986]. The result is that we can now apply many of the available models to the failure data coming from a particular product, and gradually learn which (if any) of the different predictions can be trusted.

Of course, the success of such a procedure depends upon the observed failure process being similar to that which it is desired to predict: the techniques are essentially sophisticated forms of extrapolation. In particular, if we wish to predict the operational reliability of a program from failure data obtained during testing, it is necessary that the test case selection mechanism is close to that which applies during operational use. This is not always easy, but there is some experience of it being carried out successfully in realistic industrial conditions [Currit *et al*, 1986].

It is also worth emphasising that, although we often speak loosely of *the* reliability of a software product, in fact we really mean the reliability of the product *working in a particular environment*, since the perceived reliability will vary considerably from one user to another. It is a truism, for example, that operating system reliability can differ greatly from one site to another. It is not currently possible to test a program in one environment and use the reliability growth modeling techniques to predict how reliable it will be in another. This may be possible in the future, since this is an active research area, but we currently do not even know how to characterise the 'stress' of a software environment so that we could relate one to another.

With these reservations, it is now possible to obtain accurate reliability predictions for software in many cases and, perhaps equally importantly, to know when particular predictions can be trusted: see [Littlewood, 1988] for examples using real software failure data. Unfortunately it seems clear that such methods are really only suitable for the assurance of relatively modest reliability goals. This can be seen by considering the following examples.

Table 1 shows some failure data which has been used quite widely in the literature. It shows the successive inter-failure times, in seconds of execution, for a command and control system. The data was collected during in-house testing, but this was conducted to reflect operational use. The data set is one of several collected by John Musa at Bell Labs [Musa, 1979], all of which are notable for the very great care taken during the collection exercise.

3	30	113	81	115
9	2	91	112	15
138	50	77	24	108
88	670	120	26	114
325	55	242	68	422
180	10	1146	600	15
36	4	0	8	227
65	176	58	457	300
97	263	452	255	197
193	6	79	816	1351
148	21	233	134	357
193	236	31	369	748
0	232	330	365	1222
543	10	16	529	379
44	129	810	290	300
529	281	160	828	1011
445	296	1755	1064	1783
860	983	707	33	868
724	2323	2930	1461	843
12	261	1800	865	1435
30	143	108	0	3110
1247	943	700	875	245
729	1897	447	386	446
122	990	948	1082	22
75	482	5509	100	10
1071	371	790	6150	3321
1045	648	5485	1160	1864
4116				

Table 1 Execution times in seconds between successive failures [Musa, 1979]. Read left to right in rows.

sample size, i	elapsed time, t_i	achieved mttf, m_i	t_i/m_i
40	5324	269.9	19.7
50	10088	375.0	26.9
60	12559	392.5	32.0
70	16185	437.5	37.0
80	20566	490.4	41.9
90	29360	617.3	47.7
100	42014	776.3	54.1
110	49415	841.6	58.7
120	56484	896.4	63.0
130	74363	1054.1	70.1

Table 2 An illustration of the law of diminishing returns in heroic debugging. Here the total execution time required to reach a particular mean time to failure is compared with the mean itself. The data is from Table 1, and the calculations used the Littlewood-Verrall model [Littlewood *et al*, 1973]. Similar results are obtained with other models.

Table 2 shows a simple analysis of this data. The calculations shown here are conducted sequentially in the manner that someone would use the software reliability growth models. At a particular stage in the testing the simplest question is 'how reliable is the program now?'; here this question is answered immediately following the 40th, 50th, . . , 130th failures. The answer could be framed in various ways: in this case, for simplicity, the *mean time to next failure* is calculated, here using the Littlewood-Verrall model to perform the calculations. Alongside the mttf in the table is the total execution time on test that was needed to achieve that estimated mttf.

Clearly, there is improvement in the reliability of this system, represented by an increasing mttf, as the testing progresses. However, inspection of the final column shows a clear *law of diminishing returns*: later improvements in the mttf are brought about through proportionally longer testing.

Of course, this is only a single piece of evidence, involving a particular measure of reliability (mttf), a particular model to perform the calculations (Littlewood-Verrall), and a particular program under study. Table 3 shows some failure data from a system in operational use, for which software and *hardware design* changes were being introduced as a result of the failures. Figure 1 shows the current rate of occurrence of failures (ROCOF) computed at various times in the history, using a different reliability growth model. The dotted line is fitted manually to give a visual impression of what, again, seems to be a very clear law of diminishing returns. It is by no means obvious how the details of the future reliability growth of this system will look. For example, it is not clear to what the curve is asymptotic: could one expect that eventually the ROCOF will approach zero, or is there an irreducible level of residual unreliability reached when the effects of correct fault removal are balanced by those of new fault insertion?

In both cases it is clear that, even if we could be sure that the system was going to achieve a particular very high reliability figure, the time needed to obtain this would be very high.

39	10	4	36	4
5	4	91	49	1
25	1	4	30	42
9	49	44	32	3
78	1	30	205	5
129	103	224	186	53
14	9	2	10	1
34	170	129	4	4
35	5	5	22	36
35	121	23	33	48
32	21	4	23	9
13	165	14	22	41
12	138	95	49	62
2	35	89	90	69
22	15	19	42	14
11	41	210	16	30
37	66	9	16	14
24	12	159	89	118
29	21	18	2	114
37	46	17	1	150
382	160	66	206	9
26	62	239	13	4
85	85	240	178	34
102	9	146	59	48
25	25	111	5	31
51	6	193	27	25
96	26	30	30	17
320	78	39	13	13
19	128	34	84	40
177	349	274	82	58
31	114	39	88	84
232	108	38	86	7
22	80	239	3	39
63	152	63	80	245
196	46	152	102	9
228	220	208	78	3
83	6	212	91	3
10	172	21	173	371
40	48	126	90	149
30	317	500	673	432
66	168	66	66	120
49	332			

Table 3 Operating times between successive failures. This data relates to a system experiencing failures due to software faults *and* hardware design faults.

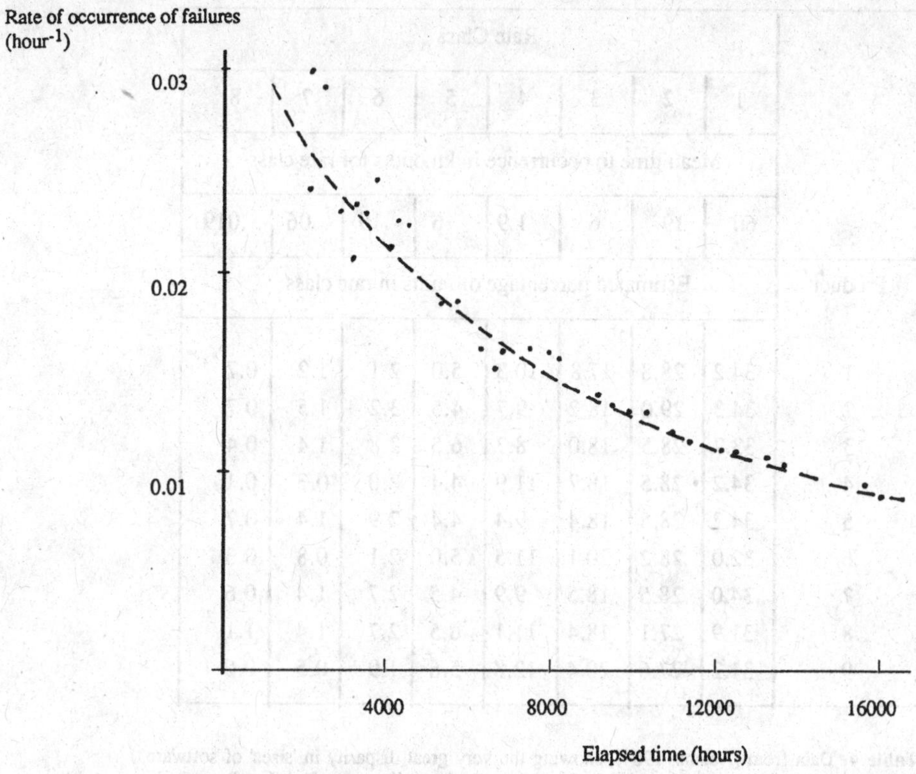

Figure 1 Successive estimates of the rate of occurrence of failures for the data of Table 2. The broken line here is fitted by eye.

This empirical evidence of a law of diminishing returns for debugging software, shown by these two systems, is supported by similar evidence from all other systems we have studied. There are convincing intuitive reasons for such results.

A plausible conceptual model of the software failure process, at least during operational use, is as follows. A program starts life with a finite number of faults, and these are encountered in a purely unpredictable fashion. Different faults contribute differently to the overall unreliability of the program: some are 'larger' than others. It is convenient to think of 'large' here as meaning that the *rate* at which the fault would show itself (i.e. if we were not to remove it the first time we saw it) is large. Thus different faults have different rates of occurrence. Table 4 shows a particularly dramatic example of this based on a large database of problem reports for some large IBM systems [Adams, 1984].

	Rate Class							
	1	2	3	4	5	6	7	8
	Mean time to occurrence in kmonths for rate class							
	60	19	6	1.9	.6	.19	.06	.019
Product	Estimated percentage of faults in rate class							
1	34.2	28.8	17.8	10.3	5.0	2.1	1.2	0.7
2	34.3	29.0	18.2	9.7	4.5	3.2	1.5	0.7
3	33.7	28.5	18.0	8.7	6.5	2.8	1.4	0.4
4	34.2	28.5	18.7	11.9	4.4	2.0	0.3	0.1
5	34.2	28.5	18.4	9.4	4.4	2.9	1.4	0.7
6	32.0	28.2	20.1	11.5	5.0	2.1	0.8	0.3
7	34.0	28.5	18.5	9.9	4.5	2.7	1.4	0.6
8	31.9	27.1	18.4	11.1	6.5	2.7	1.4	1.1
9	31.2	27.6	20.4	12.8	5.6	1.9	0.5	0.0

Table 4 Data from [Adams, 1984], showing the very great disparity in 'sizes' of software faults. Here size is taken to be the mean time it would take to discover a fault (or alternatively its reciprocal, the rate of occurrence of the fault). Adams classified the faults into eight classes according to their sizes, and the most notable aspect of the above figures is the very large differences between the 'largest' and the 'smallest. Perhaps most startling is that about one third of faults fall into the 60 kmonth class: i.e. a fault from this class would only be seen at the rate of about once every 5000 years!

For the reliability growth situation we have been considering above, we adopt a policy of carrying out fixes at each failure. Let us assume for simplicity that each fix attempt is successful (this assumption, whilst thoroughly unrealistic, does not affect the general thrust of the present argument). As debugging progresses, there will be a tendency for a fault with a larger rate to show itself before a fault with a smaller rate: more precisely, for any time t, the probability that fault A reveals itself before time t has elapsed will be smaller than the probability that B reveals itself before t, if the rate of A is smaller than the rate of B. Informally, large faults get removed earlier than small ones. It follows that the improvements in the reliability of the program due to earlier fixes, corresponding to faults which are likely to be larger, are greater than those due to later fixes.

Thus the law of diminishing returns shown in the two examples is a result of two effects which reinforce one another. As debugging progresses and the program becomes more reliable, it becomes harder to find faults (because the rate at which the *program* is failing is becoming smaller), and the improvements to the reliability resulting from these fault-removals are also becoming smaller and smaller.

It should be noted that these observations about the limits to the confidence we can gain from a reliability growth study are not in any way a result of inadequacies of the models. Rather they are a consequence of the relative paucity of the information available. If we want to have an assurance of high dependability, using only information obtained from the failure process, then we need to observe the system for a very long time. We shall look at this question more formally in the next section; suffice it to say here that no improvement in the predictive accuracy of reliability growth modelling will be able to overcome this inherent difficulty.

It might be argued, of course, that we generally do not need to rely solely upon the evidence of the failure process to gain confidence in a system. For example, we generally know a great deal about the software development methods used, or about the quality of the team of individuals who developed the system. We shall return at a later stage to the difficult problem of how such additional information might influence the confidence we have gained from direct observation of the failure behaviour of the system.

In the discussion above, there has been an implicit assumption that it is possible to fix a fault when it has been revealed during the test, *and to know that the fix is successful*. In fact, there has been no serious attempt to model the fault-fixing operation and most reliability growth models simply assume that fixes are perfect [Musa, 1975; Jelinski *et al*, 1973; Littlewood, 1981], or average out any short-term reversals to give the longer term trend [Littlewood *et al*, 1973]. It is fairly easy to incorporate the possibility of a purely ineffectual fix (simply introduce an extra parameter representing the probability that an attempted fix leaves the reliability unchanged), but the more realistic situation in which an attempted fix introduces a *novel* fault seems much harder and has not been studied to any great extent. At the moderate reliability levels for which the reliability growth models are designed, these problems may be of only secondary effect upon the accuracy of reliability estimates, but for a safety-critical application such an assumption would be rash.

The difficulty here is that the potential increase in unreliability due to a bad fix is unbounded. The history prior to the last failure, at least as this is used in current models, does not tell us anything about the effect of this last fix. Of course, in principle we could learn about the efficacy of previous fixes (although this would not be easy), and may be able to estimate the proportion of previous bad fixes. Thus we might take this proportion to be a good estimate of the probability that the current fix is a bad one. In order to have high confidence that the reliability was even as high as it was immediately prior to the last failure, it would be necessary to have high confidence that no new fault had been introduced. There seem to be no good grounds to have such high confidence associated with a *particular* fix other than to exercise the software for a long time and never see a failure arise from the fix. Eventually, of course, as the software runs failure-free after this fix, one would acquire confidence in the efficacy of the fix, and thus (taken with the earlier evidence) of the program as a whole. The question of what can be concluded from a period of failure-free working since the last fix is one we shall now consider in some detail.

3 Inferences to be drawn from perfect working

Consider the following imaginary scenario. You are responsible for the safety of a chemical plant which contains a particularly dangerous process. This process runs 24 hours a day, every day, and is controlled by a computer system. Although you have some concern about the reliability of the computer hardware, you are particularly worried about the effects of potential software failures. The vendor has used modern software engineering practices to create this software, but you do not know how these should influence your belief in the reliability of the final product they deliver. You therefore decide to discount all such information, and to base your decision as to whether it would be safe to deploy the product only on evidence which has been gathered during testing. You have some reservations about whether this testing is representative of operational use, but are prepared to suspend disbelief for the purposes of this analysis. You are told that the software operated without failure for 1000 hours in test. How confident are you about its future performance, and therefore its suitability for use in this safety-critical application?

This kind of information is the 'best news' it is possible to obtain from operational testing alone. Clearly, if there have been failures and (purported) fixes in the 1000 hours, we are once more in the context of reliability growth described earlier and our belief in the dependability of the software will be much more pessimistic.

My own interest in this problem arose in a context which involved both formal methods for the *achievement* of software reliability, and statistical methods for its *evaluation*. Several years ago I was a consultant to the 'Clean Room' project [Curritt, *et al*, 1986] at IBM Federal Systems Division, Bethesda, Maryland. The basic idea is implicit in the metaphor of the title: to create a software development environment in which it is difficult for faults to get into the software product in the first place. Thus the first stage of the 'Clean Room' involves the use of formal software development methods by the design team. These designers are not allowed to test the software (indeed, in the purest form of the 'Clean Room', they are not allowed access to computers on which to run the software!). Testing is the responsibility of a separate team whose main task is to create an environment which accurately reflects that which the software will encounter in operational use. Any problems encountered by this team are reported back to the design team, whose responsibility it is to provide solutions. An important feature of the 'Clean Room' is an attempt to concentrate the minds of the design team on 'getting it right first time': i.e. it is a methodology for the *achievement* of reliability. From our point of view the more important aspect is the careful attempt to create an 'operational environment' by the test team: from the failure behaviour of the software during testing in this environment it is possible to obtain an *evaluation* of its reliability in operational use.

This two part structure makes clear the separation of *achievement* and *evaluation* of the reliability of the software product: the formal design discipline is intended to ensure that the product will be reliable, whilst the testing scheme will enable accurate measurement of what reliability has actually been achieved. Experience of the 'Clean Room' methodology seems to demonstrate the efficacy of this separation of concerns, inasmuch as it seems to be a cost-effective way of obtaining acceptably high reliability together with measures of reliability which are shown to be accurate by later operational experience. However, in the early days, Harlan Mills, the leader of the project, posed the following interesting question: what if the 'zero-defect' design philosophy underlying the first part of the 'Clean Room' were to really work, and a program did not fail at all on test? How reliable could such a program reasonably be believed to be? Mills suggested that he would give a program which had survived failure-free for 1000 hours a 50:50 chance of surviving for a further 1000 hours. In the following we shall provide some formal support for this informal suggestion.

Let the random variable T represent the time to next failure of the program under examination, and let us assume that this program has been on test for a period t_0, during which no failures have occurred. Let us assume that the distribution of T is exponential with rate λ, and so has mean time to failure $\theta = \lambda^{-1}$. These assumptions are plausible, since we are interested only in the time to the first failure, and so do not need to be concerned about problems such as possible dependence between faults, one fault 'hiding' another, etc. In fact it is useful to think of the sequence of failures as a Poisson process, even though we shall only be interested in the first event.

We begin with the classical statistical approach to the problem, where we need to have a stopping rule for the testing. The obvious one is that t_0 is fixed and chosen by the experimenter. Thus the testing process runs until time t_o has elapsed, during which time the number of failures is represented by the random variable X. The actual value taken by this random variable, x, is recorded (in our case $x = 0$).

The classical statistical analysis then proceeds by using the data, x, to make inference about the unknown parameter θ (and so λ).

A conservative $(1 - \alpha)$x100% lower confidence interval for θ can be obtained by solving the following:

$$\exp(-t_o/\theta) = \alpha$$

that is

$$\theta_L = - t_o/(\ln \alpha)$$

Thus, for example, $t_o/3.00$ is a 95% lower bound, $t_o/9.21$ is a 99.99% lower bound, etc.

Notice that this classical approach is not primarily concerned with inference about T, the time to next failure. In fact such inference is a prediction problem, and the classical approach to prediction tends to be *ad hoc*. The usual thing to do if we wanted, say, an estimate of the reliability function

$$R(t) = P(T > t) = \exp(-t/\theta)$$

would be to simply substitute a maximum likelihood estimate of the unknown θ. This does not work here because the estimate is infinite. Alternatively, we could use

$$R_L(t) = \exp(-t/\theta_L)$$

$$= \alpha^{t/t_o}$$

as a conservative $(1 - \alpha)$x100% confidence bound on the reliability.

This discussion reveals several problems with the classical analysis. In the first place it is commonly the case, as here, that only approximate results can be obtained.

More importantly, there is the difficulty of interpreting a classical confidence bound. This problem is intrinsic to the classical view of probability which relies on the notion of repeatability. When we say $R_L(t)$ is the lower 90% confidence bound for $R(t)$, this must be interpreted in the following way.

Each time we conduct an experiment (in our case observe a program operating for a period t_o), the outcome (here the number of failures observed) is a random variable. That is, there is a chance that, if the experiment were to be repeated many times, there would be different outcomes observed on different occasions. Since $R_L(t)$ is a function of the outcome of the experiment, it also is a random variable. In our *single* experiment, therefore, we have obtained a realisation of this random variable. When we say that this realisation is the 90% lower confidence bound for the true but unknown $R(t)$, we mean that *if we were to repeat the experiment many times, calculating therefore many different values of* $R_L(t)$, *about 90% of these numbers would be smaller than the unknown true* $R(t)$. That is, when we talk about a confidence bound of this kind, our 'confidence' relates to the hypothetical calculated numbers which could be obtained from conducting many experiments. What we would like, of course, is for the 'confidence' to be about the unknown quantity or parameter which is of primary interest, here $R(t)$ (or, even better, T itself).

Finally, there is another serious difficulty about the interpretation of the bound: it is a confidence statement about something which is itself a probability statement (namely the true $R(t)$). There is no obvious way that these pieces of information about two sources of uncertainty can be combined to give us a single description of our uncertainty about the variable in which we are really interested, T.

One way out of these difficulties, albeit at the expense of creating some new ones, is to adopt a Bayesian approach to probability and statistics [de Groot, 1970]. The Bayesian analysis of our problem proceeds as follows.

Suppose that we have, in the most general case, seen x failures of the program during the period of testing t_0. The stopping rule turns out to be irrelevant in the Bayesian context (an advantage over the classical approach) and an application of Bayes' theorem gives the following posterior distribution for λ

$$p(\lambda \mid x, t_o) \propto p(\lambda).\ \lambda^x \exp(-\lambda t_o)$$

This posterior distribution can be thought of as representing our beliefs about the parameter λ after having seen the outcome of the experiment (i.e. x failures in the test of length t_o), whereas the prior distribution, $p(\lambda)$, represents our beliefs before seeing these data. Thus the use of Bayes theorem above shows how our *a priori* belief changes into our *a posteriori* belief via use of the *likelihood function* for the evidence we have obtained from the experiment, here proportional to $\lambda^x \exp(-\lambda t_0)$ because of the assumption of a Poisson process.

Notice that we can here make probability statements about λ itself. That is, we can make confidence statements about this parameter expressed as probability statements in which the parameter of interest is a random variable. This contrasts with the rather contrived interpretation of a confidence statement in the classical context, which must invoke an ensemble of experiments which *could hypothetically* have been performed, and which treats the quantity calculated from the data as the sole random variable about which confidence is being expressed. This advantage of the Bayesian approach becomes even more clear as we go on to obtain probability statements about T, the time to next failure.

To proceed further, we need to formalise the representation of our prior belief about λ, i.e. we need to decide on a form for $p(\lambda)$ above. There are good arguments [deGroot, 1970] that this should be chosen from the *conjugate family* of distributions: this is the parametric family of distributions which has the property that both posterior distribution and prior will be a member of the same family. The informal idea is that there should be a certain homogeneity in the way in which our beliefs change as we acquire more evidence about the unknown rate parameter λ. Under conjugacy, such changes are represented solely by changes in the values of the hyper-parameters of the conjugate family.

The conjugate family here is the gamma, $\Gamma(\alpha, \beta)$ where $\alpha, \beta > 0$. If we let $\Gamma(a, b)$ represent our prior belief (for some suitable choice of a, and b), it is easy to show that our posterior belief about λ, $p(\lambda \mid x, t_0)$, is represented by $\Gamma(a + x, b + t_0)$. We are now in a position to make probability statements about λ, and these are exact. More importantly, we can proceed to make probability statements about T itself:

$$p(t \mid x, t_0) = \int p(t \mid \lambda)\, p(\lambda \mid x, t_0)\, d\lambda$$

$$= \frac{(a + x)(b + t_0)^{a + x}}{(b + t_0 + t)^{a + x + 1}}$$

which is a Pareto distribution. It follows that the reliability function is

$$R(t \mid x, t_0) = P(T > t \mid x, t_0)$$

$$= \left(\frac{b + t_0}{b + t_0 + t}\right)^{a + x}$$

and in our case, when $x = 0$,

$$= \left(\frac{b + t_0}{b + t_0 + t}\right)^{a}$$

It is important to emphasise how this Bayesian approach overcomes the difficulties of the classical analysis which were discussed above. In the first place, everything here is formally exact.

More importantly, we have 'natural' interpretations of the quantities of interest. Thus the beliefs we have about T, the time to next failure in operational use, are expressed as probability statements about T, not about some other random variable as is the case in the classical context. Also, the probability statements here genuinely reflect our subjective belief about the actual single time to next failure which we can eventually observe, rather than relating to the hypothetical ensemble of repetitions of the experiment which has to be invoked in the classical case.

The naturalness of the Bayesian method is, however, bought at some price. Its subjective nature forces the user to describe formally his or her prior belief about the parameter(s); in our case this means a choice of the hyper-parameters a and b. However, it is rarely the case that we do not have some prior belief about the problem under study, and in this example it is possible to think of various sources for such belief: experience of developing similar software systems in the past, previous experience of the efficacy of the software development methodology used, etc. It must be admitted that eliciting such subjective prior belief from people in order to arrive at values for a and b is a non-trivial exercise, although there has been some recent progress in semi-automatic elicitation procedures .

It is often tempting to try to avoid the difficulty of selecting values of hyper-parameters of the prior distribution to represent 'your' beliefs, by devising instead a prior distribution which represents 'total ignorance'. Unfortunately this is fraught with difficulties. One argument here runs as follows. Since $\Gamma(a + x, b + t_o)$ represents our posterior belief about the rate, *large* parameter values represent beliefs based on considerable data (i.e. large x, t_o). To represent initial ignorance, therefore, we should take a and b as small as possible. Now $\Gamma(a, b)$ exists for all $a, b > 0$. If we take a and b both very small, the posterior distribution for the rate is approximately $\Gamma(x, t_o)$, with the approximation improving as $a, b \rightarrow 0$. We could therefore informally think of $\Gamma(x, t_o)$ as the posterior in which the data 'speak for themselves'.

This argument is fairly convincing if we are to see a reasonable amount of data when we conduct the data-gathering experiment. Unfortunately it breaks down precisely in the case in which we are interested here: when $x = 0$ the posterior distribution for the rate is proportional to λ^{-1} and is thus improper. Worse, the predictive distribution for T is also improper, and is thus useless for prediction.

Here is a possible way forward. Choose the 'pessimistic' but improper prior

$$p(\lambda) \equiv 1$$

giving the posterior

$$p(\lambda \mid 0, t_o) = t_0 \exp(-\lambda t_o)$$

which is a proper distribution. More importantly, the predictive distribution for T is also proper:

$$p(t \mid 0, t_o) = \int p(t \mid \lambda)\, p(\lambda \mid 0, t_o)\, d\lambda$$

$$= t_o / (t_o + t)^2$$

which is again Pareto. The reliability function is

$$R(t \mid 0, t_o) \equiv P(T > t \mid 0, t_o)$$

$$= t_o / (t + t_o)$$

which brings us full circle to a 'justification' for the conjecture of Harlan Mills: when we have seen a period t_o of failure-free working there is a 50:50 chance that we shall wait a further period exceeding t_o until the first failure, since $R(t_o \mid 0, t_o) = 1/2$.

It follows that if we want the posterior median time to failure to be 10^9 hours, which is about the same order of magnitude claimed for the Airbus A320 fly-by-wire system reliability, we would need to see 10^9 hours of failure-free working!

I have treated this example in some detail because it shows the great gap that exists between the levels of dependability that are often required for a safety-critical system, and that which can reasonably be inferred solely from observation of operational use of the system. Perhaps more important than these observations about the implications for an 'ignorant' observer, who is willing to take note only of observed operational behaviour of the system, is how the full Bayesian analysis shows clearly the two sources of final confidence in the system dependability. Firstly there is the prior belief of the observer (represented by the prior distribution, $\Gamma(a, b)$), secondly the likelihood function representing what was actually observed of the system failure behaviour. The relative paucity of information we can gain from the latter suggests that, to obtain an assurance of very high dependability, an observer must start with very strong *a priori* beliefs. We shall now consider briefly sources for such beliefs, and whether they can make a sufficient contribution to the final confidence in a system that we can justifiably claim that it has an ultra-high dependability.

4 Indirect sources of confidence in dependability

We have seen that if we are only prepared to take into account the evidence of actual operational behaviour, obtained over a practically feasible length of test, we shall end up with a figure for system dependability which may be several orders of magnitude worse than that needed. Can this gap be closed by using other information that may be available about the system?

It seems reasonable to expect that a safety-critical system will at least be developed using 'good practice'. Unfortunately, there is little hard scientific evidence available about the relationship between choice of software development methodologies and the resulting product dependability. Even if such evidence were available, it seems to me that its contribution to our confidence in a particular product would fall far short of what is needed. One difficulty is that such information is generic: it tells us what might be expected *on average* from the adoption of a particular methodology. The actual effectiveness is likely to vary considerably from one application to another.

We face here a problem about the nature of evidence very similar to that in the previous section: what can we infer about a particular product even when we know that it has been developed using a methodology that has *always* been 'successful' in the past? can we assume that the present application of the methodology has been successful? One way in which these questions can be formalised (at the price of some loss of realism) is as follows. Assume that n products have been developed using the methodology in the past, and that these were in some sense 'similar', so that the chance of the methodology being an appropriate one is constant. Assume further that all n were developed independently of one another, with each development having a probability p of being successful ('success' might be defined as surviving a certain specified long time without failure in operational service). Clearly this is a classical Binomial probability set-up: we are observing the number of successes, x, in n independent trials where the probability of success in a particular trial is p. We now want to carry out another trial, i.e. apply the methodology to a further development. What can we say about the chance of success in the light of our having observed $x = n$ in the first n trials? Although there is no 'correct' answer to this question, here is one way forward in the Bayesian framework. Assume that our prior belief about p is represented by the conjugate prior distribution, which is the Beta distribution, $\beta(a, b)$. This gives a posterior distribution $\beta(a+x, b+n-x)$, and so the Bayes estimate of p for a squared error loss function is the posterior mean, $(a+x)/(a+b+n)$. If we take the prior to be the uniform distribution, i.e. $a = b = 1$, we get the Bayes estimate to be $(x+1)/(n+2)$. In our case, where $x = n$, we get $(n+1)/(n+2)$.

The many assumptions which go to obtain this result can be questioned in detail, but I think that, as in the previous section dealing with a system which has not failed, the example of a formal analysis gives an indication of the difficulty. Even if we have seen only evidence of efficacy of a methodology, it would be dangerous to draw a very strong conclusion about what might happen if we apply it one more time. Certainly it would clearly be wrong to assume that the probability of success is one: to conclude that we *cannot* see a failure, merely because we have not yet seen a failure, is far too optimistic. If a practitioner disagrees with the analysis above, which gives the result $(n+1)/(n+2)$, in particular if he feels more confident than this result suggests, it is incumbent upon him to justify his belief in a similar formal way. This could be done, for example, by stating his prior beliefs in the form of a distribution; as before, it would be necessary to have very strong prior beliefs in order to justify very strong posterior beliefs in the face of evidence of this kind.

Formal methods of system development, and even formal verification of the final product, have been suggested as likely candidates for achieving and assuring high dependability in safety-critical systems [MoD 1989a, 1989b]. Here again, there is little scientific support for their absolute efficacy, or even their cost-effectiveness in competition with other procedures, and advocates of their use usually appeal to the 'obvious' need for mathematical rigour. Such appeals carry some force as a justification for arguing that the methods may be necessary, but they fall far short of justifying their sufficiency. Even if formal methods are eventually demonstrated, by case studies and experiment, to be effective for the achievement of high dependability, this still does not help with the evaluation problem. At best we shall face the problem we had earlier with general 'good practice': how to argue powerfully for the particular when we only have statistical evidence of the general.

Even a full formal verification does not allow us to claim very much for the overall dependability of the product. If we can trust the verification, we shall know that a certain class of implementation faults are not present. But we shall still worry that failures can occur because the formal specification does not accurately represent the informal requirements.

This distinction between the formal specification and the informal requirement is a particularly important one in the safety-critical context. In more mundane applications, a system developer may reasonably defend himself against the disgruntled user, who claims that his requirements have not been met, by arguing that these requirements were not spelled out in the specification (although such a defence may have no legal standing). Even in the case of a safety-critical system, it is possible that the responsibility for the specification does not lie with the system developer, and it would then be reasonable for him to adopt a similar defence. In the case of the *evaluator* of the system, however, it would be most unreasonable to ignore safety-related events stemming from the specification. Faults which compromise safety, even in ways which were not foreseen at the time the system was built, must contribute to his judgment of dependability. The point is that our notion of safety is a very general one which will often benefit from hindsight (e.g. the recognition in testing or operational use that the specification was deficient). There is usually no disagreement that a system which has killed people *should* not have behaved in that way, whereas, on the other hand, apparent departures from expected non-critical functionality can be a source of genuine contention.

In practice, of course, it is precisely those unforeseen deficiencies of the specification which present the greatest difficulty to the evaluator of the safety of a system. A formal verification against the formal specification does not contribute in any way to our confidence in the rightness of that specification.

One candidate methodology for overcoming these problems is fault tolerance through design diversity; N-version programming [Avizienis, 1985] and recovery blocks [Randell, 1975; Anderson *et al*, 1981] are the best known approaches. The intention here is that two or more versions are developed by different teams in the hope that faults will tend to be different and so failures can be masked by a suitable adjudication mechanism at run time. The concept owes much to the hardware *redundancy* idea, where several similar components are in parallel. In the hardware analogy, it is sometimes reasonable to assume that the stochastic failure processes of the different components in a parallel configuration are *independent*. In such a case it is then possible to compute the reliability of the redundant system as a function of the reliabilities of its component parts and the organising structure. As long as this independence assumption holds, it is easy to show that a system of arbitrarily high reliability can be constructed from arbitrarily unreliable components.

In practice, of course, the independence assumption is often unreasonable even for hardware: components tend to fail together as a result of common environmental factors, for example. In the case of design diversity, such an assumption of complete independence in the failure processes of the different versions seems completely implausible on intuitive grounds. Recent experiments [Knight *et al*, 1986; Bishop *et al*, 1986; Anderson *et al*, 1985] suggest that, whilst design diversity does bring benefits in increased reliability compared with single versions, these benefits are very much less than a naive assumption of completely independent failure behaviour would suggest. One reason for this is that some faults are present in more than one version. Another reason comes from some recent theoretical work [Eckhardt *et al*, 1985; Littlewood *et al*, 1989] where it is proved that, even if the different versions really are independent objects (a precise definition of this is given), they will still fail dependently as a result of variation of the 'intrinsic hardness' of the problem over the input space. Put simply, the failure of version A on a particular input suggests that this is a 'hard' input, and thus the probability that version B will also fail on the same input is greater than it otherwise would be. The greater this variation of 'hardness' over the input space, the greater will be the dependence in the observed failure behaviour of versions.

These results suggest that we certainly cannot calculate the reliability of the fault tolerant system by simply *assuming* independence of failure behaviour for component versions. We therefore have no alternative to trying to estimate the degree of dependence in a particular case. It is easy to see that if we wish to try to measure this directly, by observing the operational behaviour of the system, we are reduced to the 'black-box' estimation problem that has already defeated us [Miller, 1989]. If we wish to estimate it indirectly, via evidence of the degrees of version dependence obtained in operational use from previous projects, we are once more in the same difficulties we have seen earlier: quite extensive experience of successfully achieving low version dependence does not allow us to conclude that we shall be almost certain to succeed in the present instance.

5 Discussion

I have tried to show in the previous sections how difficult it is to obtain confidence that a system has achieved ultra-high dependability. Direct evaluation from observation of test or operational behaviour will fall several orders of magnitude short, for example, of the 10^{-9} failures/hour required of the Airbus A320 fly-by-wire system. Indirect appeals to knowledge of the past efficacy of development processes, or fault tolerant architectures, seem equally problematical. *A rational person should therefore conclude in such a case, I believe, that the actual dependability of the system is several orders of magnitude worse than is required.* Such a conclusion has serious implications for builders and users of safety-critical systems.

It should be emphasised that these results do not mean that such numbers for required dependability are *meaningless*. The Airbus figure represents a probability of about 0.1 that at least one such failure will occur in a fleet of 1000 aircraft over a 30 year lifetime [Miller, 1989]; since this safety-critical system is likely to be one of many on the aircraft, such a probability does not seem an unreasonable requirement. Nor is it the case that we could expect to do significantly better with improved mathematical and statistical techniques. Rather, the problem is one concerning basic limitations in the extensiveness of evidence: informally, in order to believe in these very high dependability levels we need more evidence than could reasonably be expected to be available.

Is there a way out of this impasse? One approach would be to acknowledge that it is not possible to confirm that a sufficiently high, numerically expressed reliability had been achieved, and instead make a decision about whether the delivered system is 'good enough' on different grounds. This appears to be the approach adopted for the certification of safety-critical avionics for civil airliners [RTCA, 1985]:

> ". . techniques for estimating the post-verification probabilities of software errors were examined. The objective was to develop numerical requirements for such probabilities for digital computer-based equipment and systems certification. The conclusion reached, however, was that currently available methods do not yield results in which confidence can be placed to the level required for this purpose. Accordingly, this document does not state post-verification software error requirements in these terms."

Even if we charitably interpret 'post-verification probabilities of software errors' to mean software failure rate, this is a surprising passage to find in such a document. It seems to mean that a very high level is *required* but that, since achievement of such a level cannot be assured in practice, some other method of certification will be adopted, *with the implication that this certification will not give confidence that the required level was met.* The remainder of the document supports this view, inasmuch as it merely gives guidelines to 'good practice' and documentation, which as we have seen fall far short of providing the assurance needed.

It might be argued that such an approach is not new. The *design* reliability of hardware systems has traditionally not been evaluated as part of certification procedures: reliability estimation has instead referred only to physical failures. Sometimes such a view was reasonable, since the complexity of the design was low and it could be plausibly argued that it was 'almost certainly' correct. In addition, there was often a fairly slow evolution of design from one product to another, so that confidence about design dependability could be carried over.

These conditions do not apply to software systems. Typically, for example, when a software-based system is used to replace the functionality of an existing purely hardware system, the new system provides more functionality and is much more complex. Thus the fly-by-wire A320 control system does not merely reproduce the somewhat limited functionality of conventional control systems, but provides extra functions such as automatic flight envelope protection. Since it would be quite wrong to assume that a design of this complexity was correct, the manufacturers quite properly demand that the total system failure rate, *including the effects of software design faults*, should be no worse than 10^{-9} per hour. The problem then, of course, is that there is no way that achievement of this requirement can be demonstrated.

Are there other ways than evaluation of achieved reliability (with respect to an appropriate class of failures) which might reasonably provide assurance that a system is safe enough to use? McDermid [1990] argues that assurance derived from 'comprehension of, and diversity in, the complete procurement process . .' is *more* fundamental than reliability. But his argument seems to depend on an acknowledged, but unquantified, relationship between reliability and such assurance: that a higher level of assurance implies greater reliability. Certainly it seems reasonable to believe that, all other things being equal, one would prefer *on reliability grounds* a product in which one had the highest level of assurance in this sense. But merely knowing that reliability increases with assurance is not sufficient to allow us to decide whether a particular level of reliability has been achieved by having a certain level of assurance. This is once again the issue of 'process' evidence discussed earlier.

It seems to me that decisions about whether safety-critical systems are 'good enough' can only be taken rationally in a framework where risks can be compared with benefits. Evaluation of risks must entail (among other things) reliability with respect to classes of safety-related events, e.g. rates of occurrence of failures. If this is not done explicitly, then it is being done implicitly. Whether the latter is acceptable will to some extent depend on the magnitudes of risks and benefits involved, as well as social and political factors. In the case of safety-critical software in automobiles, for example, an implicit procedure may be acceptable: typically small numbers of deaths are involved in individual incidents, there seems to be a social tolerance of a fairly large attrition rate for such transport, and it might be expected that design faults would be discovered (and fixed) quite quickly in operational use. For a nuclear reactor emergency shut-down system, on the other hand, such conditions do not apply, and a single incident could be catastrophic, killing thousands of people. A high confidence that such incidents will occur at a sufficiently low rate seems essential here.

The problem is that it is precisely for those systems where there is the greatest need for a quantification of dependability, because of the potentially catastrophic nature of single incidents, that evaluation is most difficult. However, the solution cannot be via the informality of 'engineering judgment' as castigated by Feynman in the quotation which heads this paper. If we are to reason about our uncertainty concerning the dependability of novel systems, and be able to communicate our reasoning to others in a scientific discourse, I see no alternative to quantifying that uncertainty. Probability is certainly not the only way in which this quantification can be carried out, but it seems certain that the difficulties we have encountered using probabilities will be encountered in different forms using other approaches. Certainly probability seems an appropriate language for conducting this debate, given its already extensive familiarity in science and engineering through concepts like reliability, although the Bayesian subjectivist flavour which seems inevitable here may be less familiar.

How can we proceed from here? One way forward might be to insist that certain safety-critical systems should only be built if the safety case can be demonstrated to rely only on *assurable* levels of design dependability. This seems to be the position adopted by the UK CEGB for its nuclear reactor safety systems [CEGB, 1982a and 1982b], who assume that the reliability of a system subject to design faults (particularly software) will never be better than 10^{-5} per demand, and normally accept only 10^{-4}. Such levels are about on the boundary of what is measurable. Of course, the safety case for the overall reactor system needs to make further assumptions in order to arrive at an acceptable dependability level: most notably about the rate at which demands are likely to be placed upon the safety system, and about the representativeness of the input cases used for the evaluation of the rate of failures upon demand. However, the natural separation of concerns here, between the stochastic process of demands, and the conditional process of safety system failures upon demands, does allow the adoption of a conservative design philosophy.

This approach was not available to the designers of the A320 fly-by-wire system, which is essentially in permanent active control of the aircraft. Although total failure of the system is not critical in level flight, it could be catastrophic during landing. In the worst case, a total loss of the system leaves the pilot with control of merely tail trim and rudder, which are the only surfaces with direct mechanical linkages. It is therefore understandable why this single electronic flight control system must be demonstrated to have an extremely high dependability, in contrast to the CEGB case. One could question why it was decided to rely on this computer system to such a high degree that it was not thought necessary to have a mechanical back-up system able to operate all main control surfaces. As it is, although the system has several *internal* modes of degraded operation, when seen as a black box it forms a single potential source for failures which leave the aircraft under rather vestigial control.

Of course, if a fully-functioning mechanical back-up had been provided for the A320, there would still remain difficulties, as there are in the CEGB argument. All the sophisticated flight envelope protection would be lost, for example, in the event of reversion to the back-up. And it must be admitted that there would be difficulties in designing the switch-over mechanism (automatic? pilot authorised?). These reservations notwithstanding, it seems to me that such a conservative design philosophy could have made the safety case a more plausible one.

It is sometimes argued that at least there is less chance of human errors (i.e. pilot errors in the case of the A320) than would be the case in a more conventional system. There is some truth in this, inasmuch as a fly-by-wire system can provide protection against certain human-induced failures, such as aircraft stall. But I think this view is fundamentally misleading. What is really happening is that we are diminishing the possibility of human errors being made by the person who is conventionally in direct control (the pilot), at the expense of increasing the possibility of failures due to human errors at the design stage. We thus have more decisions taken by the designer, trying to *imagine* all the circumstances into which the aircraft might get, than by the pilot, who actually *experiences* the specific circumstances and has to respond under tight time constraints. Whether such a trade-off results in a system that is, overall, safer than a conventional system is moot. Is it necessarily a good thing that a pilot should be prevented from manoeuvres that could damage the aircraft, in the event that he needs to escape from a dangerous situation - for example, overstressing the airframe or demanding more than rated thrust from the engines? Wrecking the engines might have primarily economic implications, but tearing off the wings is a little more final (although there are examples of aircraft surviving manoeuvres which 'should' have had this conclusion). There is probably a middle course here and it would be nice to have some scientific evidence to justify actual design decisions of this kind.

Driving much of this concern about the dependability of safety critical systems are two issues: complexity and novelty. Whenever we are concerned about a safety case we need to limit these as much as we can; unfortunately, the introduction of computer systems usually seems to increase them.

Controlling complexity and novelty can sometimes be relatively easy. Often, for example, systems involving software are built to replicate the functionality of purely-hardware systems. In cases like this it is usual to take advantage of the presence of the computer system to introduce novel extra functionality overall. It ought to be possible to provide some of this extra functionality with an assurance that the dependability of the basic functionality, originally provided by the hardware system, has not been compromised. This requires a separation of concerns between, on the one hand, the basic provision and assurance that the system will function as well as its predecessors, and on the other hand the provision of novel functionality in such a way that it does not compromise the basics *and* perhaps provides additional safeguards. Such a separation seems to be lacking in the A320 system, where basic and novel functionality are inextricably bound up in a single system.

The idea here is that complexity which is *necessary* should if possible benefit from past experience of similar systems: evolutionary change induces more confidence than discrete change. Complexity which is providing desirable, but not necessary, functionality should not be allowed to compromise the safety of the rest.

Control of novelty will often largely depend upon social and economic judgment. At present, for example, there seems to be an unfortunate tendency to build quite exotic systems to fulfil quite mundane, but safety-critical, needs. Four-wheel steer-by-wire for automobiles, for example, seems to me to offer rather questionable benefits at some extra risk over that offered by conventional mechanical systems.

In a recent paper, Fred Brooks [Brooks, 1987] has argued cogently that there is no 'silver bullet' for the problem of software engineering. Put in the terminology of this paper, he is arguing that there is no magic solution which will allow us to *achieve* arbitrarily high system dependability. My purpose has been to show that there is, equally, no silver bullet for the evaluation problem.

Acknowledgement

This work was conducted as part of the author's involvement in the ESPRIT project 3092 'Predictably Dependable Computing Systems' (PDCS).

References

Abdel-Ghaly, A.A., Chan, P.Y., Littlewood, B. 1986. Evaluation of competing software reliability predictions. *IEEE Trans. Software Engineering*, **SE-12**, 9, 950-967.

Adams, E.N. 1984. Optimizing preventive service of software products. *IBM Journal Res. and Dev.*, **28**, 1, 2-14.

Anderson, T. and Lee, P. 1981. *Fault Tolerance: Principles and Practice*. Prentice-Hall, Englewood Cliffs, NJ.

Anderson, T., Barrett, P. A., Halliwell, D. N., and Moulding, M. R. 1985. Software fault tolerance: an evaluation, *IEEE Trans Software Engineering*, **SE-11**, 12, 1502-1510.

Avizienis, A., Ball, D. E. 1987. On the achievement of a highly dependable and fault-tolerant air traffic control system, *IEEE Computer*, **20** (2), 84-90.

Avizienis, A. 1985. The N-version approach to fault-tolerant software, *IEEE Trans Software Engineering*, **SE-11**, 12

Barlow, R. E., Proschan, F., 1975. *Statistical Theory of Reliability and Life Testing*. New York: Holt. Rinehart and Winston.

Bishop, P. G., Esp, D. G. , Barnes, M., Humphreys, P., Dahll, G., Lahti, J. 1986. PODS - A project on diverse software, *IEEE Trans Software Engineering*, **SE-12**, 9.

Brocklehurst, S., Chan, P. Y., Littlewood, B., Snell, J. 1990. Recalibrating software reliability models, *IEEE Trans Software Engineering*, **SE-16**, 4, 458-470.

Brooks, F. 1987. No silver bullet: essence and accidents of software engineering. *IEEE Computer*, vol 20, 4, 10-19.

CEGB 1982a. *Design safety criteria for CEGB nuclear power stations*. Report HS/R167/81 (Revised).

CEGB 1982b. *Pressurised water reactor design safety guidelines*. Report DSG2 (Issue A).

Curritt, P.A., Dyer, M. and Mills, H.D. 1986. Certifying the reliability of software. *IEEE Trans Software Engineering*, SE-12, 1, 3-11

de Groot, M. H. 1970. *Optimal Statistical Decisions*. New York: McGraw-Hill.

Eckhardt, D.E. and Lee, L.D. 1985. A theoretical basis for the analysis of multi-version software subject to coincident errors. *IEEE Trans. Software Engineering*, **SE-11**, 12, 1511-1517.

Feynman, R. 1988. *"What do you care what other people think?" - further adventures of a curious character*. London: Unwin Hyman.

Jelinski, Z. and Moranda, P.B. 1972. Software reliability research. In *Statistical Computer Performance Evaluation*, (ed. W. Freiberger), pp 465-484. New York: Academic Press.

Knight, J.C. and Leveson, N.G. 1986. An empirical study of failure probabilities in multi-version software. In *Digest 16th International Symposium on Fault-tolerant Computing*, pp 165-170. New York: IEEE Press.

Laprie, J.C. 1988. Dependability: a unifying concept for reliable computing and fault tolerance. In *More Resilient Computing Systems* (ed. T. Anderson). London: Collins (to appear).

Littlewood, B. 1981. Stochastic reliability growth: a model for fault removal in computer programs and hardware designs. *IEEE Trans. Reliability*, **R-30**, 313-320.

Littlewood, B. 1988. Forecasting software reliability. In *Software Reliability, Modelling and Identification*, (Ed S. Bittanti) Lecture Notes in Computer Science 341, pp141-209. Heidelberg: Springer-Verlag.

Littlewood, B. and Miller, D. R. 1989. Conceptual modeling of coincident failures in multiversion software, *IEEE Trans Software Engineering*, **SE-15**, 12, 1596-1614.

Littlewood, B. and Verrall, J.L. 1973. A Bayesian reliability growth model for computer software. *J. Royal Statist. Soc.* C, **22**, 332-346.

Mann, N. R., Schafer, R. E., Singpurwalla, N. D., 1974. *Methods for Statistical Analysis of Reliability and Life Data.* New York: John Wiley.

McDermid, J. A. 1990. Issues in developing software for safety critical systems. *Reliability Engineering and System Safety.* (to appear)

Miller, D.R. 1989. The role of statistical modelling and inference in software quality assurance. In *Software Certification* (Ed B. de Neumann), pp135-152. Barking: Elsevier Applied Science.

MoD 1989a. Draft Interim Defence Standard 00-55, *Requirements for the procurement of safety-critical software in defence equipment.* UK Ministry of Defence, London.

MoD 1989b. Draft Interim Defence Standard 00-55, *Requirements for the analysis of safety-critical software in defence equipment.* UK Ministry of Defence, London.

Musa, J. 1975. A theory of software reliability and its application. *IEEE Trans. Software Engineering*, **SE-1**, 312-327.

Musa, J. 1979. Software reliability data. *Technical Report available from Data Analysis Center for Software*, Rome Air Development Center, N.Y., U.S.A.

Perrow, C. 1984. *Normal Accidents - Living with High Risk Technologies.* New York: Basic Books.

Randell, B. 1975. System structure for software fault tolerance. *IEEE Trans Software Engineering*, **SE-1**, 2, 220-232.

Rouquet, J.C. and Traverse, P.J. 1986. Safe and reliable computing on board the Airbus and ATR aircraft. In *Proceedings of Fifth IFAC Workshop on Safety of Computer Control Systems* (ed. W.J. Quirk), pp 93-97. Oxford: Pergamon Press.

RTCA, 1985. *Software Considerations in Airborne Systems and Equipment Certification.* Washington: Radio Technical Commission for Aeronautics, Doc DO178A

7

Predictably Dependable Computing Systems: An ESPRIT Basic Research Action[1]

JOHN DOBSON

Computing Laboratory
University of Newcastle upon Tyne, U.K.

JEAN-CLAUDE LAPRIE

LAAS-CNRS
Toulouse, France

BRIAN RANDELL

Computing Laboratory
University of Newcastle upon Tyne, U.K.

Summary

Predictably Dependable Computing Systems (PDCS) is ESPRIT Basic Research Action 3092. The institutions and principal investigators involved in PDCS are:

Centre for Software Reliability, The City University, London, UK;
Bev Littlewood.

IEI del CNR, Pisa, Italy;
Lorenzo Strigini.

Institut fur Algorithm und Kognitiv Systeme, Universitaet Karlsruhe, Karlsruhe, Federal Republic of Germany;
Tom Beth.

---

1 This text is an updated version of the paper which appeared in the Bulletin of EATCS (European Association for Theoretical Computer Science), vol. 40, Feb. 1990. The body of the paper is reprinted with permission of the EATCS Bulletin

LAAS-CNRS, Toulouse, France;
Jean-Claude Laprie.

Computing Laboratory, The University of Newcastle upon Tyne, Newcastle upon Tyne, UK;
Brian Randell.

LRI, Universite Paris-Sud, Paris, France;
Marie-Claude Gaudel.

Institut fur Technische Informatik, Technische Universitaet Wien, Vienna, Austria;
Herman Kopetz.

Department of Computer Science, The University of York, York, UK;
John McDermid.

The coordinating contractor is the University of Newcastle upon Tyne. Brian Randell is PDCS Project Director, who co-chairs the Project's Executive Board with Jean-Claude Laprie. The project's Technical Coordinator is John Dobson. The Action involves approximately 40 staff at the participating institutions, and lasts in the first instance for 30 months.

The objective of the PDCS Project is to contribute to making the process of designing and constructing dependable computing systems much more predictable and cost-effective than it is at present. To this end, the Project plans to develop:

(a) unifying concepts underlying dependability which should support design decisions involving trade-offs between different approaches to dependability and draw together technical work within both our own Action and other related research projects;

(b) means for the establishment and validation of dependability requirements, including those related to the timing properties of so-called "hard real-time" systems;

(c) stochastic techniques for assessing and predicting dependability, covering all means of attempting to prevent, remove and tolerate all types of faults, including design faults and deliberate attacks.

The ultimate long term objective is to produce a design support environment which is well-populated with tools and ready-made system components and which fully supports the notion of predictably dependable design of large real-time fault-tolerant distributed systems.

1. Introduction

Increasingly, individuals and organisations are developing or procuring sophisticated computing systems on whose services they need to place great reliance - whether to service a set of cash dispensers, calculate a satellite orbit, control an airplane or nuclear plant, or to maintain the confidentiality of a sensitive government database. In differing circumstances, the focus will be on differing aspects of such services - e.g. the average real-time response achieved, the likelihood of producing the required results, the ability to avoid causing failures which could be catastrophic to the system's environment, or the degree to which deliberate security intrusions can be prevented. The recently-introduced notion of **dependability**, defined in [15] as *that property of a computing system which allows reliance justifiably to be placed on the service which it delivers,* provides a very convenient means of subsuming these various concerns within a single conceptual framework. Dependability thus includes as special cases such properties as reliability, integrity, privacy, safety, security, etc. It also provides means of addressing the problem that what a user usually needs from a system is an appropriate balance of several such properties.

The great problem about dependability - as with reliability, security, etc. - is that it is a *systems issue,* since virtually all aspects of a computing system, and of the means by which it was specified, designed and constructed, can affect the system's overall dependability. Users gain little satisfaction from being assured that particular system components are functioning faultlessly or that particular parts of the design process have been carried out absolutely correctly if the overall *system* does not provide a level of dependability commensurate with the level of dependence that they have to place on it.

Moreover, realistic dependability prediction and assessment normally have to involve careful calculation of probabilities and risks, rather than naive belief in certainties. Thus they should, if at all possible, be based on stochastic models and well-established statistics, rather than simplistic assumptions, whether about the functioning of system hardware components, or the care with which system design processes have been carried out.

This discussion serves to draw out the two principal topics around which our proposed Action is centred:

- development of unifying concepts underpinning dependability as a systems issue;
- development of stochastic techniques for dependability prediction and assessment.

These topics are strongly related as the work on the underlying concepts will give a framework for determining the range of dependability measures needed, for articulating the measures, and for employing them in a predictive manner.

2. Technical Overview

In the real world, the dependability requirements that will actually be placed on a system by the various people and organisations that will be affected by it can be very difficult to identify, leave alone quantify. One major difficulty is that the value of a system's actions and the costs of its failures, whether or not expressed in monetary terms, will not in general be constant, but will instead be functions of time. Work on real-time systems addresses this difficulty, but almost invariably only simple step-functions are considered; the simplistic assumption is made that the results of the system have a constant value if obtained prior to a given deadline, and thereafter are valueless, or result in some fixed penalty.

In establishing requirements, we need, in addition, to be able to model the operational environment for a system since we can only articulate dependability issues, e.g. the consequences of failure, in terms of this environment. This poses additional problems for requirements analysis, above the normal problems of elicitation and validation. We need to be able to define, and preferably to quantify, dependability.

Another complication arises from the fact that, in very complex hardware/software systems, residual design faults constitute a major dependability problem. Much promising work is being done on the use of formal methods and design verification techniques aimed at ensuring the absence of such faults. However it seems generally accepted that though this research is, and will continue to be, of considerable value, there will for some time to come be a need to place a significant degree of dependence on systems that cannot realistically be assumed to be completely free of logical design errors. Indeed, there are good arguments, and much hard-won experience from various fields of engineering, which would indicate that no single technique for dealing with design faults will always prove fully adequate and optimally cost-effective in isolation, or in all situations.

This poses the problem of how to ally formal verification, probably concentrated on critical components, with techniques such as testing and fault tolerance, in order to obtain the required dependability of the overall system. There are currently no worthwhile guidelines available as to how best to allocate time and resources between efforts at verification, testing or the provision of design fault tolerance. A further problem is the difficulty of formalising the problem domain itself; yet this is essential if we are to gain the full benefits of formal techniques in verifying the dependability of a system. In fact, it seems unlikely that it will ever be possible to have complete confidence that the formal specifications for a complex system have been generated with absolute accuracy, and so there is a limitation on the contribution of formal approaches to the *achievement* of dependability. This is one of the reasons that we stress a systems approach, and a multi-faceted view of dependability and its achievement.

3. Objectives

Perhaps the single most important characteristic of our proposed Action is the stress we are putting on the necessity of taking a "systems engineering" approach to the above objective. Such an approach, we suggest, should aim at achieving significant, well-coordinated progress towards the following very challenging objectives:

(i) developing effective techniques for establishing realistic dependability requirements, and so producing dependability specifications against which the system design process and its resultant products can be assessed;

(ii) producing quantitative methods for measuring and predicting the dependability of complex software/hardware systems, allowing for the possible presence of design and deliberate faults as well as the occurrence of operational faults;

(iii) incorporating such methods more fully into the design process, and all its means of attempting to prevent, remove and tolerate faults, so as to make the process much more controlled and capable of allowing design decisions (and decisions concerning the actual deployment of the system) to be based on meaningful analyses of risks and quantified likely benefits; and, ultimately

(iv) producing an effective design support environment populated both with the tools necessary to facilitate practical use of such techniques and methods, and with ready-to-use families of system components with known dependability characteristics.

An important characteristic of the goal we have set ourselves is thus to facilitate increased use of quantitative assessments of system dependability. Clearly there will be limits to the extent that many process and product characteristics can be meaningfully and accurately quantified. Nevertheless, we feel that a degree of concentration on techniques which will help lay the foundations of increased use of quantitative methods is fully justified. Indeed, our view is that increased effective use of quantitative methods is a prerequisite to turning the activity of constructing large computer-based systems into a true engineering discipline.

4. Main Technical Themes

The ultimate long term objective, a design support environment which is well-populated with tools and ready-made components, and which fully supports the notion of predictably dependable design of large distributed real-time computing systems, is of course extremely ambitious, and not something one would expect to achieve within the time span of our Basic Research Action. Dependability, as we have already indicated, is a prime example of a "systems issue" and the notion of predictably dependable computing systems encompasses many different topics in computing science, such as software engineering, fault tolerance, reliability modelling, formal verification, systems architecture, etc. It is of course not practicable for a single Basic Research Action to address adequately all these areas, and we have had to be selective. Our choice of areas is affected by our analysis of the state of the art, the extent to which we believe we can advance the state of the art, and our perception of the quality of work being undertaken elsewhere. We have identified a set of six topics to which we think we can make unique and substantive contributions, and which will dovetail with other proposed and ongoing work.

These six topics are:

(i) Dependability concepts and terminology.

This topic provides the conceptual framework and unifying theme for the whole of the Action. It is concerned with the development of a range of models to be refined by other tasks within the Action, and with the creation of a common vocabulary.

(ii) Specification of dependability requirements.

This topic deals with the operational and user environments and their effect on the dependability of a system. It is concerned with the specification of dependability requirements; and in order to be able to obtain valid requirements, it is necessary to understand how, and by whom, a system is likely to be used.

(iii) Management of the design process, including support environment issues.

This topic examines the process of making a dependable system and the control that is necessary over the design and development process required in order to achieve predictability.

(iv) Achievement and assessment of fault tolerance.

This topic addresses the provision of dependability through fault tolerance. The aim is to develop a systematic and unified approach to the design of fault-tolerant systems which will facilitate the assessment of their dependability characteristics.

(v) Stochastic models and techniques for dependability prediction and evaluation.

This topic develops the mathematics, and in particular the stochastic tools and techniques, for prediction and evaluation. This mathematics will, of course, pervade the whole Action and justify the *predictability* of the techniques we propose to achieve dependability.

(vi) System components and architectures for dependability.

This topic is essentially an engineering task which will combine all the results of the previous conceptual and formal studies in producing architectures and components for real systems. The primary aim is to demonstrate the validity of the approaches adopted by showing how the models, classification schemes, and and mathematics can be refined into components and architectures.

All these topics are inter-related; for example, work on evaluation must reflect all the different development technologies that can be used in producing a predictably dependable computing system. However, certain of the relationships are much more important than the others, particularly where one task provides the conceptual underpinning for another. We have therefore grouped these six topics into three distinct tasks within the Action. Again, resource limitations have forced us to postpone some investigations until a later phase of the Action, but the task structure is not expected to change. These tasks will now be described in the following sections of this paper.

5. Task A : Dependability Concepts and Terminology

This task is concerned with the problem of understanding a system as a whole, and its relation to its environment and the organisation whose purposes it serves. Thus important individual themes are modelling the environment, understanding the interplay between the system and its environment, and understanding how to abstract real-world human concerns into rigorous notions of dependability. The aim is to provide a basis for confidence that the abstractions do in fact capture the connotations of such terms as 'reliance', 'verification and validation', 'security', and 'fault'. The original work on the definition of the concept of dependability [15] will be revisited and updated where necessary to incorporate further understanding.

Subtask A.1 : Framework and Taxonomic Principles

Work recently carried out at Newcastle [7] and further refined by the Alvey ANSA Project [3] has shown that it is possible to develop a framework which can be used to define a *range of formal models*, each formal model dealing with a particular aspect of the problem under investigation and at a particular level of abstraction. For example, as shown in [6], a communications application can be described with the aid of four formal models: of system composition, of system behaviour, of messages, and of communication. The advantage of the framework is that it provides a means of relating the formal models together so as to show that they all represent separate facets of the *same* underlying system. Using this framework, the Action will create a *related* collection of formal models which will be used to provide the formal basis of the methods and tools to be developed.

A major component of the framework will be a set of taxonomic principles. Classification is a human activity, and therefore the principles on which it is based must derive from the human purposes for which the classification is required. In the case of classifying concepts related to predictably dependable computer systems, we intend to study ways of classifying the various dependability attributes such as performance, reliability, safety, security and so on, and to expose the underlying concepts, particularly with respect to the various fault possibilities and failure modes.

Subtask A.2 : System Fault Tolerance.

A system level view of fault tolerance [2] seeks to provide tolerance to faults of design and to operational faults at all relevant levels of the system. A coherent architectural approach will be investigated, seeking to exploit general mechanisms for error detection, error signalling, adjudication and error recovery. By such means, we hope to harmonise current design fault tolerance schemes, such as N-version programming and recovery blocks, and also to make use of various existing techniques for tolerating operational faults, so as to achieve a very general architecture for fault tolerant systems appropriate for a broad range of application areas (e.g. distributed, real-time, embedded, critical). In its application to fault tolerance, the framework will incorporate and refine existing structuring techniques such as ideal components, exception handling, generalised adjudicators and recoverable actions. The primary goal will be for the framework to describe a unified design structure for a fault-tolerant system, which ideally could be synthesised with respect to dependability requirements and analysed to provide guarantees of dependability provision (subject to an appropriate fault model).

One component of this framework will be a systematic approach to software fault tolerance by combining formal techniques of algebraic specification with formal models of exception handling. The work will start by consolidating previous work at Paris-Sud on construction of robust programs [5] which has resulted in systematic techniques for constructing robust programs, using exception handling, from algebraic specifications. These techniques and tools will be extended to deal with other software fault tolerance mechanisms such as recovery blocks. This work will involve collaboration between groups specialising in algebraic specifications and in fault tolerant software.

6. Task B : Specification and Design for Dependability

There are two distinct major threads to this task. The first thread is concerned with understanding the principles involved in constructing a development environment for predictably dependable computing systems. Any design support environment must espouse a model of both the design process and design decision-making. Further, in order to achieve *predictable* dependability it is necessary to have control over the design and development process. Control requires the ability to measure (and influence) the process. Whilst it is possible to make some measurements on products produced early in the life cycle [9] we need for control purposes to be able to make measurements with incomplete and inconsistent specifications. For this, and other reasons, we believe that much of the predictability and control in producing dependable systems must stem from process metrics and metrics derived from early product representations. In order to measure facets of the development process and intermediate products we need to have accurate formal models of the activities undertaken during the process.

A rational process for the design of predictably dependable systems must start with an explicit statement of the relevant dependability requirements. Thus the objectives of this thread are twofold:

(a) to provide the basis, in terms of process models and possibly some project support environment interface definitions, which would render feasible the production of the infrastructure of a design environment for the predictable production of dependable computing systems; and

(b) to develop a framework and a set of procedures for expressing the relevant dependability requirements in a form that is consistent with a validation procedure at some later phase in the life cycle, and to provide a set of techniques in order to derive these dependability requirements from the context of the enterprise whose needs the computer system is to serve.

The second thread is to explore a number of issues concerned with system specification and design that are of particular importance for dependability and which have largely been ignored by the main stream of formal specification techniques. There will be two distinct aspects of dependability that will be examined as part of this thread: one particular focus will be the specification of the timeliness requirements of complex distributed real-time systems, concentrating on the fundamental concepts and measures which must be contained in any requirements specification language; and the second investigation will be concerned with the proper specification of requirements concerning safety and security

Subtask B.1 : Effects of Operational Environment on Dependability

The modelling technique we have mentioned above emphasises and forces consideration of the various kinds of constraint that have to be observed by the product once it is inhabiting its operational environment. It is a frequent informal observation that some operational environments are more stressful to products, even software products, in ways that are not easy to state precisely but appear to be related to the nature of the enterprise using the product. For these reasons, the operational environment of both process and product must be studied. Issues to be examined include identification of environmental factors that affect the dependability of a system, assessment of the sensitivity of a system to these factors, determination of means of controlling these factors, and allocation of responsibility to ensure the factors are in fact controlled.

Subtask B.2 : Specification and Design for Timeliness.

During design, objects of interest (e.g. hardware components, control algorithms, data representations, ...) are refined into a set of sub-objects, along with their interactions. These sub-objects together have to adhere to the overall requirements of the original object. This refinement method, well established with respect to functional requirements, will be extended to handle the timing requirements. We are investigating the following questions: How can one derive timing requirements for sub-objects given the "global" timing requirement? What is a good strategy for resource allocation in a distributed system, such that the specified timing requirements are met by design and the given architectural constraints are observed?

The three most critical aspects of timeliness requirements are response time, transaction rate, and the relevance of data. Only the first of these three aspects are dealt with by current requirements analysis methods, and even this treatment is not really adequate. The required timing behaviour of a real-time computer system is determined by the dynamics of the application the system is to interact with, and perhaps control. Therefore, in the requirements phase the following timing attributes of the application environment must be explored: the maximum tolerated time interval between the stimuli and the corresponding responses; the minimum time interval between the activation of two successive instances of hard real-time transactions; and the time-dependent validity of real-time data. If any one of these three fundamental timeliness requirements is missing it is not possible to proceed with a rational design of a hard real-time system with the proper performance characteristics.

Subtask B.3 : Dependability Requirements.

We plan to approach the general problem of dependability from two separate directions. First, the general concept of dependability is being examined in order to see how it can be specialised to generate particular requirements. Secondly, and independently, we shall focus on these particular requirements and see how they can be generalised to dependability as a more abstract concept.

Guidelines for producing structured specifications of dependability will be given, addressing the issues of (a) proper service, (b) conditions under which an error becomes a failure, and (c) improper service. An important feature will be the elicitation of (a) the cross-couplings between the above items, and (b) the ways of associating objectives to the various facets of dependability (reliability, availability, safety, security etc.) either through qualitative indicators or through quantitative metrics.

In particular, models of safety and security have to be established that are reasonably comprehensive, whose scope is well understood, and which can underpin statements of requirements. It seems infeasible to create a single model of security that covers all possible intuitive aspects of security, but we believe it is feasible to produce a set of related models each one covering a different aspect of security. Methods for risk/cost analysis have to inform the development of the security models. Changes in requirements and the resulting changes in a system are dangerous points in the life-cycle of a system as new features may inadvertently breach existing security mechanisms. Thus one should strive for a class of models where properties of a system will provably survive under system changes, and where it is possible to analyse the effects of changes.

Subtask B.4 : Requirements and Constraints on Software Engineering Environments for Dependable Systems.

The development of predictably dependable computing systems places additional requirements on Software Engineering Environments (SEEs). The current approaches to this problem are far from satisfactory. The two most serious problems are:

(a) existing work, e.g. [8], has exposed conflicts between the needs of predictable dependability and normal SEE requirements, but has not resolved the conflicts; and

(b) the current approaches to supporting the design of dependable systems are based on the notion of extending existing SEE interfaces, rather than defining them anew.

This task will consider models of the design process, both as a means of providing a control model for environments and as a basis for qualitative indicators which can be used to predict dependability. Existing work on process models has been carried out both as part of software engineering in general and as part of SEE developments (e.g. the Alvey ASPECT and IPSE2.5 projects). Whilst there are promising signs in this work none of it yet offers an adequate basis for supporting design decision making and other aspects of control in a SEE. In particular, issues of timeliness and security are often not well addressed.

Some work has been done on process modelling, mainly in the context of project support environments, but the available notations are inadequate for the purposes identified above. There is therefore a need to improve existing notations. This process needs to be supported by suitable metrics. The work will be based on existing models developed in the UK and elsewhere and will proceed by experiment and case study. For example, when a new formalism is proposed, its capability will be validated by using it to (try to) model a number of different approaches to producing dependable systems.

7. Task C : Dependability Prediction and Evaluation

This task is concerned with the basic techniques for measurement and prediction which justify the use of the word "predictable" in the title of this Research Action. As such it pervades the whole programme and will, during the execution of the work, parallel the research into methods of *achieving* dependability. Particular attention will be paid to the application of these techniques to fault-tolerant systems and software and to issues of validation.

Subtask C1 : Dependability Modelling and Evaluation.

Recent work [17] [4] has increased our understanding of some of the basic concepts, clarifying issues such as (a) diversity and independence of software, (b) the relation between failure process and software activity, and (c) the behaviour of adjudication mechanisms; but further advances are needed. Our work will be targetted on the following areas:

- the relationship between process and product with respect to diversity and independence;
- the impact of development methodology, and operational environment, on properties of individual programs drawn from a population of programs;
- incorporation of experimental results to refine the models;
- extending the models to cover adjudication mechanisms as well as the underlying fault-tolerance mechanisms (recovery point establishment and restoration, runtime synchronisation, etc.).

The software reliability measurement and prediction problem which has been most studied in the literature concerns the reliability growth taking place during fault removal. With a few exceptions, such as the work reported in [12], existing models vary greatly in their accuracy (see below) and in the plausibility of the underlying assumptions, and are therefore of dubious applicability to systems in operational use. An aim in this task will be to develop models with less stringent assumptions and models directly aimed at the whole of the operational life, thus incorporating evolution in the specifications. It is expected that this approach will have two benefits: unsophisticated potential users are more likely to find these attractive; and it is likely that such models will be robust (i.e. not too sensitive to deviations from modelling assumptions).

The reliability growth models in the literature vary greatly in their accuracy. Some techniques are now available [1] which allow a user to decide, for a particular source of failure data, which of the models is giving the most accurate results. These ideas will be developed, particularly by investigating the ways of reducing the variability ("noisiness") of predictions. An important bonus from this work will be ways of improving model predictions in quite general ways: essentially by using an analysis of past performance on a particular data source to reduce predictive errors. Such adaptive methods have already shown great potential for simple short term predictions [1] [16]; it remains to be seen whether they will work in a wider class of situations.

Dependability models incorporating both hardware and software failures are not common practice, in spite of the user's interest in getting results representative of the behaviour of their systems, which are of course composed of both hardware and software. We plan to extend the preliminary work reported in [14] and to determine models accommodating both hardware and software failures when considering both stable dependability and dependability growth. In doing so, emphasis will be placed on the analysis of the underlying assumptions, and so it is proposed to use the techniques of direct analysis of accuracy mentioned above. Again, it may be possible to improve the output of such models by means of an analysis of past performance.

Subtask C.2 : Timeliness Analysis.

An important aspect of the dependability of a system is its capacity for performing within acceptable timing limits, particularly in the face of fluctuating demand and resource availability. The objective will be to develop mathematical tools for the assessment, prediction and improvement of that capacity. The methods employed will be those of probabilistic modelling, analysis and optimisation [18]. Existing models for evaluating the effects of congestion, interference and faults on performance [13][10][19] will be generalised and made more applicable, and new models will be constructed and investigated.

In addition, there are some problems of performance analysis where worst-case, deterministic models are more tractable and more easily interpreted than probabilistic models. This is especially true when considering peak load demands on a system, associated with stringent timing requirements. Questions of worst possible execution time of critical tasks and their appropriate schedules will be examined.

Subtask C.3 : Statistical Assessment of Fault Tolerance.

The provision of fault tolerance mechanisms in a system introduces additional problems in evaluating the dependability of the system. These problems are mainly concerned with determining the validity of the fault hypotheses and assessing the effectiveness of the various aspects of fault tolerance (such as error detection and recovery). Validation methods will be studied, concentrating on two forms of statistical testing:

a) statistical testing of systems with respect to functional inputs, aimed at estimating the reliability of software components or systems. The approach will consist in deriving the test inputs from a Markov model of the functional specification, and we intend to apply it to both conventional (non fault-tolerant) software as well as to fault-tolerant software;

b) statistical testing of systems with respect to inputs that are specifically processed by fault-tolerant systems, namely faults. This form of testing, sometimes referred to as fault injection, is aimed at estimating the coverage of the error processing and fault treatment strategies, at different phases of design and construction.

Both of these forms of statistical testing provide a means of fault forecasting which complements approaches based on probability modelling, and of course contribute to fault removal. An expected spin-off will be to identify design rules for fault-tolerant systems which facilitate validation (cf. design for testability).

Subtask C.4 : Security Evaluation.

Most current work on security is qualitative in nature. We hope to investigate ways of measuring and predicting the actual achieved operational security of systems. The objective is to obtain measures, similar to those which are currently available in certain contexts for operational reliability, such as the rate of occurrence of security violations, and the probability of survival for a specified time without such violation. At an abstract level, security can be seen as simply a particular aspect of dependability. However, such a view does not always reveal the important issues which arise from the intentionality implicit in security violations. These differences will drive the investigation in a number of ways. Current testing for security shares the drawback common to all testing procedures: that they may be efficient for *achievement* (of reliability, of security), but do not in general allow for *measurement* because the test case selection is not representative of operational use (or, in the case of security, of deliberate misuse). Possible approaches might be into the possibility of creating test case generators which emulate operational security-sensitive environments, or to try to develop methods for Bayesian subjective reasoning to elicit formal measures of expert belief in system security. Since such subjective belief will, for a rational individual, be influenced by information about actual security (mis)behaviour, it may prove possible to combine these two strands.

Subtask C.5 : Ultra-high Dependability.

Achievement of figures such as the oft-quoted 10^{-9} failures per hour (for a safety-critical avionics program) is hard; it seems even harder to *assure* that it has been achieved in a particular context. We intend to investigate this assurance problem from below: essentially by trying to determine the limits to what is measurable by current (and immediate future) techniques. This work will involve incorporation of human belief using formal methods of elicitation [11][20], study of the limitations of what can be achieved by testing, and examination of the likely benefits of special architectures.

8. Conclusion

Perhaps the main conclusion to be drawn is that, although much research has been, and is continuing to be, undertaken on the multi-faceted problem of system dependability of complex hardware/software systems, comparatively little progress has been made on drawing all the relevant research threads together.

The notion of setting up a collaborative Basic Research Action aimed at this issue captured the imagination of a number of major European research groups working in dependability, software engineering, and distributed real-time systems. Each of these groups was already in close contact with several of the other groups. However, the set of groups as a whole have, like the set of topics that need to be addressed, not been brought closely together before. In fact the very phrase "Predictably Dependable Computing Systems" which we have adopted to characterise our general objectives, and the idea of a design support environment for such systems, make this situation all too apparent.

Our belief is that such design support environments, if cost/effective, and applicable to distributed real-time systems, could be of tremendous value. However it is clear that their development will not be feasible until much research has been carried out. This must be research not just in topics such as dependability requirements analysis, fault avoidance, fault forecasting, etc., but more importantly in the task of combining the results of such work so as to create a true "systems engineering" approach to dependability.

This view caused us to put very considerable effort into the task of preparing an Action which does indeed attempt to cover, and to bring together, all the many major issues involved in the real-world dependability problems of large computer-based systems. Equally, we put considerable work into the task of identifying what basic research aims are now appropriate and timely, and to plan their coordinated investigation. We hope that the plan that our Action envisages of a programme of basic research producing results which should be of considerable value in themselves, will also constitute a significant step towards the ultimate objective.

9. Progress to Date

The Action started according to contract in May 1989. During the first six months, staff have been recruited, two plenary workshops have been held in addition to a number of task-specific ones, and technical work on the tasks described above and also on setting up the project infrastructure has got under way. In order to aid communication within the project, an electronic bulletin board has been created, based on the Unix newsgroup facility in order to try to compensate for at least some of the dependability problems associated with European electronic mail. A Technical Report series has been initiated which will publish original PDCS research work and reprint PDCS papers originating within the Action but first published elsewhere.

A major open workshop was held on May 15-17 1990 at LAAS, at which the results of the first year of the Action were disseminated. One hundred persons attended, originating from ten countries. The contents of the first year report is given hereafter.

Anyone wishing to be put on the PDCS mailing list and receive the Technical Reports as they are published, should write to Nick Cook, Computing Laboratory, University of Newcastle upon Tyne, Newcastle NE1 7RU, U.K. (email : Nick.Cook@newcastle.ac.uk).

Acknowledgements

The named authors of this paper are not, of course, the sole creators of the words it contains. We are grateful to our many colleagues in the Action for their contributions to the proposal, the Technical Annex, and the project papers, all of which have provided raw material for our selection.

Contents of the first year report

Volume 1: Dependability concepts and terminology

Summary and Conclusions

W.C. Carter, J.E. Dobson, J.C. Laprie, B. Randell

I- Dependability: Basic Concepts and Associated Terminology

J.C. Laprie (LAAS-CNRS)

II- PDCS from a Designer's Viewpoint

W.C. Carter (University of Newcastle upon Tyne)

Volume 2: Specification and design for dependability

Chapter 1: Fault tolerance

Summary and Conclusions

J. Arlat, C. Beounes, A. Bondavalli, F. Di Giandomenico, M. Gaschignard, M.C. Gaudel, K. Kanoun, J.C. Laprie, D. Powell, L. Simoncini, L. Strigini

I- Software Fault Tolerance

L. Strigini (IEI-CNR)

II- Diversification from Algebraic Specifications

M. Gaschignard, M.C. Gaudel (LRI-Université de Paris Sud et CNRS)

III- Adjudicators for Diverse Redundant Components

F. Di Giandomenico, L. Strigini (IEI-CNR)

IV- Definition and Analysis of Hardware-and-Software Fault-Tolerant Architectures

J.C. Laprie, J. Arlat, C. Beounes, K. Kanoun (LAAS-CNRS)

V- Failure Classification with respect to Detection

A. Bondavalli (CNUCE-CNR), L. Simoncini (Universita' di Reggio Calabria)

Chapter 2: Timeliness

Summary and Conclusions

N. Audsley, A. Bhattacharyya, A. Burns, G. Fohler, H. Kantz, H. Kopetz, J.A. McDermid, W. Schütz, R. Zainlinger

I- A Design Methodology for Predictable Hard Real-Time Systems
G. Fohler, H. Kantz, W. Schütz, R. Zainlinger (Technische Universität Wien)

II- Real-Time System Scheduling
N. Audsley, A. Burns (University of York)

III- A Test Strategy for the Distributed Real-Time System MARS
W. Schütz (Technische Universität Wien)

Chapter 3: Software engineering environments

Summary and Conclusions

E.S. Hocking, J.A. McDermid, Qi Shi

I- Integrated Project Support Environments: General Principles and Issues in the Development of Dependable Systems
J.A. McDermid (University of York)

II- Security Policies for Integrated Project Support Environments
J.A. McDermid, E.S. Hocking (University of York)

Volume 3: Dependability prediction and evaluation

Chapter 1: Reliability and Availability Modelling

Summary and Conclusions

J. Arlat, C. Beounes, S. Brocklehurst, N. Fenton, M. Kaâniche, K. Kanoun, J.C. Laprie, B. Littlewood, G. Pucci

I- Recalibrating Software Reliability Models
S. Brocklehurst, P.Y. Chan, B. Littlewood, J. Snell (City University)

II- The KAT — Knowledge-Action-Transformation — Approach to the Modelling and Evaluation of Reliability and Availability Growth
J.C. Laprie, K. Kanoun, C. Beounes, M. Kaâniche (LAAS-CNRS)

III- Dependability Modelling and Evaluation of Software-Fault Tolerance: Recovery Blocks, N-Version Programming, N Self-Checking Programming
J. Arlat, K. Kanoun, J.C. Laprie (LAAS-CNRS)

IV- On the Modelling and Testing of Recovery Block Structures
G. Pucci (University of Newcastle upon Tyne)

V- Deriving Structurally Based Software Measures
N.E. Fenton (City University), A. Melton (Kansas State University)

Chapter 2: Security Evaluation

Summary and Conclusions
T. Beth, J. Dobson , D. Gollmann, A. Klar

Security Evaluation Report: Concepts and Terminology
T. Beth, D. Gollmann, A. Klar (EISS-Universität Karlsruhe), J. Dobson (University of Newcastle upon Tyne)

References

1. A. A. Abdel-Ghaly, P. Y. Chan and B. Littlewood, "Evaluation of Competing Software Reliability Predictions", *IEEE Trans. on Software Engineering* **SE-12**, pp. 950-967, Sept. 1986.

2. T. Anderson and P. A. Lee, *Fault Tolerance: Principles and Practice* , Prentice Hall, 1981.

3. ANSA, *ANSA Reference Manual, Release 01.00*, 1989.

4. J. Arlat, K. Kanoun and J.-C. Laprie, "Dependability Evaluation of Software Fault Tolerance" in *Proceedings of FTCS-18* , Tokyo, June 1988, pp. 142-147.

5. M. Bidoit, M.-C. Gaudel and G. Guiho, "Towards a Systematic and Safe Programming of Exception Handling in Ada" in *Proc. 3rd Joint ADA Europe/ADA-TEC Conference* , The ADA Companion Series, Cambridge University Press, Brussels, Belgium, June 1984, pp. 141-152.

6. J. E. Dobson, "Modelling Real-World Issues for Dependable Software" in *High Integrity Software* , C. T. Sennett, Ed. Pitman, 1988.

7. J. E. Dobson and M. J. Martin, "Modelling the Real Issues in Dependable Communications Systems" in *Safety of Computer Control Systems (SAFECOMP 1986)* , W. J. Quirk, Ed. Pergamon Press, Oxford, 1986, pp. 123-128.

8. GIE EMERAUDE, "Requirements and Design Criteria for Tool Support Interface (EURAC) No. MA112B.8" , 1987.

9. N. E. Fenton and R. W. Whitty, "Axiomatic Approach to Software Metrication through Program Decomposition", *Computer Journal* **29**, 1986.

10. E. Gelenbe and I. Mitrani, "Modelling the Execution of Block Structured Processes with Failures" in *Mathematical Computer Performance and Reliability* , G. Iazeolla, Ed. North-Holland, 1984.

11. P. C. Humphreys and W. McFadden, "Experiences with MAUD", *Acta Psychologica* **45**, pp. 51-69, 1980.

12. K. Kanoun and T. Sabourin, "Software Dependability of a Telephone Switching System" in *Proc. 17th IEEE Int. Symp. on Fault-Tolerant Computing (FTCS-17)* , Pittsburg, PA, July 1987, pp. 236-241.

13. P. J. B. King and I. Mitrani, "The Effect of Breakdowns on the Performance of Multiprocessor Systems" in *Performance'81* , F. J. Kylstra, Ed. North-Holland, 1981.

14. J.-C. Laprie, *Towards an X-ware Reliability Theory* , LAAS, December 1986.

15. J.-C. Laprie, "Dependable Computing and Fault Tolerance: Basic concepts and terminology" in *Proc. 15th IEEE Int. Symp. on Fault-Tolerant Computing (FTCS-15)* , Ann Arbor, Michigan, June 1985, pp. 2-11.

16. B. Littlewood and P. A. Keiller, "Adaptive Software Reliability Modelling" in *Proc. 14th IEEE Int. Symp. on Fault-Tolerant Computing (FTCS-14)* , 1984, pp. 108-113.

17. B. Littlewood and D. R. Miller, "A Conceptual Model of Multi-Version Software" in *Proc. 17th IEEE Int. Symp. on Fault-Tolerant Computing (FTCS-17)* , Pittsburgh, June 1987.

18. I. Mitrani, *Modelling of Computer and Communication Systems* , Cambridge University Press, 1987.

19. I. Mitrani, "Multiprocessor Systems With Reserves and Preferences", *Queueing Systems Theory and Applications* **2**, pp. 245-259, 1987.

20. G. Shafer, *A Mathematical Theory of Evidence* , Princeton University Press, 1976.

8

SOFTWARE CERTIFICATION PROGRAMME IN EUROPE - SCOPE

W.Ehrenberger*, A.Roan+ and P.Robert+

ABSTRACT

With the increasing spread of software the problem of software quality has become important to the broad public. So the idea was born to guarantee software at a standardised quality to all those, who are not software specialists or who do not want to spend effort in investigating the quality of a specific product. The presence of software quality should be made visible through a specific label that could be attributed to the qualified products: the certificate for software, or the software quality sign.

The basic difference to other areas where high software quality is needed, such as aviation, nuclear power or compiler construction is, however, that no validation can be enforced and that no generally applicable standards, such as BNFs exist. In the target area of SCOPE a software product description has to form the basis for certification.

Following the lines of such thoughts the CEC has granted an ESPRIT project for outlining the basis for a European Software quality sign.

During its first phase the project has done several case studies; it has created a data base for taking over their intermediate results and allowing easy access from all partners. Existing software certification schemes have been studied. A certification model has been produced that assumes two different views from the customer's point and four classes of rigour for certification. In addition to the technical aspects some legal questions have been studied. Another point was the possible structure of a European Software Certification Organisation.

Some open problems have been identified that should be solved during the second phase of the project. Among these are the question of granting the certificate on the basis of operating experience, the question of making aspects of software ergonomy mandatory and what to do in case of changes of a certified product.

---

* GRS, Forschungsgelände, D - 8Ø46 Garching
+ Vérilog, 15Ø, Rue Nicolas Vauquelin, F - 31 Ø81 Toulouse

THE PROBLEM AND THE IDEA

With the increasing spread of software to various areas of our life the demands on its quality naturally have increased. This was due to several reasons:

- the enlarged responsibility of software: both in chemical plants, in road, rail and air trafic systems, in robots and in nuclear power plans software has occupied more and more responsible tasks;
- the increased frequency of use of software: things that have been done manually or mechanically during the past are now to a certain degree software controlled and software is employed for typing purposes, in book keeping systems, in hotel reservation systems, for making technical drawings and in computer games;
- the increased publicity of software: during the past it was largely only the specialists in their companies who had to work with software or software contolled items, but now the spread becomes such that the wide public has to deal with it.

Whereas safety responsible software applications have been subject to regulations for a long time already - see e.g. /IEC 880/ or /Radio Technical Commision for Aeronautics/, the software for the other areas and its quality has been largely left to the market forces. This was to a certain contrast to other areas of technology, e.g. civil egineering. In Germany e.g. it was during the 1920s already that several quality associations were founded, whose members committed themselves to produce and sell according to certain quality standards only. Thereby the uninformed customer could be sure that the product he bought, met well defined minimum quality requirements; a brick e.g. had a certain minimum stability. The products of the members of such a quality association were entitled to a specific quality sign enabling customers to distinguish them from normal ones.

Now the idea was born to provide such a quality instrument for software as well. Software with a certain quality should be visible at a glance and the customer should be able to identify quality software in contrast to "normal" software. This idea lead to the project SCOPE, "Software CertificatiOn Programme in Europe", whose aim it is to identify the conditions under which a certificate for a specific quality may be granted.

In contrast to the already existing certification activities for compilers or telecomunication software SCOPE does not aim at software for clearly specified tasks, but at general purpose software. The tasks for the software that is envisaged by SCOPE and its capabilities are defined by its customer or producer and are fixed in a user manual, product description or functional specification. The software quality sign or certificate shall make clear that the software will meet what the desriptions promise and hopefully ensure that the customer will not get disapointed.

This contribution shows some of the problems and findings of the SCOPE project. Due to the large number of project participants and the considerable time of working up to now it was impossible to treat all aspects of the project with equal clarity. Therefore a rather subjective selection has been made, highlighting some points only. A more balanced description of the so far achieved results is given in /Robert and Roan/.

THE SCOPE PROJECT

Partners

Following the obove mentioned idea 11 partners from 7 European Countries have suggested the SCOPE project and have got the grant to work on it by the Commission of the European Communities. The consortium comprises industry, research institutions and academia. It is shown in Figure 1.

The project results must lead to an internationally recognised standard in order to be meaningful. Therefore it was clear from the begining that the project could not be carried out among its partners only, but would need publicity and a good cooperation with the standardisation organisations of the various countries. Therefore appropriate connections have been activated. Figure 2 shows some of the existing relationships, both in the various countries and on the international level. The intent for publicity was also the incentive for the conference ASP-90, that contains many contributions from SCOPE.

Investigated Items

An important aspect of working was to follow different approaches to the problem of software certification:

- investigate how the problem of software quality and software certification was dealt with in other areas,
- make a certification model based on theoretical, considerations (top down branch),
- investigate certification possibilities by means of case studies (bottom up branch).
- investigate the legal questions of software quality, certification and product liability.

The first approach lead to a state of the art report that is publicly available /SCOPE Consortium 1/. It became clear that the approach of the German Gütegemeinschaft Software /DIN 66285, Knorr/ was in the intended area. Its characteristic is that it is based on an evaluation of the delivered product. In contrast to this approach others rely on the way the product is made. See e.g. /Hummel/.

prime contractor	partners
	Atomic Energy Agency Winfrith United Kingdom
	City University London United Kingdom
	Dublin City University Dublin Ireland
	ElectronicCentralen Hörsholm Denmark
	ERIA Madrid Spain
Vérilog Toulouse France	ETNOTEAM Milan Italy
	Gesellschaft für Mathematik und Datenverarbeitung St.Augustin Germany
	Gesellschaft für Reaktorsicherheit Garching Germany
	Glasgow College Glasgow United Kingdom
	Strathclyde University Glasgow United Kingdom

Figure 1: Members of the SCOPE Project

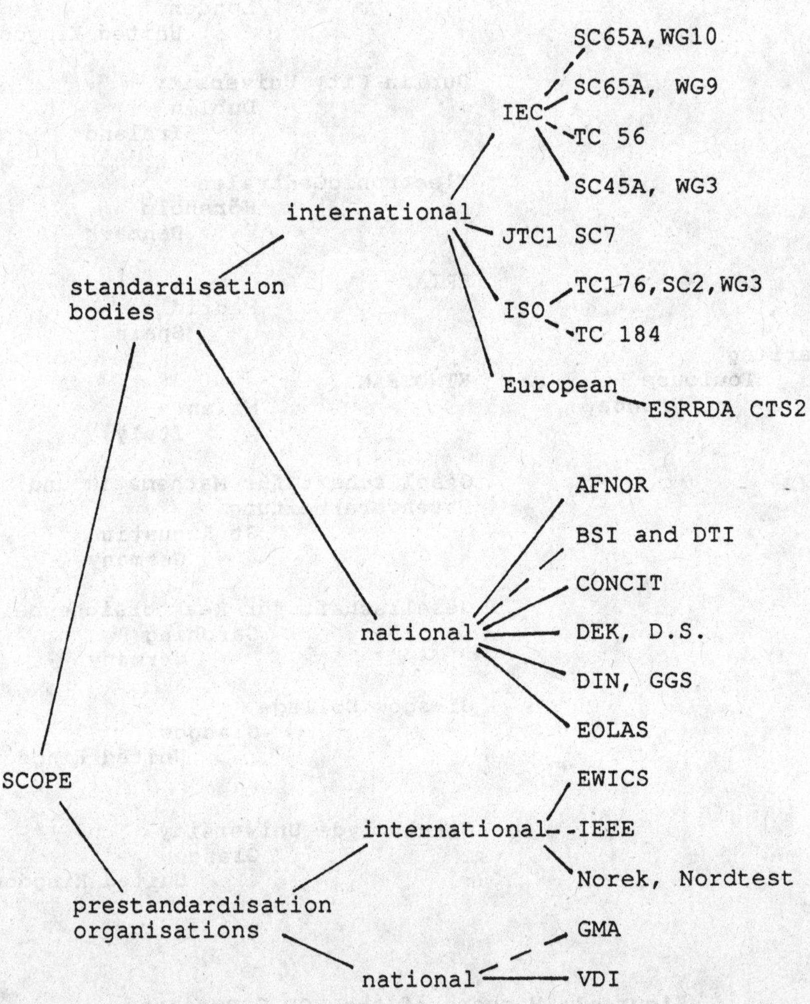

Fugure 2: Connections to Standardisation Organisations

The case studies that should provide experience with certification questions dealt with

- a medical data base system /Moynihan and O'Connor/,
- a business software system /Agostoni, Caliman and di Ventura/,
- a nuclear power plant operator information system /Bors and Kersken/,
- a power plants' performance monitoring system /Neil and Bache/,
- a documents management system /Hunter, Kirkwood and Rae/,
- a tool for analysis of programs.

The case studies had different major aims before the background of certification: investigating static analysis techniques, specification methods or data collection problems.

The underlying progams were developed in different languages. Some were complete already before SCOPE started, others were developed in parallel to the certification efforts. On the basis of the experience gained Certification Bricks were defined. These Bricks will be used as parts of a final certification model.

Another objective of these case studies was data collection about software validation. The data were stored in a data base that had been established on the basis of the REQUEST data base /Ross/.

In one of the project parts the legal implications of software malfunctions and the questions of certification have been investigated. In order to get a fairly international view on the problems both the British legal system and the French one have been considered. Results have been reported in /Lloyd and Wilson, Wilson and Lloyd/. Preliminary results are:

- the difference between the two legal systems is not large, regarding software quality requirements,
- the customer has a right to get a useful product but the product is allowed to contain some defects,
- several aspects of liability come into play,
- software is a product, not a service,
- certification may lower the manufacturer's risk.

THE CERTIFICATION MODEL

Technical Aspects

The top down approach for a certification model started with the aspects of software quality and the related metrics in general. See /Hausen and Cacutalua/ and the working papers of /de Neumann and A. Wingrove/. The software quality attributes identified as being relevant in this respect were:

Product Operation
- Correctness
- Reliability
- Efficiency
- Integrity
- Usability

Product Revision
- Maintainability
- Flexibility
- Testability

Product Transistion
- Portability
- Reusability
- Interoperability

Based on this four attributes were considered particularly important for certification:

Workmanship
Correctness
Reliability
Efficiency.

During the discussions in the project it turned out, that two types of views were reasonable:
- the strict view: certification of actual service against specified service;
- the broad view: certification of actual service against expected service (fitness for purpose).

In addition to these there were thoughts about several classes of software quality: Classes A to D, A being the strongest and D the weakest. The following table from /SCOPE Consortium 2/ shows what documentation is needed and what techniques are used in order to verify the mentioned four attributes.
Thereby it is understood that each group requires the certification bricks from all lower groups as well in addition to its own bricks.

Possible Shape of a Certification Organisation

General

At present at least two schemes exist that could be taken as some basis for a possible organisaion on software certification: the scheme according to the EOTC (European Organisation for Testing and Certification) and its suborganisation ECITC (European Committee for Information and Telecomunication technology Testing and Certification) and the scheme from the GGS (Gütegemeinschaft Software). Figure 3 gives an English translation of the German interpretation of the first scheme. The characteristic is a two level organisation: a

	Workmanship	Correctness	Reliability	Efficiency
D	user-documentation check list	user-documentation	code, specification testing	testing specification testing
C	code project doc. check lists metrics	specification functional-test	code specification testing	code specification testing
B	QA documents process metrics ISO 9000	project doc.-review white box - test	code specification testing	code specification testing
A		project doc.-review, white box - test	code specification testing	code specification testing

Table 1: Documents and Techniques for the four certification groups for the simple Certificate from /SCOPE Consortium 2/

national one and a Europen one. In order to balance the powers properly it has also become quite complex. The scheme of the GGS is depicted in Figure 4.

A particularity of the software that is considered in the SCOPE project is the user or manufacturer given specification: This is in contrast to the case of ECITC, where conformace to certain standards e.g. from the telecommunications area or from computer languages is sought after. In the SCOPE case it is not sufficient to give test packages to the individual Test Labs that enable them to test for conformity. Since each specification is different, it is important to supervise the individual test labs form a central institution in order to ensure equal quality of the certificates over a required period of time through all the individual countries.

A Large Scheme

Figure 5 gives an adaptation to the needs of softwre certification according to manufacturer specifications. In that figure the line on test packages from Fig.3 has been exchanged against a line on supervision. This supervision requires an

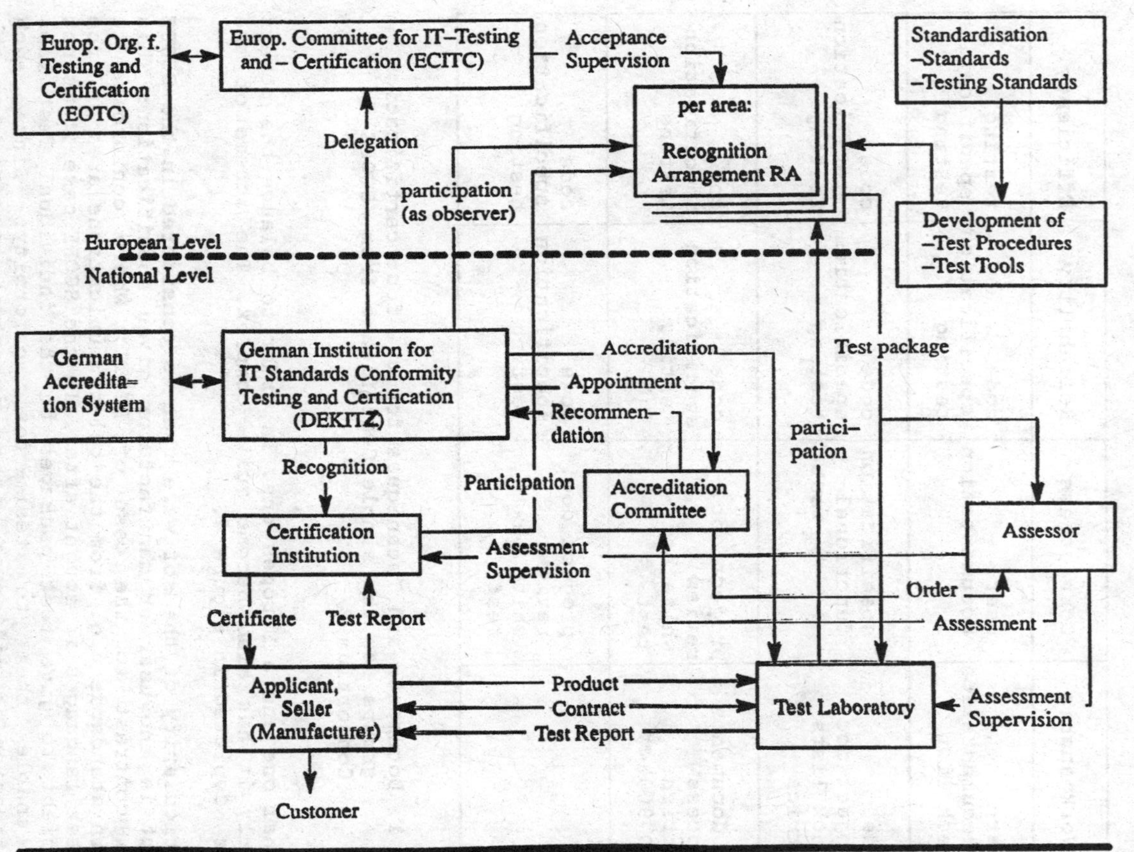

Fig. 3: German Scheme for IT Standards Conformity Testing and Certification (sector committee IT)

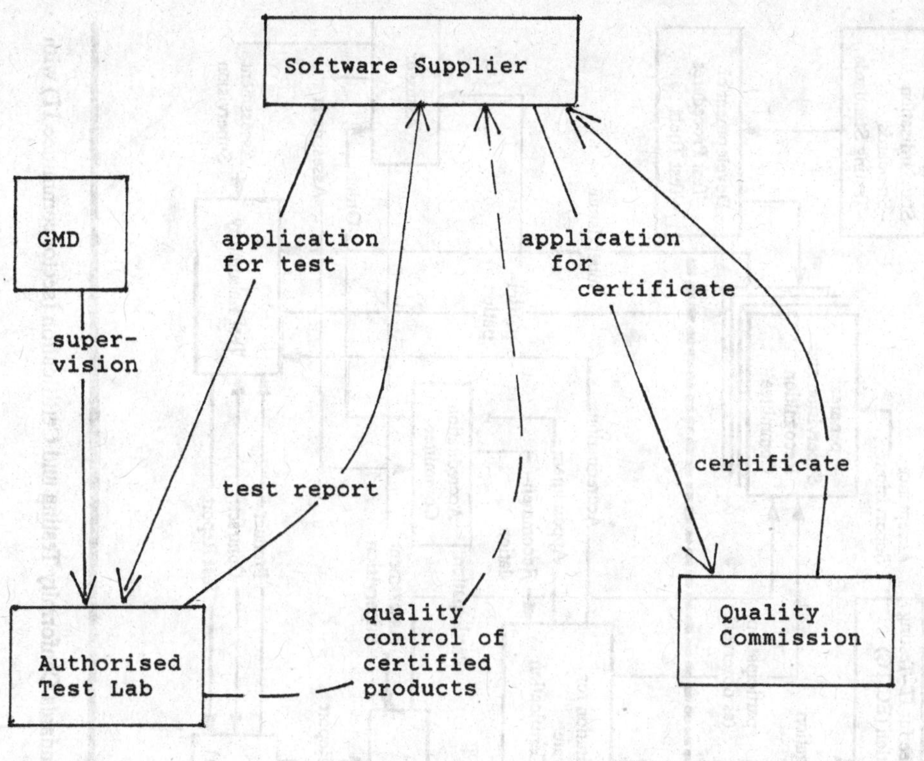

Figure 4: Mode of Working of the Gütegemeinschaft Software

acting body on the European level, here represented by the supervision and recognition committee for a particular area. This committee would be responsible for certificate equality within its area. The idea behind having serveral such committees is that it might be necessary to separate business applications from industrial software etc., because of the needed specific test equipment and detailed knowledge of the application area.
In contrast to our case here, just a recognition arrangement per area would be sufficient in the case of IT certification according to standards. On the other hand the software certification activity could well be appended to the existing organisation of the ECITC. Also the production of standards and test procedures and tools would remain the same as in the already established body.

On the national level an organisation about software testing and certification would be required. That organisation would

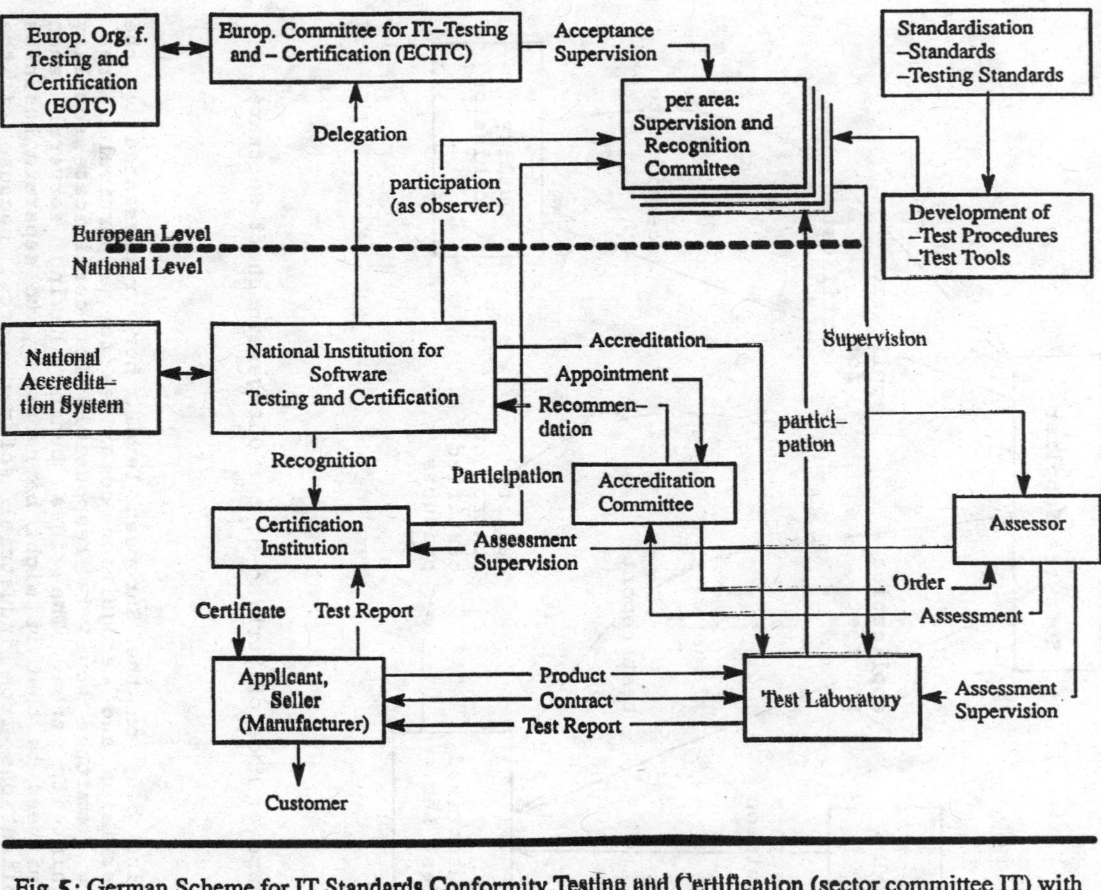

Fig. 5: German Scheme for IT Standards Conformity Testing and Certification (sector committee IT) with minimum adaptations

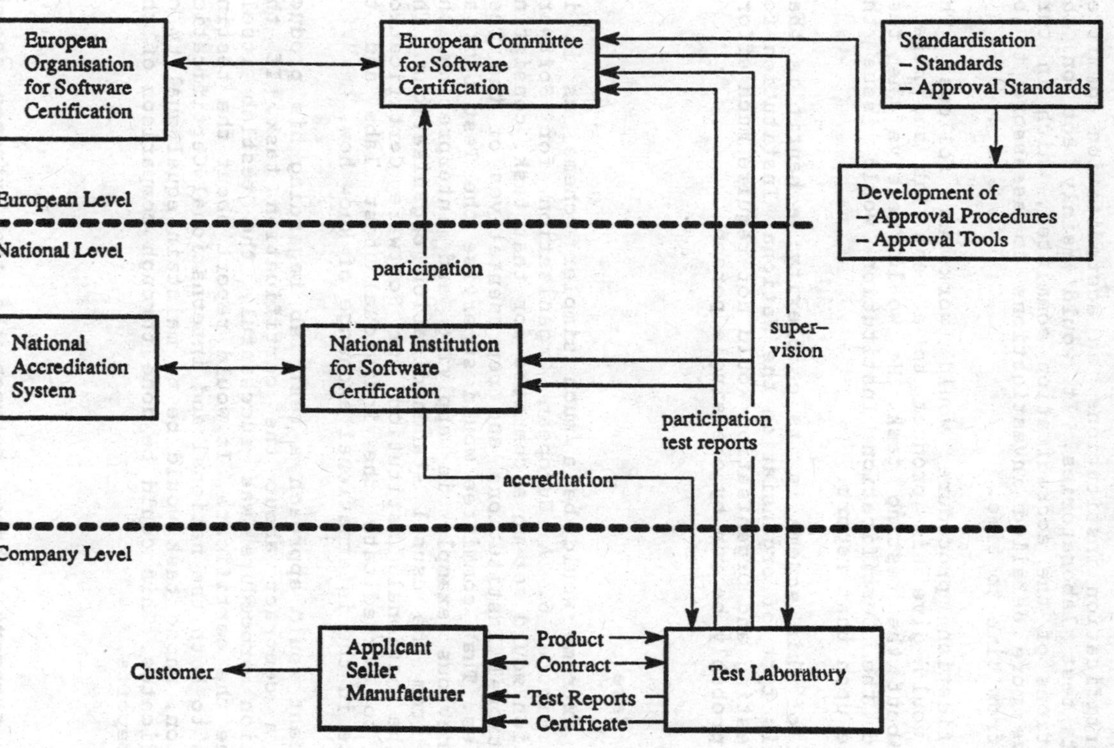

Fig. 6: Minimum Scheme for Software Certification

install certification institutions, an accreditation committee and permit test laboratories. It would mainly act on the recommendations of the accreditation committee, which in turn would leave more detailed investigations to assessors to be appointed from time to time.

The certification procedure would work as follows: The applicant would give his product to a test lab and make a contract about the testing task. He would receive the test report and the Certification Institution would issue the certificate upon that report.

A drawback of this scheme is its complexity; a benfit is that through this type of organsiation the National Institution for Software Testing and Organisation would not require much effort and could probably be run by one single person.

The Modest Case

The other extreme would be a much simpler scheme, as it is given in Figure 6. A European Organisation for Software Certification would set up a committe for that task, consisting of the National Institutions and representatives of the Test Laboratories. That committee would supervise the Test Labs as in the previous example in applying and interpreting the standards from the ususal standardisation organisations. The task of the national institution for Software Certification would be to accreditate the individual test labs and to participate in the international exchange of know how.

The applicant would approach a test lab regarding his product and make a contract about the certification task. If the certification procedure was successful, the testlab itself could issue the certificate. It would report about the testing procedures to both the national and international Certification Organisation, whose task would be to maintain equal quality of all certificates. This could be done through comparison of the received reports.

Other

There are numerous schemes between the two extremes shown. since the individual European countries are very different in both their sizes and their structures, it is probably not desireable to prescribe too much, but leave it to the individual case how things should be organised.

PHASE II OF THE PROJECT AND OPEN QUESTIONS

During the second phase of the project more organisations will participate. The aim will be a workable standard about a European Software Certification Scheme. The aspects found in phase I need be brought together: the legal questions, the case study outcomes and the theoretical results based on software quality attributes and metrics.

Among the yet open questions range the following items:

- re-certification; what has to be done if a certificate was already issued and some changes to the software have been made? is a completely new certification required? ... a partially new certification?

- branch specific certificates; is it reasonable to issue separate certificates for software for different branches: for lawyers, for farmers, for shop keepers, for travel agencies etc.?

- user interfaces; for the uninformed human user of a computer system the user interface is very important; should the achievements of software ergonomy be a mandatory part of all good quality software?

- certification on the basis of operating experience; probabilistic reasoning suggests that large positive operating experience wîth a certain product could replace some Bricks of the certification procedure; whow could this be cast into rules?

- how long should a certificate last? Is it reasonable to have it indefinitely, even if technology or legal surroundings change?

CONCLUSION

Most of the aspects of the SCOPE project have been dealt with in a rather subjetive manner in this contribution. Readers, who are interesed in a balanced description of the so far achieved results are referred to /Robert and Roan/. Various details on the project and its findings are published in the conference proceedings of ASP-90 and in the numerous intermediate reports which can be ordered from their authors.

ACKNOWLEDGEMENTS

The authors express their thanks to all members of the consortium, who have contributed to the above mentioned results both during many discussions and in their papers. They thank for their engaged and successful efforts in view of a European Software quality sign. They thank in particular the Commission of the European Communities for having granted the ESPRIT project SCOPE number P 2151, the responsible official, Mr.D.Callaghan and the reviewers of this project Messers Cicu and Rienstra for their engagement and many helpful remarks.

REFERENCES

AEA Technology and Strathclyde University
Database Definition: Data & Database Issues
Report in the SCOPE Project
SC.90/009/AEA.STC/T 1.3.1.RP02. Feb 1990

G.Agostoni, P.Caliman and D.di Ventura
Assessing Quality for Business Oriented
Software: An Experience on an Application
Supoported by a Relational Data Base
in: Approving Software Products (ASP-90),
Elsevier, September 1990

A.Bors and M.Kersken Interaction of Man and Tools in Static
Analysis
in: Approving Software Products (ASP-90),
Elsevier, September 1990

F. Copigneaux Software Process and Product Certification
in B.de Neumann edt, CSR Conference: Software
Certification, pp 23 to 42, Sept 88, Elsevier

DEKITZ Deutsches Institut für Normung, Deutsche Koordinierungsstelle für IT-Normenkonformitätsprüfung
und -zertifizierung (DEKITZ)
Akkreditierung als Prüflaboratorium auf dem
Gebiet der Informations-und Telekommunikationstechnik durch die Deutsche Koordinierungsstelle
für IT-Normenkonformitätsprüfung und -
Zertifizierung (DEKITZ), Informationspaket für
den Antragsteller, Berlin, 1990, INF.P.01.90

DIN 66285 Deutsches Institut für Normung
Anwendungssoftware Prüfgrundsätze, Vornorm 1985,
Norm 1990

R.Lindermeier and F.Siebert Proposals for the Organisation of
final Software Black Box Tests
in: Approving Software Products (ASP-90),
Elsevier, September 1990

I.Lloyd and R.Wilson Software Quality - Some Legal Issues
in: Approving Software Products (ASP-90),
Elsevier, September 1990

G.Knorr The Gütegemeinschaft Software - A Major Concept
in the Certification of Software Quality
in: Approving Software Products (ASP-90),
Elsevier, September 1990

H.Hummel The Life Cycle Methodology for Software Production and the Related Experience
in: Approving Software Products (ASP-9Ø), Elsevier, September 199Ø

H.L.Hausen and N.Cacutalua Defining a Method for Software Certification
in: Approving Software Products (ASP-9Ø), Elsevier, September 199Ø

R.B.Hunter, K.B.Kirkwood and A.K.Rae Experiences of Automated Data Collection from Software Development Projects
in: Approving Software Products (ASP-9Ø), Elsevier, September 199Ø

IEC 88Ø International Electrotechnical Commission
Software for Computers in the Safety System of Nuclear Power Stations
Geneva, 1987

B.de Neumann and A. Wingrove Experiences with producing a Computerised Software Certification Tool
in: Approving Software Products (ASP-9Ø), Elsevier, September 199Ø

several working papers of the SCOPE project
1989 and 199Ø

T.Moynihan and N.O'Connor
Towards a Method for Evaluating the Quality of a User-Oriented Functional Specification
in: Approving Software Products (ASP-9Ø), Elsevier, September 199Ø

Radio Technical Commission for Aeronautics
Software Considerations in Airborne Systems and Equipent Certification
RTCA/DO-178A, 194

P.Robert and A.Roan The SCOPE Project: an Overview
in: Approving Software Products (ASP-9Ø), Elsevier, September 199Ø

N. Ross High level Data Model Design
REQUEST/STL-nfr/111/S3/DC-RP/Ø1.2, August 1989
Atomic Energy Agency, Winfrith

SCOPE Consortium 1 Software Certification: State of the Art
SCOPE/R 1.1.1.1./RL/Ø1, SC.89/Ø66, Sept.1989

SCOPE Consortium 2 Certification Model - final report
SCOPE SC.9Ø/Ø31/ECT.jb/T1.1.1.2/RP/Ø3, July 199Ø

R. Wilson and I.Lloyd   First Report on the Legal Aspects of SCOPE, SCOPE/STH/T 1.1.5/Report/DL/ØØ, August 89

Third Report on the Legal Aspects of SCOPE SCOPE/STH/T 1.1.5/Report/DL/Ø2, May 199Ø

9

METKIT

Nicholas Ashley - BRAMEUR
October 1990

Abstract

The purpose of this paper is to present the mid term progress of METKIT, a collaborative project part-funded by the Commission of the European Communities under the second phase of the ESPRIT programme.

Introduction

The European software industry is slowly becoming more aware of the need to employ measurement to help understand and thus control software development. Although software development is becoming more methodical, the uptake of measurement is not as advanced as it should be. This is due to a variety of reasons, not least because of the lack of suitable teaching material to promote the use of measurement in software engineering.

The present situation is that an organisation wishing to set up a software engineering measurement programme has very little guidance on what to do and usually has unrealistic expectations. A major reason for this is that there has been very little effort to transfer the most promising research work in measurement to the very people who need it, namely software practioners. This has led to a climate of scepticism by software managers to the relevance and benefits of measurement. The aim of METKIT is to redress this situation.

Overview of METKIT

The primary objective of METKIT is to develop an educational package to promote the use of measurement in software engineering throughout Europe. In other words, METKIT will produce measurement courses and supporting materials tailored to the specific needs of industry and academia, using a variety of educational techniques and media.

At present there is much confusion amongst the software community as to the meaning of such terms as metric, measure and measurement. An aim of

METKIT is to remove this unnecessary confusion by providing consistent and unambiguous definitions.

It should be stressed that METKIT will not be conducting further research into software engineering measurement neither will it be producing the type of courses already commercially available. Rather it will harmonise existing reasearch, knowledge and experience to produce a comprehensive package which will teach Information Technology personnel and academic students the benefits and uses of measurement in software engineering. To help achieve this harmonisation, METKIT has formed links with and utilised the work done on other ESPRIT projects, including REQUEST, MUSE, TRUST, COSMOS, SCOPE and MERMAID.

The METKIT consortium consists of five industrial partners from France, Germany and the UK, a German Research Institute, one academic partner from the UK and an Italian company specialising in educational technology. The eight partners are :

- BRAMEUR (UK) - project co-ordinator
- British Telecom Research Laboratories (UK)
- Sema Group (UK)
- South Bank Polytechnic (UK)
- Dida*El (Italy)
- GMD (Germany)
- SES (Germany)
- Verilog (France)

The project began in February 1989 with a budget of 47 person years effort, and is due to be completed in January 1992. The project is now at the half-way stage, in terms of elapsed time, effort expended and plans.

Project Philosophy

One of the original aims of METKIT was to provide a unified set of metrics by which it would be possible to measure software quality attributes, such as reliability, maintainability, usability, etc. Early on in the project it became clear that it would not be desirable or feasible to provide such a unified set. This decision was influenced by feedback from the European software industry which revealed that organisations need to tailor metrics to suit their particular development methodologies and development environments.

To meet the needs of the European Software Industry, the METKIT philosophy to software engineering measurement advocates :

- a goal-driven approach, in contrast to the all too familiar approach of collecting data without having clearly defined goals on why the data is being collected and what to do with the information

- a rigorous approach to measurement based on the fundamental ideas in measurement theory.

- a classification of entities associated with software development in terms of products, processes and resources.

Development Strategy

The overriding approach to developing METKIT is to ensure that it meets the needs of industry and academia over the next five to ten years. To help ensure that this is the case, METKIT is using an iterative refinement approach to enable the involvement of potential users of the package throughout its development. At the start of the project, the METKIT consortium carried out an industrial survey throughout Europe, USA and Japan to determine the current practices and future requirements for using measurement in software development. An academic survey was also carried out to determine the current extent of the teaching of software measurement in academia and to assess the need for educational materials. These surveys were performed by conducting postal surveys using questionnaires, interviews and holding workshops. Specifically, answers were sought to four questions :

- who needs to be trained ?
- what needs to be taught ?
- what type of educational media needs to be used ?
- how should the package be structured ?

The industrial survey revealed that organisations want to use measurement to improve cost estimation, to determine productivity, to predict reliability and control development. Industry would also like guidelines on how to set up and run a measurement programme.

The academic survey revealed that software measurement is taught widely in academic software engineering courses, but there is insufficient educational material on software measurement. The future needs of academia were for flexible materials which advocate a goal-driven approach to software engineering measurement, supported by demonstration tools. The materials needed to be flexible in the sense that courses can be constructed to cope with variable time constraints.

To help ensure that METKIT meets the needs of industry and academia both now and in the future, a METKIT Users Panel has been established in the UK. The aim of the User Panel is to ensure the METKIT package reflects the needs of industry and academia and to participate in beta testing the courses. It is planned to expand the Users Panel, both within other METKIT partner countries as well as within academia.

Figure 1 depicts the development strategy.

Figure 1 - Strategy

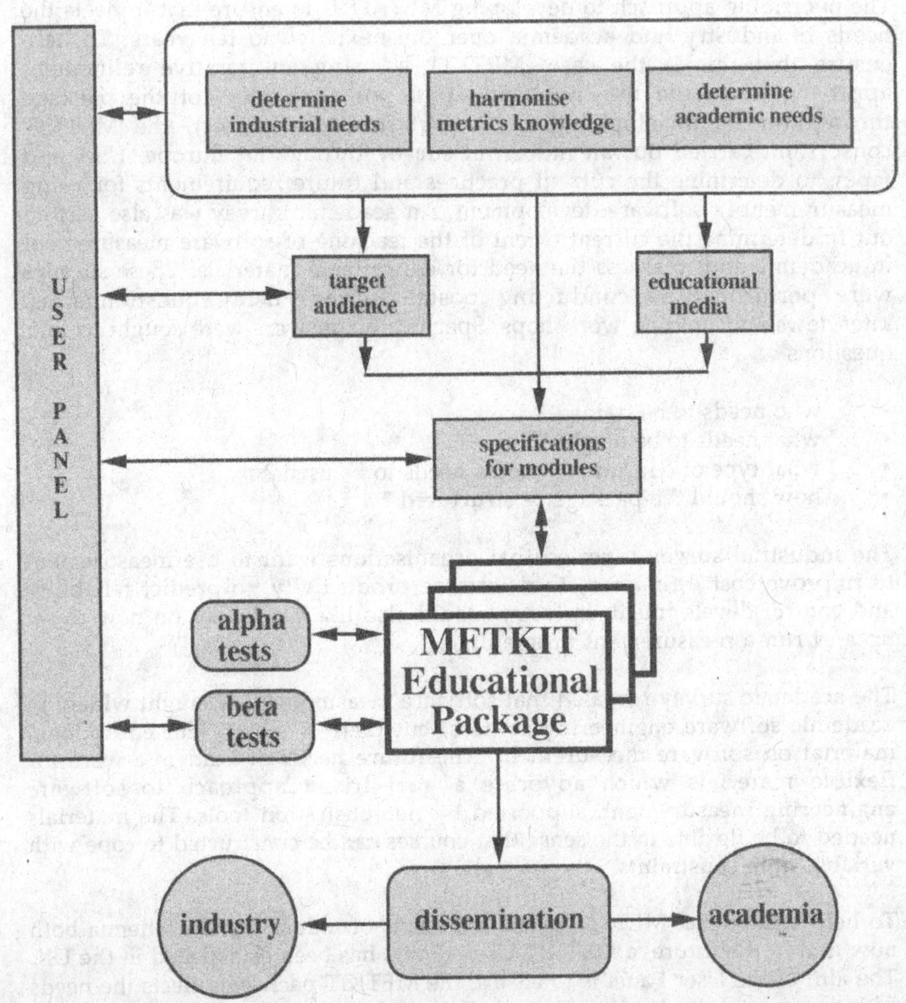

Structure of METKIT

The industrial and academic surveys revealed that the METKIT educational package should be able to satisfy the following criteria :

- take account of future changes in software development
- be expanded without the need for extensive changes to the structure
- allow parts of a course to be in different media
- support interval training
- allow organisations to structure their own courses
- be integrated into an organisation's own courses
- allow an organisation to introduce their own measurement tools
- support variable time constraints imposed by users and educators.

To meet these requirements it was decided that METKIT should consist of a set of modules together with supporting materials. Educators will then create courses by putting together a sequence of modules. It will be possible for an organisation to select specific modules from the total structure, in order to meet specific learning needs.

Each module may be studied relatively independently from other modules, as long as the student has the necessary prior knowledge and skills for that module. The duration of each module will be between one and four hours.

The modularity of METKIT will allow courses to be changed by enhancing, adding and discarding modules.

Target Audience

Based on the requirements of industry and academia, the METKIT package will be aimed primarily at three target groups :

- **managers** (including chief executives, project managers, QA managers)
- **software engineers** (including developers, QA personnel, planners and estimators)
- **academic students** (post graduates and under graduates).

This is only a part of the total possible audience for the METKIT package, which includes independent testers and certification bodies, tender evaluators, auditors, and users. The scope of the METKIT project, given the time and effort constraints, could not effectively target all possible audience groups. To attempt to do so would result in incomplete and relatively ineffective educational courses. Other target audiences will be catered for in the post ESPRIT stage of development.

To encourage the use of software engineering measurement, a major target group will be managers. The industrial survey confirmed opinions that, without managerial support and commitment for implementing a measurement programme, there will be little chance of such practices being adopted and hence little need for education of other groups.

Academic students are also seen as an important group because they will be the software engineers of the future, and therefore need a sound appreciation of software engineering measurement.

It should be noted that educators will also be a target group in the sense that METKIT will be providing training programmes for educators to enable them to use the METKIT package.

Educational Media

In order to meet the needs of a wide range of potential user groups, METKIT will use a range of educational technologies and techniques and will be developed in the following media :

- teacher-mediated with supporting text and slides
- rule-based CAL (Computer Aided Learning) system
- hypertext, running under the Apple Macintosh
- video
- interactive video
- audio cassette.

The majority of modules will be developed using a teacher mediated educational environment with slides. This decision was influenced by the fact that slides are widely used and popular in both industry and academia and that text and slides are relatively cheap and easy to change. This is an important factor when using an iterative refinement development process where a series of prototype modules need to be produced, tested and enhanced. It is envisaged that if the courses prove to be popular, they will then be translated into other educational media and other languages.

It should be noted that not all media are appropriate to the three target groups. For example, the industrial survey confirmed opinions that senior managers would not be prepared to use a CAL system to gain an awareness of the importance of using measurement to understand and control software development.

Some modules will be developed in more than one media. For example, the high level awareness module for managers will be available as a video, audio cassette and as slides with supporting text.

Initially, all courseware will be developed in English. On completion of beta testing the courseware, it is planned to translate a selection of the courseware into French, German and Italian.

Contents of METKIT

The METKIT educational package will consist of a suite of modules and supporting materials which can be structured into courses and covering the following areas :

- **modules for managers**
  - A teacher mediated awareness module whose objective is to convince managers of the importance of using measurement as a management tool to understand and control software development.
  - A teacher mediated module explaining how to set up and run a measurement programme.
  - A video explaining the importance and benefits of using measurement as a management tool to control software development.
  - An audio cassette tape explaining the importance and benefits of using measurement as a management tool to control software development.
- **modules for software engineers**
  - A teacher mediated module explaining the scope, applicability and benefits of software engineering measurement.
  - A teacher mediated module describing the benefits of using measurement to understand and thus control software projects.
  - A teacher mediated module describing the concepts of measurement in a non mathematical way and illustrated by examples in everyday life.
  - A teacher mediated module describing what atributes of software development can be measured and how they can be measured.

- A teacher mediated module providing an overview of the current industrial practices in using software engineering measurement and covering such issues as tools to support measurement activities and standards and certification.

- A set of modules on cost estimation explaining how to set up a cost estimation programme and perform cost estimates. The modules will be supported by a case study to show how to implement a cost estimation metrics programme.

- A rule-based Computer Aided Learning system to learn about measurement in quality assurance.

- An interactive video to learn about using measurement to assess the usabiliy of a software system.

- **modules for academic students**

  - A teacher mediated module providing an introduction to software engineering measurement.

  - A teacher mediated technical module on the theory of measurement.

  - A teacher mediated module describing what attributes of software development can be measured and how they can be measured, paying particular attention to data collection and analysis.

  - A teacher mediated module providing an overview of the current industrial practices in using software engineering measurement and covering such issues as tools to support measurement activities, standards and certification.

  - A teacher mediated module on complexity metrics relating to the structure of software.

  - A teacher mediated module dealing with the classification of entities associated with software development, into products, processes and resources.

  - A teacher mediated module on the state-of-the-art of measurement applied to distributed systems, including concurrent and object oriented systems.

  - A case study to enable students to apply software metrics to analyse industrial data using computer-based tools.

- A prototype hypertext system, running under Apple Macintosh, for academic students to learn about the theory of measurement.

- **support material**

  - A set of educators guides which provide guidelines for teachers who will give the courses.

  - A text book providing a comprehensive description of software engineering measurement and a theoretical foundation of measurement theory. The text book will be consistent with the courseware modules.

  - A text book on using measurement to assess the usability of a software system.

  - A text book for managers providing guidelines for setting up and running a measurement programme based on a pragmatic approach to measurement.

  - A tool sampler containing a variety of demonstration and educational versions of measurement tools will also be developed as an aid to the teaching of software measurement; for example, to enable students to get hands on experience when carrying out case studies. The tools will consist initially of demonstration versions of commercially available tools and educational versions of tools owned by partners in the METKIT consortium. Tools developed by METKIT partners include :

    - Logiscope (Verilog) - a static analysis tool

    - QUALMS (South Bank Polytechnic) - a tool to analyse the structure of software and produce measures relating to this structure

    - ATHENA (BRAMEUR) - a usability assessment tool

    - PC CALC (SES) - a cost estimation tool.

  - A bibliography database of software metrics papers.

  - A computer-based glossary of terms.

Figure 2 depicts the METKIT educational package.

Figure 2 - METKIT Educational Package

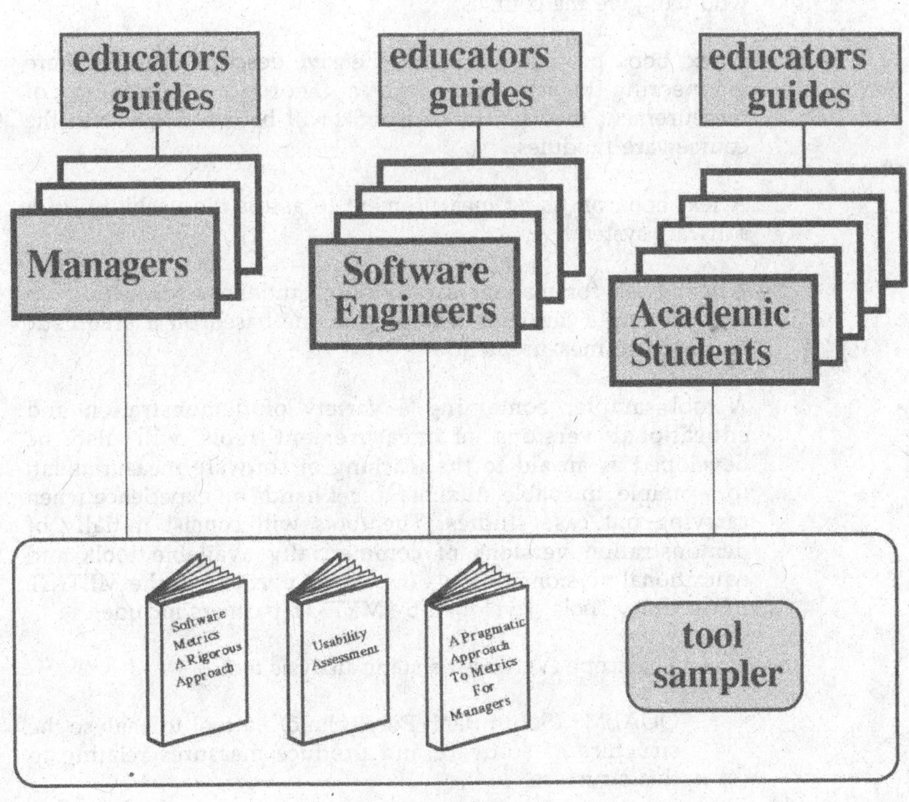

support materials

Assessment

The modules have been specified in such a way that it will be possible to quantifiably measure how much a student has learnt from taking a particular module.

Main Outputs To Date

METKIT has produced the following major project documents :

- a report on European industrial practices in using measurement in software development and their future needs
- a report on academic current practices and needs in teaching software measurement
- a state-of-the-art report in software metrics
- courseware for the high level awareness module for academic students entitled **Introduction To Software Engineering Measurement**
- specifications for the courseware modules
- a classification scheme for software metrics encompassing all stages of software development which provides a framework into which particular metrics can be placed and subsequently analysed
- a bibliography database of software metrics papers
- a glossary of terms.

Dissemination Activities To Date

The marketing of METKIT is a vital activity, especially as the success of METKIT will be judged by how many organisations and academic institutions use METKIT. To help ensure METKIT reaches the widest possible audience across Europe, the following dissemination activites have been performed :

- holding an academic workshop to explain the specification and design of academic modules
- holding an industrial workshop to promote METKIT
- presenting papers on METKIT at various conferences

- partners promoting METKIT both within their organisations and externally

- distributing the METKIT brochure to 1500 industrial and academic organisations.

Quantitative Aims Of METKIT

By the end of the project, it is expected that the following quantitative aims will have been met :

- over 100 educators will have been trained to use the METKIT educational package

- over 200 students will have been trained in the fundamentals of software engineering measurement

- over 100 senior managers will have taken the managers awareness course

- over 200 software engineers will have taken a course for software engineers

- over 2000 software personnel, external to the METKIT consortium, will have been made aware of METKIT through courses, workshops, seminars, brochures, etc.

The Future

The future milestones for METKIT are as follows :

- December 1990 - completion of prototype modules for managers
- December 1990 - completion of awareness modules for software engineers
- April 1991 - completion of alpha testing industrial courseware
- July 1991 - completion of alpha testing student modules
- May 1991 - METKIT textbook on software measurement
- October 1991 - completion of beta testing industrial courseware
- January 1992 - completion of dissemination activities.

The ESPRIT funded project is only the first development stage of METKIT. It is intended to continue dissemination activities and the modification and enhancement of the METKIT package after the end of the funded stage in order to :

- meet the requirements of a wider range of audience types
- translate courses into other educational media

- continue translating courses into French, German and Italian
- develop additional courses.

The long-term aim is to make METKIT a commercially available product by January 1993.

10

NEW APPROACH TO SOFTWARE COST ESTIMATION

PETER KOK
VOLMAC Nederland BV
P.O. Box 2575
The Netherlands

ABSTRACT

Why do the cost estimates of software development projects so often differ from the actual costs? This article is focussed on this question. An answer and a possible solution to this problem will be provided. The solution is based on an analysis of the problems with regard to the present generation models and is being developed within the MERMAID project.

INTRODUCTION

Despite the ample availability of methods and software packages that support the preparation of an estimate for a software development project, cost estimation is still a very complicated activity. Research has shown that the reliability and accuracy of such tools is limited [Heemstra, 1989], [MERMAID, 1989]. Besides, only a limited number of organizations makes use of a systematic method for the preparation of a project estimate. In a large number of cases one is unable to answer questions like: 'What were the costs of this project?' and 'What is the productivity of this team?'. Several sectors (among others the building trade and the hotel and catering industry) have been using historical project data for the preparation of their project estimates for years now and they are able to estimate the costs within a margin of 10%. Such a basis is often lacking in an estimate of a software development project, also because adequate tools for the recording and the analysis of historical project data are lacking.

This paper provides a concise overview of the problem analysis of the MERMAID project, which was published in the January issue of Journal of Software Research [Kok, 1990]. Subsequently the architecture and the functionality of the MERMAID toolset are discussed. This prototype supports project managers during their preparation of a cost estimate, in which they are able to make extensive use of historical project data. Due to the unique flexible design, the toolset can be used in the administrative as well as in the industrial sector.

Due to a number of developments the importance of accurate estimates is increasing. In the first place, these last few years, systems have been implemented that support corporate processes which can no longer be performed without automated systems. Take for example the payments between banks and the complex process control within factories. Since in a large number of cases automation was considered the only solution, a cost estimate only had a restricted influence on the decision making process. The software to be developed in the next years will mainly be used to start up new services and to optimize existing services. The costs begin to play an important part within the selection of the different alternatives, since the technical possibilities have increased and because the necessity to automate these processes is obviously less.

In the second place the software industry is becoming more and more 'grown-up'. Today the purchasers of software products and software services no longer accept things they would have accepted five years ago. This development does not only have consequences for the 'cost estimation' field, but it concerns all aspects of software engineering. The software products market is slowly shifting from a demand market to a supply market. Characteristic to a supply market is the increasing competition. A result of this trend is the increase of the number of fixed-price contracts. In this type of agreement a precise estimate is of vital importance to the supplier, because an overrun of the budget would be at the expense of the profit margin. The professionalization of the field is also reflected in the increasing attention to the effectiveness and the efficiency of the development process. The collection of historical project data and the use of a project budget are consequences of this trend.

THE MERMAID PROJECT

The ESPRIT II project MERMAID was started in October 1988 on a budget of 45 person-years and it will be completed in October 1992. The aim of the MERMAID project is to support project managers in the field of cost estimation, resource modelling, risk analysis and progress monitoring, by means of the development of the MERMAID toolset. The first version of the MERMAID toolset (MARK 1) is now in its implementation stage and will be delivered to the CEC by the end of this year. This prototype is an implementation of part of the MERMAID results and its main objective is to validate MERMAID concepts. The MARK 1 toolset will be tested in practice, among others by commercial organizations. The evaluations and the results of research are the basis of the MARK 2 toolset that will be delivered by the end of the project. Next to the basic concepts from the MARK 1 prototype this toolset will consist of the additional project management tools (resource modelling and risk analysis).

PROBLEMS

Most cost estimation models (COCOMO, FPA) were developed at the beginning of the eighties by collecting and analyzing data from a large number of projects. In such analysis an algorithm is produced, in which the required effort is a function of a number of product attributes and process attributes. The collected project data serve as testcases to verify and refine the algorithm. To evaluate a model as 'acceptable' several standards have been employed within the field. The standard for the detailed COCOMO model was for example 'the actual costs are within a margin of 20% of the estimates for 70% of the number of projects'. The data that have been used by the different researchers in order to specify the costs models can be considered obsolete where the software industry is concerned. Moreover, the data originate from several organizations; there is no guarantee that the same counting and measuring procedures have been used.

A difficult issue within the field of cost estimation with regard to software research is the 'calibration' (to calibrate means adjusting the constants and/or parameters within the algorithm) of the standard cost models. Several studies have demonstrated that the use of an uncalibrated model is not advisable, since the results are very inaccurate. Obviously, for the development of a system using a fourth generation language within a small organization other productivity figures must be used than for a COBOL application within a complex bureaucratic environment.

Heemstra [Heemstra 1989] has demonstrated that a large number of organizations (profit as well as non-profit) in Holland hardly or never use budgets or cost estimates. These organizations are either not interested or unable to put a price tag on the software that has been developed on their own account. It has been shown that a lot of the organizations that do prepare estimates do so without systematic methods or tools.

When one realizes that estimation models are hardly used in practice and that several researchers have demonstrated that the accuracy of such models is limited, the following essential question arises: **'What is wrong with the existing estimation models?'**.

This question can be answered simply by analyzing the aim of the present generation models and by comparing them to the demands a project manager makes of a cost model for the purpose of project estimates and cost management.

The aim of the present models is to model all factors from the entire universe that can be of influence to the costs of system development. In such models two types of factors are incorporated (see Figure 1). The first type (for example lines-of-code) models the deviation between different projects within the same environment. The second type explains the differences between environments. These last mentioned factors (productivity for example) are necessary because the models are applied in several different branches and organizations. Before a model can be used to estimate the project costs within a certain environment, these last factors must be provided with a value; this is called 'calibration'.

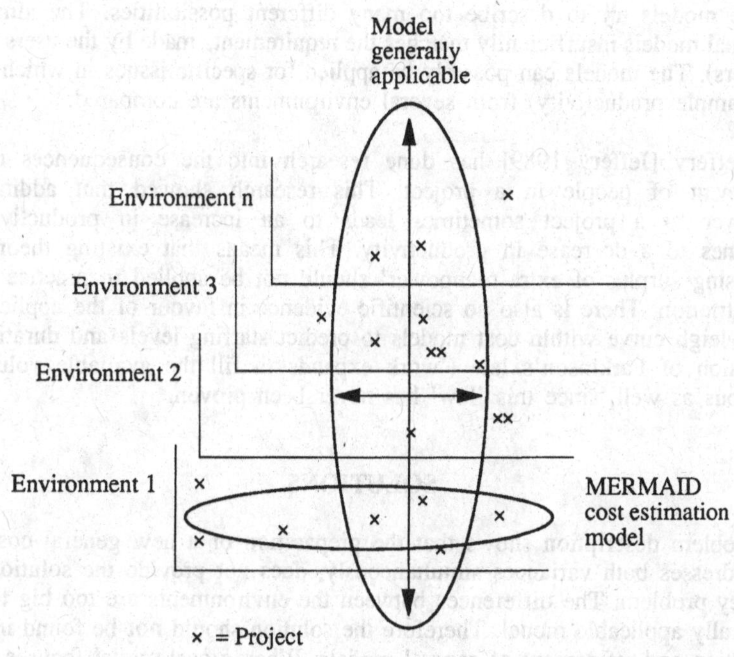

Figure 1 The domain of cost models

However, practice shows that an estimation model is often used by a project manager to make and monitor the planning and forecasts of his or her project. The most important requirements to such a model are reliability and accuracy of the estimate for the next stage or for the entire project. The model is therefore used to determine the differences between projects within one organization or department.

Thus, this analysis shows that the present generation of models tries to model both variances (between projects and between environments), while in practice only the differences between the projects are of importance.

The number of factors required to explain the differences between environments is huge and the factors are often correlated, which makes the models instable (in other words: a difference within a specific cost driver has an unwanted strong influence on the final result). Assigning a value to these factors within a specific situation is difficult. The present generation of models is too complex and the differences between the organizations are too large to be able to incorporate them in one model.

From this we can conclude that the inaccurate results are partly due to the fact that the models try to describe too many different possibilities. The aim of the traditional models insufficiently matches the requirements made by the users (project managers). The models can possibly be applied for specific issues in which aspects (for example productivity) from several environments are compared.

Ross Jeffery [Jeffery 1989] has done research into the consequences of extra deployment of people in a project. This research showed that adding extra manpower to a project sometimes leads to an increase in productivity and sometimes to a decrease in productivity. This means that existing theories like 'decreasing surplus of extra manpower' should not be applied in practice without any restriction. There is also no scientific evidence in favour of the application of the Rayleigh curve within cost models to predict staffing levels and duration. The application of Parkinson's law ('work expands to fill the available volume') is dangerous as well, since this 'law' has never been proven.

SOLUTIONS

The problem description shows that the preparation of a new general cost model that addresses both variances simultaneously, does not provide the solution to the accuracy problem. The differences between the environments are too big to model a generally applicable model. Therefore the solution should **not** be found in further elaboration and refinement of general models. When a cost model focuses on only one of both variances there is a good chance that the reliability and the accuracy of the prediction will increase considerably. It is obvious, that the model should be restricted to the differences between projects within an environment, because in actual practice this question has top priority.

The MERMAID approach is not a successor of a generally applicable model, but it supports a project manager with regard to producing and monitoring cost estimates within a certain environment. This option has very far-reaching consequences.

Contrary to the present generation of models that are based on relatively obsolete data from different environments, within the MERMAID approach a model will be generated in a dynamic way; use will be made of statistical techniques, based on the most recent data. Next to the data of the project for which a cost estimate is produced, use is made of historical project data that have been collected within a certain environment, with the aid of specific, environment-dependent definitions. These definitions correspond with the working method of the organization and they direct the data collection process. The MERMAID approach provides the organization with the opportunity to adjust the model to the specific characteristics of the organization, while the present generation of models often forced an organization to work with predefined variables (metrics).

The application of a 'local' model, based on a homogenous database will probably lead to considerably less factors that influence the costs. This simplifies the use of the model.

An important parameter that influences various models is the 'lines-of-code' metric. When models which contain such metrics are used at the beginning of the software development development lifecycle, this metric has to be predicted. However, there is no proof that people are better in predicting lines-of-codes than in predicting costs. The MERMAID approach therefore avoids estimating the cost on the basis of estimated factors instead of measured factors. This philosophy is based on the ideas of DeMarco [1982]. In his book DeMarco states that it is impossible to estimate or manage projects without measured data [metrics=knowledge]. In addition, he introduces 'phased-based estimation'. MERMAID has adopted this approach. The MERMAID approach is based on one or more standard life cycles within an organization. A life cycle consists of a number of sequential milestones. A milestone is a moment when a(n) (intermediate) product is delivered. Such a(n) (intermediate) product, for example a system proposal or a functional design, has its own metrics (units of measure) that can be used for cost estimation. Consequently MERMAID propose to use different metrics at different times. In this way the actual values of the previous phase can be used to estimate the next phase.

The dynamic use of statistical techniques has two more advantages. In the first place it is possible to provide accuracy intervals for each prediction. This provides the project manager with an indication of the accuracy. Moreover, the models can provide information about the quality of the model within a specific situation. The quality of the model is tested by comparing the forecasts of all historical projects with the realized costs. This information indicates the suitability of the model and is an indication of the reliability as well. Such indication of the applicability of a model within a specific situation is lacking in existing models.

The MERMAID approach does not consist of statistical techniques only, because these cannot be applied in any situation. For example:

The start-up phase.
The statistical models require at least 5 projects before any prediction can be made. When an environment is redefined, many project data is missing. For the first projects within an environment other techniques are therefore necessary.

Tender support
At the beginning of a project the required quantitative information that enables you to perform statistical techniques successfully is often missing. Techniques, based on qualitative information (for example estimation by analogy) are therefore necessary.

Deviating projects
It is possible that the statistical techniques cannot be used in a project that strongly deviates from the historical projects with regard to certain aspects

Within the MERMAID approach the principle of 'analogy' is applied for these situations. An estimate based on this technique requires only one analogous project. The project for which an estimate has to be made is compared with one or more historical projects on a number of aspects. By assigning relative values to the aspects (for example this system is 20% more complex than the previous system) an estimate can be deduced.

THE MARK 1 TOOLS

The MARK 1 toolset is one of the achievements of the MERMAID project. This toolset is the first implementation of the MERMAID approach to cost estimation. The selection of MARK 1 functions is influenced by the limiting conditions (man-hours and elapsed time) of the project and the available knowledge and experience within the consortium. The MARK 1 toolset is the first prototype, while the aspects of the MERMAID approach that were not selected have been transferred to MARK 2. In general it can be stated that the models of MARK 1 are based on limited research. The subjects which require intensive research will be part of the MARK 2 toolset. These tools will be delivered by the end of the MERMAID project.

The MERMAID tools are aimed at organizations engaged in project-based software development within a relatively stable environment, according to a life cycle in which several milestones can be distinguished. One must also be willing to invest in data collection, because the MERMAID approach is based on historical data. The tools support the project manager when he is estimating the required effort for the next phase and for the entire project, with the aid of the principle of analogy and statistical techniques. Additional support is provided in the form of product size predictions, accuracy intervals, progress monitoring and feedback on the quality of the predictions. The acquired results can be used within in several stages of the project. First the results can be used to draw up tenders, project proposals, etcetera. Subsequently the result can be used as a basis and as a target for the project manager. The tools can also support the project manager with regard to revisions of the estimate, for example in case of extension, and to change the product specifications.

For the development of the MARK 1 toolset the MERMAID consortium has made use of a SUN 3 workstation, the semantic database PCTE and an object oriented extension to C. During the development much attention was paid to the interaction with the user and to the definition of the different interface protocols. The user friendliness of a tool is one of the most important acceptance factors and therefore it is important for the overall success when the basic concept is: SUCCESS = QUALITY * ACCEPTANCE. The project uses the interface protocols to make the models and methods less dependent of the hardware- and software environment. The database interface makes it possible to approach the database as objects instead of as entities and relationships. The current interface supports the PCTE implementation, but with a minimum effort it can be adapted to another DBMS. Basically it is possible to adapt the present Objective C-interface to one of the 'de facto' industrial standards. However, further research is required to establish if such a user interface meets the requirements made by the MARK 1 models.

The Estimation Base is the central issue in the MARK 1 tools. This repository for metric definitions and estimation data is one of the mechanisms used to integrate the various tools. The structure of the Estimation Base is represented in figure 2.

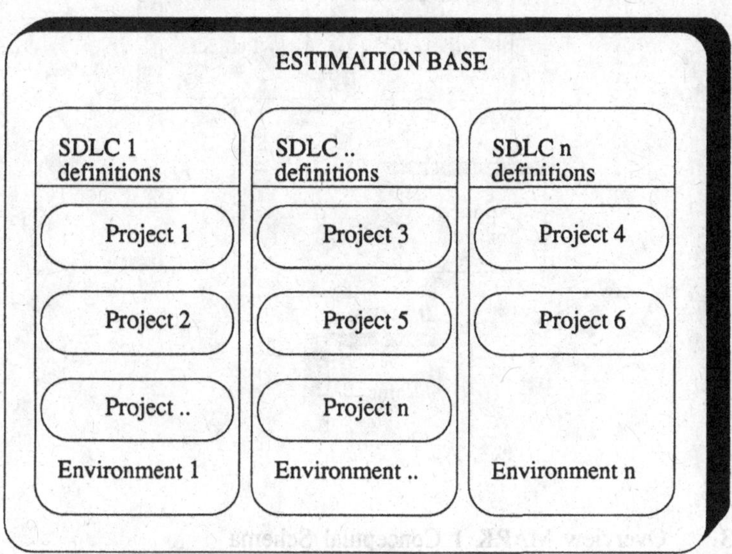

Figure 2 Structure of the Estimation Base

The Estimation Base consists of one or more 'environments', depending on the number of Software Development Life Cycles (SDLC) used within the organization. An SDLC is a life cycle in which use is made of sequential milestones. An 'environment' consists of definitions and of the historical data of several projects.

The definitions refer to a SDLC and its milestones and to the attributes which must be collected when a project has reached a milestone. The data consists of the collected measurements with regard to a specific milestone and the estimation figures (predictions, assumptions) generated by the different estimation tools.

The data are stored according to a kind of metamodel of an SDLC. This is necessary, because the user of the MARK 1 toolset has the possibility of changing the definition of each 'attribute'. Besides, new milestones and cost figures can be added to the toolset. Figure 3 displays a strongly simplified representation of the conceptual model on which the Estimation Base is implemented.

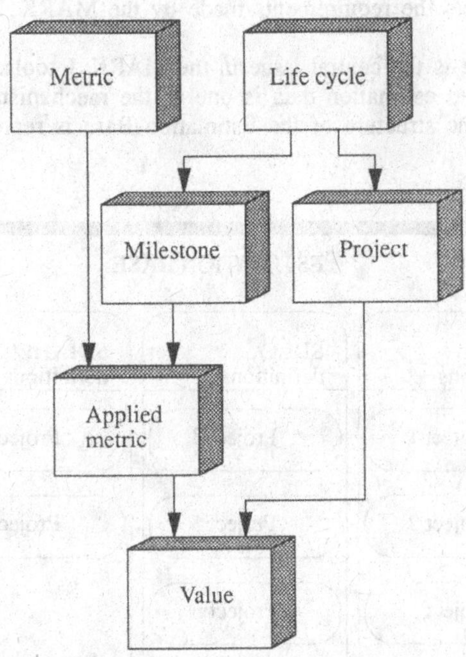

Figure 3 Overview MARK 1 Conceptual Schema

The MERMAID toolset consists of 8 different tools which have been combined in a 'workbench'. Figure 4 provides an overview of the architecture of MARK 1. As the overview shows, all tools make use of the centrally registered definitions and project data that have been stored in the Estimation Base.

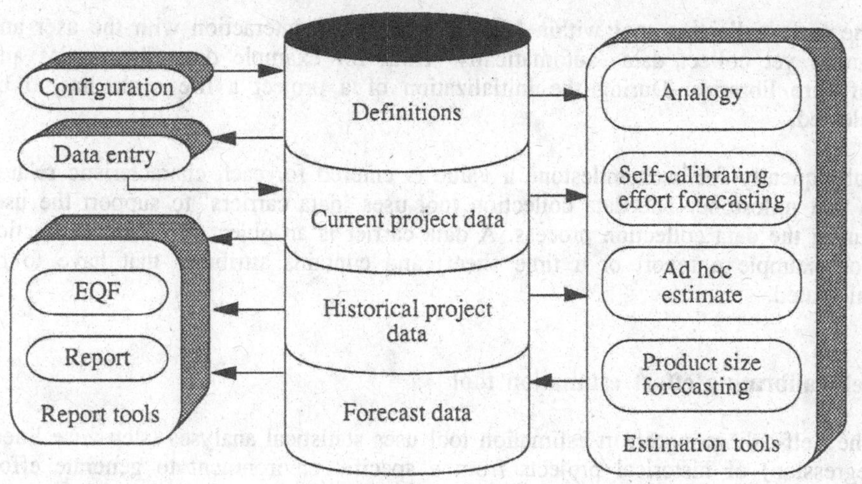

Figure 4 MARK 1 Architecture

These eight tools can be described as follows:

Configuration tool

The life cycle and the definitions of milestones and the characteristics to be collected that are used within a certain environment are user-defined and are added to the Estimation Base by means of the configuration tool. This tool must be used at least once, because the data collection process uses these definitions. Once the data has been stored, this tool is only used when the local working method changes, due to which for example certain data can not be collected anymore. A fundamental change (for example a life cycle modification) generally results in the definition of a new environment.

The influence of this tool makes it necessary that the user of the configuration tool (for example employees of the Quality Assurance department) has a thorough knowledge of the local system development procedures.

Data collection tool

The Data collection tool within MARK 1 works in interaction with the user and cannot yet collect data 'automatically' from for example data dictionaries and software libraries. During the initialization of a project a life cycle has to be selected.

Subsequently for each milestone a value is entered for each characteristic related to that milestone. The data collection tool uses 'data carriers' to support the user during the data collection process. A data carrier is an object from actual practice (for example a report or a time sheet) and contains attributes that have to be calculated.

Self-calibrating effort estimation tool

The Self-calibrating effort estimation tool uses statistical analyses (step-wise linear regression) of historical projects from a specific environment to generate effort estimates. These techniques provide more accurate predictions than the present generation of models, because they make use of local data that have an unambiguous meaning, are never obsolete and 'automatically' adjust the parameters and constants within the model.

This tool provides an estimate of the effort required for the next phase and for the project as a whole. Besides, additional information is provided in the form of accuracy intervals and the quality of the model.

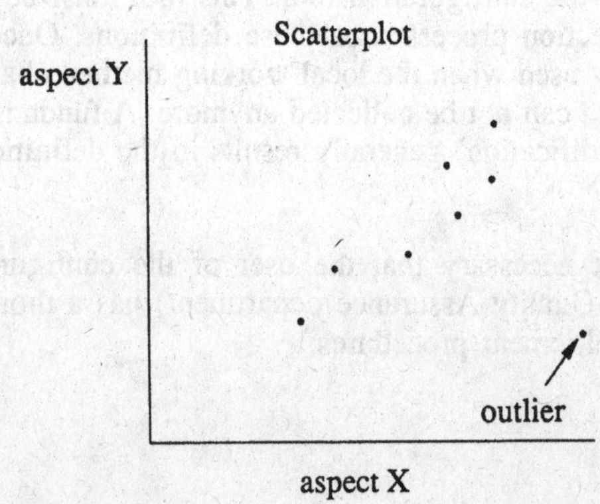

Figure 5 Example of an scatterplot to detect outliers

The user can choose for an automatic selection of the 'cost factors' or he can select a number of characteristics to be used to generate a prediction. Use is also made of the method that has been developed within the ESPRIT I project REQUEST, to detect outliers that are causing disturbances [Kitchenham, 1990] (see Figure 5).

Analogy tool

The analogy tool implemented within MARK 1 does not cover all aspects of analogy. Within MARK 1 the project manager makes 'models' for each project. In a later stage these can be used for the analogy tool. Existing models can be used as a base as well, and they can be adapted to the user's wishes. After the selection of one or more analogous projects all relevant factors are assessed during the estimation; they are provided with a relative value with regard to the analogous project. This results in predictions of effort and duration.

Product sizing tool

The Product sizing tool provides the opportunity to predict the future product size on the basis of counts from specification documents. The unit of the product size and the kind of 'predictive' factors are of course fully user-definable in the configuration tool. The results can also be used as input for the analogy tool.

Report tool

With the aid of the report tool various reports can be produced. The emphasis is on the information for each milestone.

Ad-hoc estimate tool

This is a simple tool with which the project manager can add manually performed (external) estimates and adjustments to forecasts to the Estimation Base. With this tool the local expertise can be recorded.

Estimation Quality Factor Tool

Within the MERMAID approach a project manager is stimulated during the development path to produce cost estimates several times. As a feedback mechanism within MARK 1, MERMAID has chosen the estimation quality factor (EQF) of DeMarco [1982]. The EQF tool provides an algorithm that reflects the efficiency of the estimation sequence. With this feedback the project manager is provided with an indication of the quality of the predictions.

FUTURE

In the second phase of the MERMAID project attention will be focused on the development of the MARK 2 toolset. In this stage intensive use will be made of knowledge technology, because this is a useful addition to the data oriented approach in MARK 1. Still, MARK 2 will not become an expert system, but a decision support system. The architecture of MARK 2 will be an extension to that of MARK 1. The most important fields in which the contribution of knowledge technology may yield better results are:

- Risk analysis
- Resource modelling
- Analogy forecasts
- Support of the use of statistical techniques.

The well-known concepts within the field of risk analysis are the checklist containing risk factors and the method in which the risk is described as 'the product of the chance that the risk occurs and the actual damage' [Boehm, 1989]. MERMAID is undertaking research to expand these methods and to integrate them with cost estimation by making use of local expertise.

Considering the fact that no resource model can make a reliable and accurate statement with regard to the capacity required for a project and the consequences of restrictions with regard to staffing levels and duration, it is probably impossible to describe the relationship between effort and duration a parametric model. The MERMAID project shall examine the possibilities of integrating local expertise with the local data.

In estimation by analogy using qualitative information is very important. The project manager uses this information and is therefore a vital link. Applied knowledge technology is one of the means available to MERMAID to provide support for this complex problem.

Despite the fact that statistical techniques can be applied very usefully in the estimation of project costs, this cannot be done in just any situation. The MERMAID project will investigate the possibilities of supporting the user with knowledge technology in the use of parametric models.

In future the stand-alone cost estimation tools will slowly disappear. Besides the obvious integration with other project management tools, this type of tool is very appropriate for implementation within an IPSE. One of the major advantages of such an environment is the possibility of automatic (objective) product- and process attribute collection. The fact is that many of these characteristics are generated by the different CASE tools and stored in a generally accessible repository. The future project manager will no longer have to depend on the quality of the procedures to be able to collect data manually.

ACKNOWLEDGMENTS

The author acknowledges the contribution to this paper from all the members of the MERMAID consortium, Volmac (the Netherlands), City University London (United Kingdom), National Computer Centre (United Kingdom), University College Cork (Ireland) and Data Management (Italy). The MERMAID project is partially funded by the Commission of the European Countries as part of the ESPRIT II programme (ref. P2046).

REFERENCES

1. Boehm, B.W., Tutorial on Software Risk Management. 11th Conf on Software Engineering, 1989.

2. DeMarco, T., Controlling Software Projects: management measurement and estimation. Yourdon, New York, 1982.

3. Heemstra, F.J., Hoe duur is programmatuur. Kluwer, Deventer, 1989.

4. Jeffery, D.R., Time-sensitive cost models in commercial MIS environments. IEEE Trans of Software Engineering, 198, SE-13 ,7.

5. Kitchenham, B.A. en Taylor, N.R., Software project development cost estimation. The Journal of Systems and Software, 1985, no. 5.

6. Kitchenham, B.A., Pichard, L.M. en Linkman,S.J., An evaluation of some design metrics. Software Engineering Journal, 1990, 5, no.1.

7. Kok, P.A.M. en Kitchenham, B.A., Enhanced support for cost estimation of software development, Journal of Software Research, 1990, no.1.

8. MERMAID, Comparative evaluation of existing cost estimation tools. ESPRIT II project P2046 MERMAID, Available via: VOLMAC, P.O. Box 2575, 3500 GN Utrecht, The Netherlands, 1989.

11

COSMOS* - COST MANAGEMENT WITH METRICS OF SPECIFICATION

NORBERT FUCHS
Alcatel Austria - ELIN Research Centre
Ruthnergasse 1-7
A-1210 Wien
Austria

ABSTRACT

COSMOS is an ESPRIT II project with the aim to develop a tool, supporting management decision making during the development of complex real-time systems.

COSMOS supports cost management decision making providing objective, measurable information, that is extracted during the software development lifecycle. This is achieved by applying the theory of software metrics on formal and semi-formal development methods, from the early definition phase through to the final acceptance of the system. Special emphasis will be on the early phases in the software life cycle.

1. INTRODUCTION

The ESPRIT II project COSMOS was launched at summer 1989 with a budget of 45 manyears. COSMOS will end summer 1993.

The aim is

- to extract measurable information from system representations early in the software life cycle (e.g. formal specification, design, code),
- to use this information to support cost management decision making,

* COSMOS is supported by the CEC under ESPRIT II Project 2686 COSMOS and by the Austrian "Innovations- und Technologiefond".

- to provide state of the art tools and methods for the collection of measurable information and subsequent analysis and
- to demonstrate the validity of these methods and tools during industrial observation studies.

The theoretical bases for this project is the graph-theoretically model of structured programming described in papers by Fenton, Kaposi and Whitty ([1], [2]). In this theory programs are represented by special directed graphs called flowgraphs which are derived from the formal notation of a system by tools. This tools are called language frontends and we will see the importance of these tools later.

For structured programs the building blocks of the corresponding flowgraph (so called prime flowgraphs) should belong to a certain set of prime flowgraphs, e.g. the so called Dijkstra graphs which in fact represent the elements of structured programming (sequence, decision, iteration).

The process of dividing a flowgraph into his basic elements (prime graphs) is called decomposition and results in a decomposition tree. This is a unique representation of how to combine prime flowgraphs for getting a certain flowgraph. Based on this decomposition tree we are able to evaluate software measurements. Once metric values are agreed for the set of prime flowgraphs and basic operations one may construct global measures of things like complexity, or testability, in a systematic and objective way.

It should be pointed out that all these measurements are based on objective characteristics of formal notations of a software system. So, this is one of the most important differences to other tools concerning cost management.

2. THE COSMOS ARCHITECTURE

The architecture of the COSMOS tool can be seen in Figure 1. There are two main parts: the technical part (the Core Metrics Tool (CMT) plus the Language Interfaces) and the Management Support Interface (MSI). This bisection of the architecture can be found within the consortium also: computer scientists on one hand and people with management background on the other side. The coming together of this different kind of background and knowledge makes the project so fascinating and hopefully fruitful.

The CMT (Core Metrics Tool) together with the Language Interfaces are of main interest for this paper and will be discused in more detail in the following sections.

The MSI (Management Support Interface), as second part of the system, is responsible for the way how the results of the measurement part are presented to the users. As there are very different groups of users for this tool - managers, software engineers, quality assurance

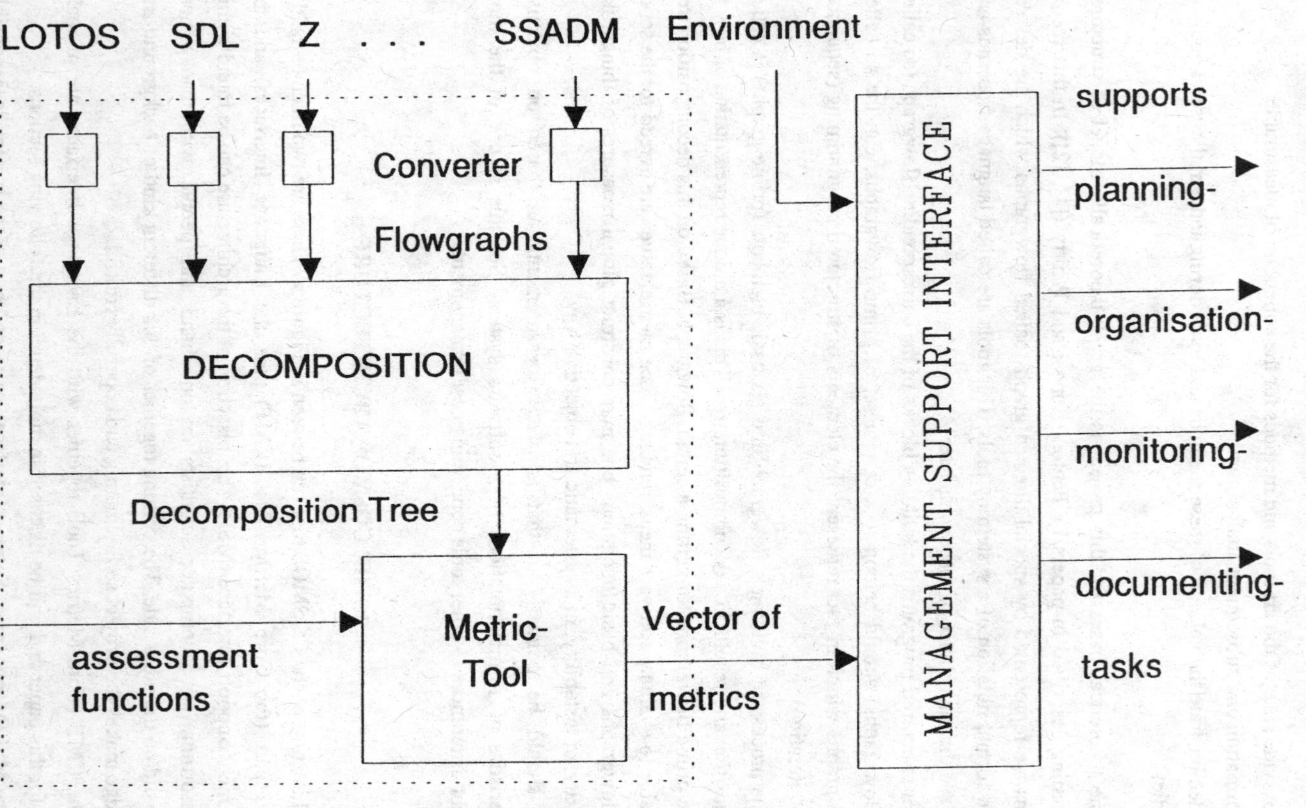

Figure 1. COSMOS Architecture

people - this is a very sensible task. Here we find a combination of a lot of different disciplines like computer science, business science, software ergonomic, psychology. You can get an example of the kind of user interface in Figure 2.

3. LANGUAGE INTERFACES

The Language Interface is this part of the tool which makes the mapping from the actual program to the corresponding flowgraph. Of course this frontend has to be build new for each language (specification-, design-, programming-). It is quit easy to imagine how an interface for a language like PASCAL should look like. But much more problems arise during transferring the experience with such interfaces to the area of specification languages. So, we decided to start with prototyping a language interface for a specification language which seems to be very general on one side and really different to implementation languages on the other side. Also for practical reasons - experience and projects available - we have chosen LOTOS (Language Of Temporal Ordering Specification).

LOTOS is one of two formal description techniques developed within ISO for the formal specification of open distributed systems, and in particular for those related to the OSI (Open System Interconnection) computer network architecture. In the meantime the LOTOS specification language has become ISO standard and is one of the most promising formal description languages ([3]). LOTOS has two components. The first component deals with the description of process behaviours and interactions, and is based on a modification of the Calculus of Communication Systems (CCS), which was developed at the University of Edinburgh. The second component deals with the description of data structures and value expressions and is based on the abstract data type language ACT ONE.

When mapping LOTOS specifications to flowgraphs we investigate basic constructs of the process part of the language. At the moment the whole data part is ignored. We are mainly interested in structural elements viz. behaviour expressions (BE), which are essential components of a process definition.

A graphical representation is defined for each BE of basic LOTOS. A graph has one startnode and one stopnode. We have taken other symbols in order to differ between start-/stopnodes and "normal" nodes (i.e. nodes which are between start- and stopnodes). We have used a black circle enclosed by a white circle to express start- and stopnodes and a simple white circle to sign the normal nodes.

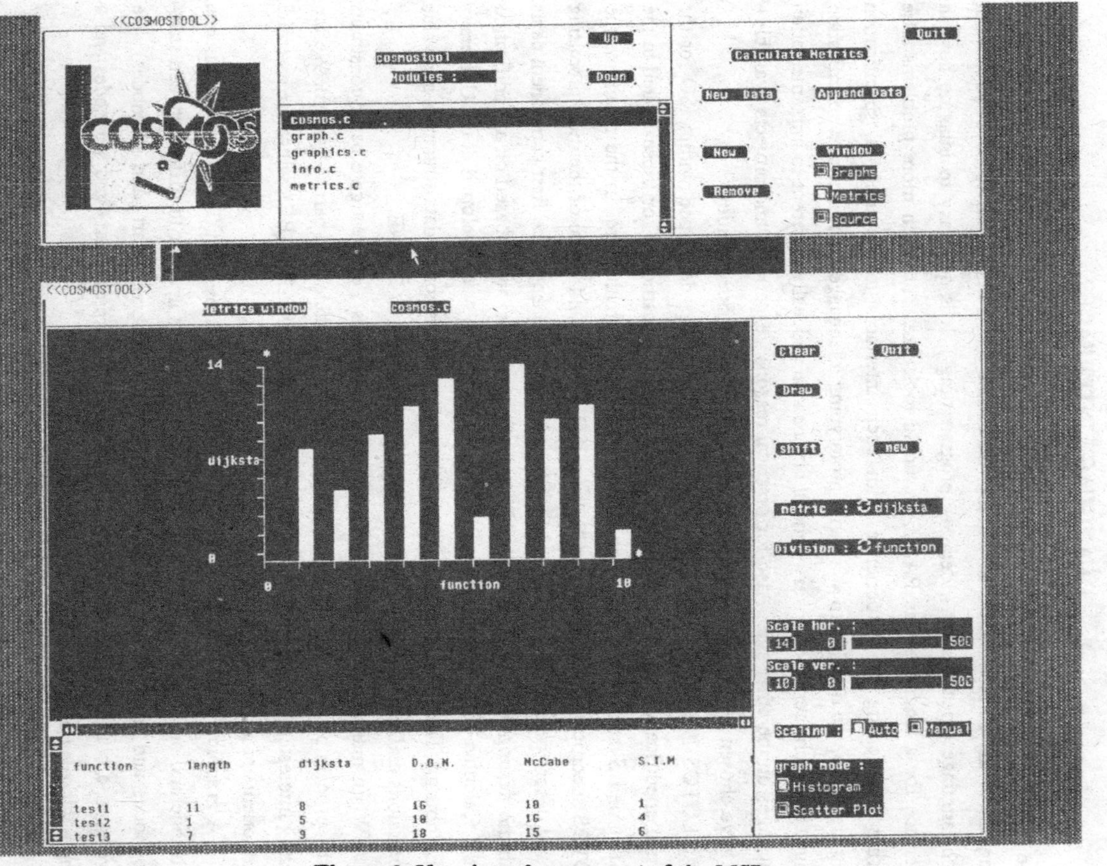

Figure 2. User interface as part of the MSI

In the following examples the symbols B, B1, B2 stand for any BE, i for the LOTOS internal event, g, g_1, ..., g_n, h, h_1,...,h_m, f_1,...,f_j for LOTOS gates, x for a variable of sort t and p and q for processes.

In order to maintain the required bijectivity of the mapping we would need for each basic operator one prime to map to. But the restriction which is demanded by ourselves is that we do not want to use too many new primes otherwise the use and interpretation of general metrics would be of no worth.

Of course a lot of LOTOS constructs can be mapped straight forward. Here we don't want to list them all. So, we try to show on hand of one example where the problems are. If we investigate two constructs: the choice-statement - which corresponds to an if-statement - and a parallel composition - which means that two behaviour expressions run in parallel.

choice parallel composition

Figure 3.

The idea to map both constructs to the same flowgraph structure is straightforward. Nevertheless we loose the information about the different meaning (complexity, ...) of the constructs. Investigating LOTOS into more detail you find that there are even more constructs which are candidates for mapping to the same "if-structure".

Because of this loosing of information and missing bijectivity we were forced to initiate so-called prime descriptors. In fact these descriptors are a kind of additional information which we put to a startnode of a prime graph. The primes to which we are mapping more than one of the basic operators will be marked with these descriptors. Naturally the same descriptor, which is 'joined' the prime, identifies always the same operator. So we have saved our required bijectivity because the mapping has become unambiguous again.

In our example the result can be seen in Figure 4.

Figure 4.

This is an easy example. Investigating LOTOS we found the necessity to introduce even more information in addition. The result was the definition of a descriptor as a letter together with a set of numbers. So, e.g. for a synchronization construct this number could mean the number of gates over which is synchronised (see Figure 5).

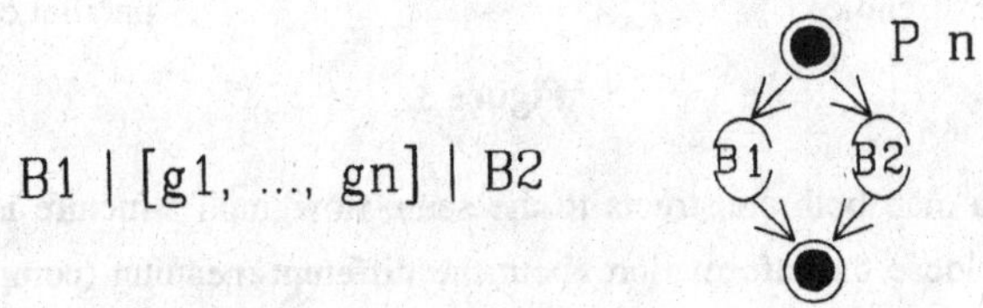

Figure 5.

A complete list of all the descriptors used can be found in [4].

4. THE CORE METRICS TOOL (CMT)

As mentioned above, the theoretical base of the project was brought in by one of the partners (Goldsmiths' College) as result of a UK Alvey project (SE069). The project is documented in [5]. An implementation of this theory can be found in [6] under the name QUALMS. This tool allows to decompose a flowgraph into his primes and to apply a certain set of metrics to this decomposition tree. It was decided by the COSMOS consortium to take this tool as a base for the development of one part of the future COSMOS tool, the CMT.

Two major changes have been planed in the first phase of the project.

- As a result of the implementation of the LOTOS language interface the underlying theory had to be extended. The new defined descriptors (see chapter 3. Language Interfaces) had to be introduced and the decomposition algorithm had to be proved. This task is done and ended with only minor changes to the theory of decomposition [1]. The result is described in more detail in [4].
- The second major change was the separation of the calculation of metrics from the decomposition algorithm. We introduced a language which helps to formulate a metric. Also an interpreter for this language was developed as part of the CMT. This allows the user to experiment with new metrics in an interactive way and see the results of his "own" metric immediately.

5. PROBLEMS AND FUTURE DIRECTION

After the implementation of the first language interfaces using this technique we did make first experiments in form of a workshop about interpretation of software measurements. The result can be seen in [7]. The main lesson we learned was the sensibility of the different software measurements on the decisions we maid during defining a certain language interface. As a result we even can say that the success of the COSMOS tool will depend on the formalisation and standardisation of these decisions.

So, the logical next step is to define general rules how to map different programming languages to this extended flowgraph model. This will be done in the near future by defining classes of constructs and their corresponding mapping and descriptors.

6. ACKNOWLEDGMENTS

The COSMOS partners are:

- Ing. F. Hirdes, COSMOS Management Office, TechForce B V, Niels Bohrweg 11, Leiden, The Netherlands.
- Dr. N. Fuchs, Alcatel Austria-ELIN Research Centre, Ruthnergasse 1-7, A-1210 Wien, Austria.
- Dr. K. Tse, Nijenrode, The Netherland School of Business, Straatweg 25, 3621 BG Breukelen, The Netherlands.
- G. Duenas, Telefonica Sistemas, S.A. Sor Angela de la Cruz 3, 28020 Madrid, Spain.
- A. Pengelly, British Telecom Research Labs, Martlesham Heath, Ipswich 1P5 7RE, United Kingdom.

- Dr. R. Whitty, COSMOS Office, Department of Mathematical Studies, Goldsmiths' College, 25 St James, New Cross SE14 6NW, United Kingdom.

6. REFERENCES

1 Whitty, R W, Fenton, N E and Kaposi A A, Structure programming: a tutorial guide, Software and Microsystems, vol.3, no.3, pp54-65, 1984

2 Fenton, N E, Whitty, R W and Kaposi, A A, A generalised mathematical theory of structured programming. Theoretical Computer Sciences 39, pp 145-171, 1985

3 Brinksma, E., Information processing systems - Open systems interconnection - LOTOS - A formal description technique based on the temporal ordering of observational behaviour, International Standard ISO 8807

4 Fuchs, N, Stainer, S, Assessing feasibility of formal specification language and model - extension of the flowgraph model, COSMOS Project Report COSMOS/Al/WP1/TEC89011.2, TechForce BV, Leiden, Netherlands

5 Fenton, N E, Software metrics: theory, tools and validation, Software Engineering Journal, vol.5, no.1, pp.65-78, 1990

6 Bache, R, Leelasena, L, QUALMS: a tool for the analysis and measurement of software structure, Glasgow College, Cowcaddens Road, Glasgow G7, UK

7 Fuchs, N, Lockhart, R, Stainer, S, Summary of an Workshop on Interpretation of Software Measurements, COSMOS Project Report COSMOS/Al/WP1/REP/5.2, TechForce BV, Leiden, Netherlands

12

THE SOFTWARE PRODUCTIVITY EVALUATION MODEL - AN ESPRIT PROJECT

PETER COMER

ADVANCED SOFTWARE TECHNOLOGY,
Via Benedetto Croce 19,
000142 ROMA, ITALIA

ABSTRACT

The goal of the Software Productivity Evaluation Model (SPEM) project was to build an 'a-posteriori' evaluation model of software development productivity for use across the spectrum of the software development industry. Development cost models have been reviewed and classified, salient cost and quality 'drivers' have been identified, and the measurement techniques and data definitions for the drivers reviewed and collated. A preliminary phase, to test data definitions, collection procedures, etc, was specified and performed, and the results studied. A second phase, incorporating the lessons of the first, was defined. The second phase included new data definitions, collection procedures, and new data verification and analysis techniques. Data has been collected, verified and analysed from 30 industrial projects. The 30 projects have been entered into a database. Cost and quality 'drivers' in the collected data have been analysed for their importance and a prototype productivity evaluation model has been built.

INTRODUCTION

SPEM, CEC ESPRIT Project No. 1527, started at the beginning of May 1987 and was planned to finish at the end of April 1990. In the event, it finished at the end of July 1990. It was supported by the European Commission through its ESPRIT initiative, which matches the funds devoted by the partners. The project partners were: Fuigi Italiana/AST (Italy, Prime contractor), Sema-Metra and Verilog of France, AEA Technology of the UK, O.Dati Espanola and Sofemasa of Spain.

The goal of the SPEM project was to build a general 'a-posteriori' software productivity model and to base it upon data collected from projects spread across as wide a range of the software industry as possible. The project, as planned and executed, had two phases. The first phase was to define a draft productivity model and to test the model by collecting and analysing data. A second phase to refine the data collection and analysis procedures, collect data, refine the productivity model, collect more data and validate the final productivity model.

The rest of this paper concentrates on the second phase. The major tasks (data definition, data collection, productivity model building and validation) will be described below and, in addition, some lessons learned and major results of the project will be presented.

SOFTWARE DATA DEFINITIONS & DATA COLLECTION

Data Collection Tools

From data collection experience in the first phase of the project it was clear that the software development data schema had to be revised with particular attention to:

* entity and attribute definitions,
* model consistency and structure,
* quality data requirements,
* inclusion of static analysis data within the schema,
* comparability data,
* practicality of collecting each data item.

Two reports were produced for the second phase; a Data Definitions document and a Data Collection Manual. In the Data Definitions document the individual data definitions were grouped under six entities:

* Project,
* Requirements,
* Staff,
* Development environment,
* Development method,
* Product.

The document concentrated on the individual data definitions rather than the overall structuring of the complete set. This was not a risk for the project, there was no great need to concentrate on overall structuring of the complete set of data definitions due to the 'a-posteriori' approach to the data collection. Other ESPRIT projects, REQUEST and SCOPE for example, have been forced to give considerable attention to this area.

Turning to the Data Collection Manual, the aim was to organise the data collection into as logical a structure and easily implemented task as possible. The order and the clarity of the forms was carefully considered, to try to minimise the work of the data collector when completing the forms. The size of the data collection manual was deliberately controlled to exclude data definitions. There was two reasons for this; firstly, the data collector should be encouraged to have already studied the data definitions document and only in extremis need to refer to written definitions, secondly, a thin data collection manual reassures both the data collector and the data provider.

In addition to the data collection manual a static analysis tool was used to complete the collection of product data. The metrics collected were:

* number of statements
* number of comments
* number of operators
* number of operands
* hierarchical complexity
* structural complexity
* cyclomatic number
* system testability.

The SPEM project thus had a practical selection criteria applicable to any project before it was possible to collect data from it: the software must have been written in one of the languages capable of analysis by the static analysis tool used. This particular selection criteria was the largest complication to finding projects and to collecting data.

Data Collection Meetings

Efficient data collection became identical, in practice, with minimising the number of data collection meetings needed to collect the data. The ideal was just one meeting for the data collection manual and one meeting for obtaining the static analysis data. This was generally not possible; the data required were not always immediately available and this meant that generally a second (sometimes third) meeting had to be arranged for the data collection manual. Following meetings were always harder to arrange; although always easier with respect to the provider's understanding of the data and preparedness for what was wanted.

The requirement for static analysis data meant installing the static analysis tool, running checks on it and then running the data provider's code through it. This, typically, took two or three days and each new environment brought its own set of problems. Multiplying the figure of two or three days by the number of projects gives an impression of the resources that were used to collect the product data.

THE SPEM MODEL

Data Verification

The data verification procedure had of two distinct steps.

The first step was termed 'single dataset verification' and consisted of checks for missing values, for typographical errors - which just might have been right, and for inconsistent replies. Single dataset verification was just about practical with the limited resources available, even though it involved a considerable amount of cross-checking with either the provider or the collector. It was made harder when it was postponed. Invariably, the datasets where verification was postponed seemed to cause the most problems when eventually verification was done. It was not always possible to verify data as soon as it was loaded - there were always other tasks calling for attention. The task was always in conflict with the available time.

The second step was termed 'multi-dataset verification', where checks were based on trend analysis. Trend analysis was very useful to easily identify questionable data points although it proved harder than single dataset verification because of the work involved in going back to the provider or collector once again, to check data thrown into question by the analysis. Thorough multi-dataset verification was a practical impossibility (even for a database of only 30 projects) given the time and resource constraints that applied.

The Model Building

The model was built using the first twenty datasets that were collected and the model was validated with the final ten. The task can be roughly broken down into the following steps:

- classify the projects,
- calculate a 'standard cost' function,
- determine standard values of environment parameters,
- validate the productivity indicator,
- determine the productivity estimators.

That the task was limited by the size of the database and the range of the data available can be seen by the conclusions made by the people involved in building the model and presented below:

* 'too few 'iterations' (not enough projects),

* not enough product-related parameters,

* not enough cost drivers,

* need to refine determination of standard values and normalisation of associated cost drivers,

* include other variables (eg. team motivation).

LESSONS ON DATA COLLECTION

It remains to say something about the experience that has been learnt with reference to software data collection. The following lessons are no more than an attempt to make some of the experience a matter of record before it is lost permanently and no importance should be inferred from their priority.

In particular, the collection of <u>effort</u> data by SPEM caused concern to many data providers; many of the providers were concerned when they realised they were being asked to disclose what they felt was sensitive information. For a surprising number of data providers it was difficult to obtain effort figures per phase because the records available weren't separated in that manner. Conversely, effort data per staff division was not a problem. This situation may have arisen because, probably, existing effort data collection systems have been created exclusively with accounting/financial motives.

Data on the product was collected via the data collection manual and via a static analysis tool. The installation of the static analysis tool as part of each data collection was a not an easy task. Although it was obviously necessary for the data it provided, it consumed considerable effort and restricted the range of potential data providers. Use of automatic data collection tools will grow - the work done on productivity modelling highlighted more product data as an area for further model development - knowing how to use them optimally will be the key to efficient data collection in future projects.

The data collection manual, in response to strong representations, included a list of which data items it was mandatory to collect and which data items were optional. This list proved to be irrelevant during the data collection - the providers were not motivated by what was seen as essentially a problem for the data collector.

For scalar measurements, five-point or three-point scales allowed people to go for the middle of the range - one provider blatantly always chose the middle of the scale and then improved his answer by one division! Providers, in general, had to be reminded to spend enough time thinking about each rank in a scale, and looking at the 'comparability data', before replying.

Classifications did not cause any problems provided both collector and provider understood the definitions.

Numerical scales, unit measurements, caused few problems as long as both collector and provider understood the definitions and the comparability data.

RESULTS AND EXPLOITATION

At the start of the project the Technical Annex declared that the aims of the project were;

to develop, use and validate a prototype of a new model of software development productivity,

to construct, formalise, and offer as a standard, data definitions and data collection procedures <u>proved</u> as usable on software projects,

to contribute to the measurement, comparison, management and improvement of software development productivity in an industrial context,

to contribute to the awareness and understanding of software productivity models and modelling, throughout the software development industry,

to cooperate with other projects in the metrics and models area, aiming at creating a mutually beneficial synergy with them.

The first two points have been certainly been achieved. The productivity model should allow;

the measurement of software development productivity across a spectrum of software application areas,

comparison of the software development factors of any specific project with a general database of such factors, to support more accurate planning and prediction on following projects, supported by evidence from a database of existing projects.

The data collection should allow;

> the Data Definitions and the Data Collection Manual to be offered as a standard to international bodies and offered as a standard for other metrics projects. With a small amount of editing it could possibly be exploited commercially as a data collection tool for the software development industry,
>
> the Database to be offered as a starting-point to other metrics projects and exploited commercially as a database of anonymous projects from the software development industry.

At the present time, July 1990, there have already been approaches from other projects with respect to the data definitions, collection manual and database.

The progress on the remaining points is less easy to comment upon. Certainly, in connection with other ESPRIT projects, SPEM has benefited from their experience and, as indicated in the previous paragraph, SPEM hopes that other projects will benefit from it. The other two points are more dependent on the attention given to them by individual partners. In Italy, Fuigi Italiana/AST runs a one-day course specifically to inform people about the aims, the progress and the results of the SPEM project. The situation with other partners is not clear - with the exception of AEA Technology, in the UK, where it is known that AEA has promoted Spem along with its other projects in software metrics.

The experience gained from SPEM provides a firm basis on which the project partners can expand, and on which it is hoped the maturity and applicability of software metrics technology can be demonstrated to the European software industry. One ESPRIT II project aimed specifically at being a 'missionary', in a practical sense, to the software industry is Project No. 5494, AMI - Application of Metrics in Industry, in which Advanced Software Technology intends to make a major contribution. AMI has one major deliverable, the Metrics User's Handbook, which will incorporate information on metrics standards and metrics teaching within the European Community. It is hoped that the AMI Handbook will quickly become a *de facto* European standard on which to evaluate the status of metrics absorption in the software industry.

In conclusion, it only remains to express on behalf of Fuigi/AST and all the partners, the thanks of the project to; the data providers, other metrics projects, bodies such as CSR, and last but definitely not least, the European Commission and Project Officer, at Brussels.

13

SOFTWARE CERTIFICATION

A A WINGROVE

Centre for Software Reliability

ABSTRACT

Certification of products by independent assessment has been established for many years. Awarding a 'certificate of conformity' or a 'seal of approval' is regarded generally as providing some form of guarantee of quality and reliability. Software certification poses particular difficulties, if only because of the impossibility of measuring every characteristic and mode of behaviour of a computer program.

Differing perceptions of software certification are discussed together with the factors which may influence the certification process. A model of a possible certification method is developed with comments on the possible methods and tools which might be used.

INTRODUCTION

The commonest perception of certification is that it gives some form of guarantee, generally of reliability in its widest sense. At least, it is assumed that the risks of failure are reduced where certification involves some form of independent assessment.

The process of Certification, awarding an independent certificate or 'Seal of Approval' formally attesting fulfilment of conditions and requirements, has been established for very many years. Most examples of certificated products that come to mind are hardware, physical objects that can be observed, analysed and measured. Contemporary examples range from 'Seals of Approval' for domestic goods to 'certificates of airworthiness' for aircraft.

Software, particularly when we mean computer programs, poses unique problems when we consider how it may be certified in the same sense as hardware. This is because it is impossible to measure all the characteristics and modes of behaviour of a software product. Nevertheless, some software is already subjected to a form of independent assessment [1,2]; language compilers [3] and communications protocols [4]for example.

CERTIFICATION

In essence, certification is simply the award of a certificate attesting to conformity with some defined attribute. The process of certification has three components;

(a) identification of the attribute(s) to be assured
(b) verification of the attribute(s)
(c) award of the certificate of conformance

Certification of a product is generally perceived as giving some confidence that a product is as described and can be relied upon. In fact, the certificate only attests conformity with the specific attributes which have been identified as of interest.

To be of any real value, certification of a product needs to cover all the essential attributes which make the product capable of satisfying its specified requirements in an operational environment. The principal parties having an interest in product certification will be the producer and the user. Thus, for the certificate to be trusted, it is also necessary for the certificate to be awarded by an independent third-party.

Certification that a product conforms to its specified requirements in an operational environment may not always be sufficient. There may be considerations of fitness for purpose, safety and conformance to regulations and standards which are not explicitly mentioned in the specifications. We might, therefore, consider two forms of certification - basic certification and extended certification.

Basic Certification **would assure the conformity of the product with its descriptions and specifications. Whilst this is perfectly adequate for a large number of products it begs the question of whether the requirements specification is correct and complete. In other words, the product may be 'made right', but it is not the 'right product'.**

Extended Certification **would be appropriate where use of a product raises questions of fitness for purpose, safety or conformance with regulations and standards, not explicitly addressed in the product requirements specification but which may be implicit in the nature of the product or its use. In such cases, basic certification may have to be extended by a deeper consideration of the product specification and application.**

PERCEPTIONS OF CERTIFICATION

General

It is inevitable that software product certification will be viewed in different ways. The perception of users (consumers, customers), producers (manufacturers), general public, legal community, evaluator, will all differ according to their involvement with software. It is almost certain that all will see certification as some form of guarantee. But just exactly what that guarantee is and the perception of its worth will differ from group to group and person to person.

If it so difficult, why should we wish to see a method for certifying software? Software has a reputation for unreliability and its increasing use in critical applications is a growing cause for concern. There is an overwhelming need for the development of software products - software engineering as it is sometimes called - to gain the respectability already earned by other engineering disciplines. Of itself, certification does nothing to improve software engineering. But software engineering must improve if software products are to be certified.

At present, computer programs come with little or no warranty as to the fitness of the program for use. Indeed, it is usual for 'off the shelf' (and even 'made to measure') software to be accompanied by comprehensive disclaimers, often seeking to limit even the statutory consumer protection which may be available. The fact that most software is only licensed for use, and not purchased, by the user helps further to confuse the issue. In the few areas where producers of software do show concern, certification may be part of the answer to the growing effects of consumer protection legislation and litigation for third party damages.

SOFTWARE

'Software' can be a very confusing term. Commonly, one finds that 'software' is used to denote computer programs: 'hardware' is the computer, 'software' the programs which run on the computer. In real life, 'software' encompasses much more than the electronic manifestation of the logic and data which bring a computer to life.

The development of a program, from initial requirements to the final code which is loaded into a computer, involves the creation of a series of specifications, manuals, listings and test results. The definition of software used in this paper covers the totality of documents, code and test results which contribute to a working program. To avoid confusion, this totality will be referred to as the 'software product'. The individual components of the software product (e.g.: design specification, user manual, source code listing, development plan etc.) will be referred to as 'product parts'.

Software products can be grouped in three major development classes:

packages - where the program development is aimed at a multiplicity of unknown clients. The significance of this is that the 'user requirements' are initially set by the producer, not the user.

projects - which are developments contracted for a single client. Often referred to as 'bespoke software', the client has full opportunity to influence the user requirements.

systems - which are developments (usually projects) where the program and its processor are embedded within hardware. Usually, these developments involve integrated digital and analog techniques and are subject to real time constraints.

Defining the conformance criteria by which software should be certified is very much more difficult. Ideally, the criteria should be measurements, made against written specifications of what the product will do under specified conditions of use, that is, the normal user environment. In some circumstances, for instance where safety is critical, it may also be necessary to specify what the product will not do. However, the very nature of software makes even these few conditions impossible to meet.

Programs are extremely complex and, other than in trivial applications, are impossible to test exhaustively for every change of state. Many software attributes have no established measures against which the success of a test might be judged. The logic of a program may not always be clearly identifiable against a specification, even when it is correct. Specifications are rarely unambiguous. Requirements may be incomplete, and on occasions, wrong! There is no such thing as a 'normal use environment'. The list of difficulties may seem to be endless.

But in the real world of software development, compromise is possible. Without attempting perfection, considerable progress can be made towards a framework of software certification which will, at least, provide economic levels of assurance commensurate with all the risks involved in the use of the software in any particular application. Use can be made of the most appropriate state-of-the-art tools and methods to attest conformity of the software product with specific design requirements and attributes.

At the lowest level, where safety is not an issue, the certification process may provide no more than a "Seal of Quality". This would give assurance to the user that a well defined development methodology had been used, the product had been adequately tested, would do what it was supposed to do under defined conditions of use and would be supported in service if things went wrong.

At the other end of the scale, with high risk safety critical applications, certification would provide specific guarantees that under strictly defined conditions of use, certain attributes would be present, as specified, and that particular malfunctions should not occur. With the current state-of-the-art it would not be possible to give a total guarantee against any eventuality, particularly where ultra-high reliability is demanded. Nevertheless, with independent test and assessment of software products, levels of product assurance will be possible that are far higher than are currently accepted.

The challenge is to define a framework for software certification that is flexible, economic in application and generally acceptable. The framework must provide:

- for any form of software in any application
- for software within systems
- independent assessment and test
- guarantees of quality, limited only by definition
- guarantees of defined, specific aspects of functionality

The key recognition must be that certification can never give all-embracing guarantees. Certification will always be given on the basis of closely defined parameters, derived from particular needs and for particular applications. These limitations need to be fully understood by everyone concerned, users, customers, manufacturers, assessors, legal representatives and the general public. Without this understanding, the role of certification will be misinterpreted and this will swiftly be followed by the process becoming discredited.

The User/Customer

The principal perception of Certified Software to a user will be that of a guarantee - firstly, that the software will perform as described and secondly, that it will not fail in normal use. The use of the words 'described' and 'normal' needs explanation.

The performance (or functionality) of software is usually described in technical terms through one or more specifications. Where the software has been specifically commissioned by a customer, the requirements specification and a functional specification should have been agreed with the manufacturer before full development started. This would provide a definition of what the software is supposed to do.

However, where software is sold (licenced) as an off-the-shelf product, the customer usually has no access to requirement and functional specifications in the technical sense. Information is usually only available in the form of sales and technical brochures, is limited in scope and often presented in glowing terms. In this case, the customer (who may not be the user) will form an impression of the performance of the software from its description. That impression will include any ambiguities that are present and will be biassed by the positive aspects of the product stressed as selling points.

Every user will have their own concept of a normal use environment and it is rare to find sales literature qualifying the performance of a program with conditions for its use. However, one positive benefit of certification may be that manufacturers will be driven to a clearer and much more accurate exposition of what their product actually does and would ensure that the customer agrees before using the product that it is suitable for the purpose for which it is being acquired. This will lead to a much clearer recognition of both the capabilities and limitations of software and will avoid much of the disappointment that often accompanies its use.

A customer who buys a certified product should not be surprised if it costs more than a competitor product which is not certified. The extra cost will be justified by the expectation that the certified product is, in some way, superior. Above all, the customer will expect the manufacturer (or an agent) to support a certified product in the event of any problems. It may be expected that the manufacturer will indemnify the user against any consequential loss occasioned by the use of the product and that the certificate will provide protection against third-party claims for damages.

The Producer/Manufacturer

The views of the producer (or manufacturer) of software are likely to be the most diverse of all those concerned with certification. Some perceptions will come from the manufacturer's intimate knowlege of the problems in producing software economically, others from the need to gain a competitive 'edge' in the marketplace.

On the positive side, a certificate could signify a superior product which would sell better. Independent assessment would provide a further layer of test and checking for errors that may have remained undiscovered during development. This could provide a defence against second and third party claims in the event of failure. The product would be better defined since it would be certified against specifications.

Against these advantages would be the cost of certification and the delays incurred in bringing the product to the marketplace. To facilitate certification, changes to established methods of design and development may be necessary. There would be doubts regarding the loss of confidentiality in having to provide the certifying authority with all the details of the product. There would need to be a thorough assessment and evaluation of the risks involved in using the software, the consequences of failure and the penalties which may be involved. Finally, the manufacturer would need to be convinced that the customer (and possibly the public) understood fully the limitations of the certification.

The Public/Third Parties

It is very probable that the general public will have little knowlege of the limitations of a certificate awarded to software. Like the user, the main perception will be that of a Guarantee against failure, a Certificate that the product is reliable and safe.

The Legal Community

The view of certification that will be taken by the legal profession [5] will be constrained by the legislation which relates to software. Examples of such legislation are Copyright, Product Liability and Consumer Protection laws, reinforced by the legal Judgements made in relevent cases.

There is, as yet, little experience from litigation concerning software other than on alleged infringement of copyright. The legal problems that are related to certification are much more likely to arise from failure of the software in some degree. Claims for economic or financial loss, damage, injury or death which are allegedly caused by the failure of a certified software product could be expected from users or when a member of the public is involved, as a third party, in an incident.

Three possible problem areas can be cited. First, is software a product or a service? Second, where defence against claims of negligence involves showing conformity with 'best practice', how will best practice be judged? Third, how can the responsibility for the failure of a certified product be apportioned, for instance, between the producer, sub-contractors when they are involved, and the assessor?

The Independent Evaluator

Clearly, the independent evaluator (eg a 'test house') will see certification as a valuable source of work and will build an organisation suited to the needs of the task. This will involve suitably qualified staff who are familiar with the problems associated with a range of applications, the availability of suitable standards, tools and techniques and the economic costs associated with the process.

One particular cause for concern will be the possibility of being deemed to be responsible when certified software fails.

FACTORS WHICH MAY HAVE AN INFLUENCE ON CERTIFICATION

There are many factors which will need to be considered in the construction of a software certification process. They can be conveniently discussed under three headings:

- factors which derive from the use of software
- factors associated with development
- consideration of software as part of a system

Software in use

Application: The application to which software is directed will determine the level of certification which may be necessary. Many applications are grouped within 'industrial' boundaries (eg business, finance, engineering, medicine, transport etc.), each of which may have a distinct 'culture'. These cultures already have particular development methods, standards, preferred computers and programming languages, all related to the particular problems that are met. The same software product (eg a spreadsheet program) may be used in quite different ways with quite different levels of risk in use and consequence of failure within different sectors.

Use environment: The environment in which a program will be used is extremely difficult to control or define. The principal problem will be to decide a representative environment for certification. For instance, how might one certify a safety control system working under emergency conditions?

Risks and consequences of failure: The consequences of software failure vary widely, from minor irritation to human or environmental disaster. A need to assure a low probability of failure for a software product will have a profound effect on the cost of certification.

Host computer: Programs may be may be run on more than one computer and under more than one operating system. This may involve multiple certifications of the same product.

Maturity: Maturity will be important in considering both applications and products. Can experience of the same or similar applications help to guide the certifier?

Is the product already in use, with user experience to draw on? Is the product similar to another product that has already been certified - for instance, is it only a new version?

Expertise of user: Most programs (and documentation such as handbooks) will be used by a wide range of users - naive to expert. The difficulties, both perceived and actual, met by such a range of experience will be quite different for the same product.

Support of producer: The level of in-service support available from the producer may have an influence on the integrity of a product. Support will vary from minimal (for a low-cost commercial package) to continuous on-site support for complex one-off commissioned applications.

Software development

Experience of producer: The experience of a software producer should be considered. The maturity of the organisation, skill of the staff, development methods employed, familiarity with the application, are all factors which have been shown to influence product quality.

Interaction with the customer or user: Beside the support for a product provided by a producer, the level of interaction with the customer (who may not be the direct user!) in formulating the requirements is an important factor.

Commercial constraints: The quality of the final product will be influenced by a number of commercial constraints. The principal of these are budget (and profit), timescale and the consequences of risks, any of which may influence the design, development methodology, level of testing and support for a product.

Methodology used: A wide range of development methods are in use, some mature with recognised standards, some newly emergent. Particular methods may be preferred by particular software sectors; eg in the UK, SSADM for governmental administrative applications, CORE for avionic applications etc. The maturity of the methodology (in terms of experience and results achieved) may influence the scheme of certification required.

Programming language: Programs are implemented in a wide variety of languages and a certification process must be able to accomodate the use of any of them in a product. Some applications may require the use of more than one language - for example, real time applications are often a mixture of a high order language (HOL) and assembler. A language may be particularly suitable for a particular application, eg FORTRAN for engineering, COBOL for business, C++ where object oriented programming is appropriate, ASSEMBLER where speed of execution or storage space are vital. One extremely important issue for certification is the restricted range of languages for which tools, such as static analysers, are available.

Software in systems

Minimum system: A program must be associated with a processor before it can be used and this will form a minimum system. Most usually, the program will be loaded into a computer but it is not uncommon for a program to be an integral part of a processor - a computer on a chip.

Typical systems: More usually, the computer and program will be managed by an operating system and will interact through peripheral equipment (hardware) with an operator and other equipment such as mass storage devices, viewing screens, printers, plotters etc. In some applications it will be necessary to ensure that peripheral equipment is included as an integral part of the certification process.

Complex systems: The most difficult problems of certification will be met with complex, computer based systems. These systems involve computer control of electronics, devices which may be mechanical, hydraulic or pneumatic, processes or plant, the functionality of which may be inseparable from the functionality of the software. In these cases, it may not be possible to emulate the controlled parts of the system so that the software can be certified on its own.

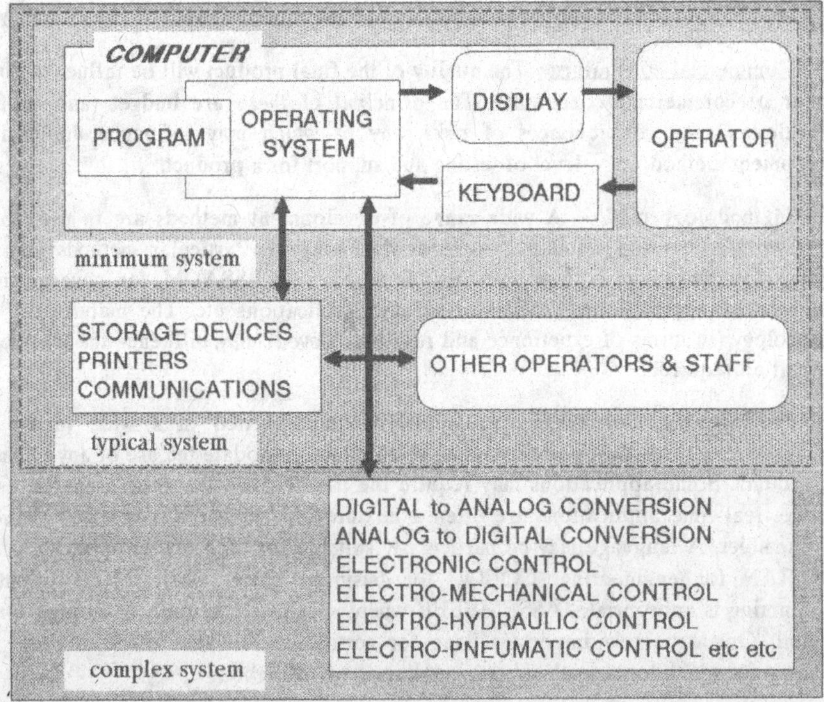

Figure 1. Minimum, Typical and Complex Systems

SOFTWARE ATTRIBUTES

An attribute is defined as an inherent characteristic (a distinguishing trait, quality or property) of an object. In general, software characteristics may be associated with the development process, the product or its performance. Over the years, considerable efforts have been expended in attempting to relate a range of software attributes to measures by which they may be defined. Decomposition of attributes into their constituent metrics has proved to be a very difficult task. Not least of these difficulties has been a lack of agreement on metric definitions and a great deal of confusion on what might be important and what is not. A selection of discussion on attributes and metrics will be found in references [6] to [17].

Software certification is all about identifying important attributes and assuring their conformance with requirements and specifications. Consequently, a key task in setting up a software certification scheme will be defining attributes and their associated metrics which can be unambiguously assured by some method or other. Before any metric can be incorporated into a certification method, its utility and repeatability will need to be demonstrated in a real environment. The Esprit SCOPE project [18] is undertaking just such a task, using real projects as certification test-beds. Of course, if some certification scheme was set up, the range of metrics available, together with the methods and tools by which they could be assessed, would be continually evolving.

Examples of attributes which might need to be assured are:

- correctness (does the functionality match the requirements?)
- reliability (how often does it fail?)
- availability (can it be used when needed?)
- integrity (can the system be corrupted?)
- security (can unauthorised users gain access?)

It can be argued that some attributes, often cited as important, would have little general value in certification unless specifically cited as a requirement. Examples of these are:

- efficiency
- extendability
- flexibility
- interoperability
- maintainability
- portability
- testability
- usability

Arguments will rage as to what is of value and what is not. Certainly, some of the measures which are decomposed from these attributes are common to both groups. The key principle must be not to accept or reject a metric (or its parent attribute) until its utility in certification has been thoroughly tested.

SOFTWARE CERTIFICATION STATE-OF-THE-ART

At present, most software 'certification' relates to the quality of the development process rather than the conformance of the final product. There are a few exceptions, notably compiler certification and the approval of communications protocols. This paper is principally concerned with the ability to certify software products. It is, therefore, necessary to recognise that process quality tells us nothing directly about the product. To certify the product it is necessary to measure its characteristics and performance against some defined requirements and functional specifications.

This is not to say that process control and certification are not important and have no place in a scheme of certification directed towards the finalproduct. Indeed, it might be said that no software development of any significant complexity could be undertaken without a rigid adherance to some established development methodology based on a scheme of quality managementand assurance - eg ISO 9000, IEEE STD-730, AQAP-13 etc. Nevertheless, it must be emphasised that even the most rigorous adherence to methods such as these will not be sufficient to assure the final product. In many cases, further assessment, measurement and testing of software products will be required before a certificate can be awarded.

Some suitable techniques [40] are already available. These form the starting point for a model certification process which would cover many current applications of software. Other tools and techniques, at present being researched and developed, will become available as time goes on. These more advanced methods will allow further extensions and development of the certification process to cover a wider range of software applications or to give higher levels of assurance.

ASSESSMENT METHODS AND TOOLS

General

This section will not attempt to deal comprehensively with all the methods and tools which are currently available, and which might be used for certification. Some are described in references [19] to [39]. Essentially, the assurance of software attributes during certification is no more than a thorough and independent verification and validation (V&V) of the product. Indeed, this represents one of the fundamental problems of certification - the cost of repeating a significant portion of the development process.

The methods and tools discussed here will only be described in generic terms. It is stressed that there are many variations of methods and tools which might be suitable. The ultimate choices will depend on a combination of versatility, effectiveness and cost of use for any particular product or application.

Sources of software failure

Since the essential purpose of certification is to reduce, within economic bounds, the probability of product failure to as low a figure as possible, it is worth considering briefly, the sources of software failures.

Failure is defined as the termination of the ability of an item to perform a specified function. Normally, the specification referred to is the Requirements Specification. It is important to note that if the reference specification contains an mistake, and that mistake causes a 'malfunction', then that malfunction cannot be classified as a failure! Although the behaviour may be considered wrong (by the user), the system may be performing its specified function. This is a particular problem, related to the different perceptions of the producer and user, which would be addressed by Extended Certification.

A program (or system) failure is the result of a software or hardware fault causing an error (incorrect processing state) which, in the absence of any recovery mechanism will lead to failure. Note that failure may not always be detected when it occurs. Also, that the presence of a fault does not necessarily result in either an error or a failure; a software fault will remain dormant until the particular part of the program in which it lies is used. Figure 2 shows the sequence of events leading to failure.

Assuming that the Requirements Specification is correct, faults can be introduced at any subsequent stage in the development of the product. Where the product is essentially a program, then the fault may be caused during design, coding, integration or documentation. A well disciplined development methodology will try to provide safeguards against faults occurring. These safeguards will include:

- a good design method
- structured development
- reviews and audits
- Quality assurance
- use of standards
- competent staff
- good management

etc. etc.

Continual checks will be made during development to verify that the requirements for each phase have been met and to validate that the results of the development meet the requirements. It is the implementation of this process of verification and validation (V&V) which certification seeks to check by the assurance of attributes of the resulting product.

Methods and Tools

The main methods used in certification are;

- inspections
- audit
- assessment
- analysis
- test

Most of the certification process will concentrate on three aspects of the product,

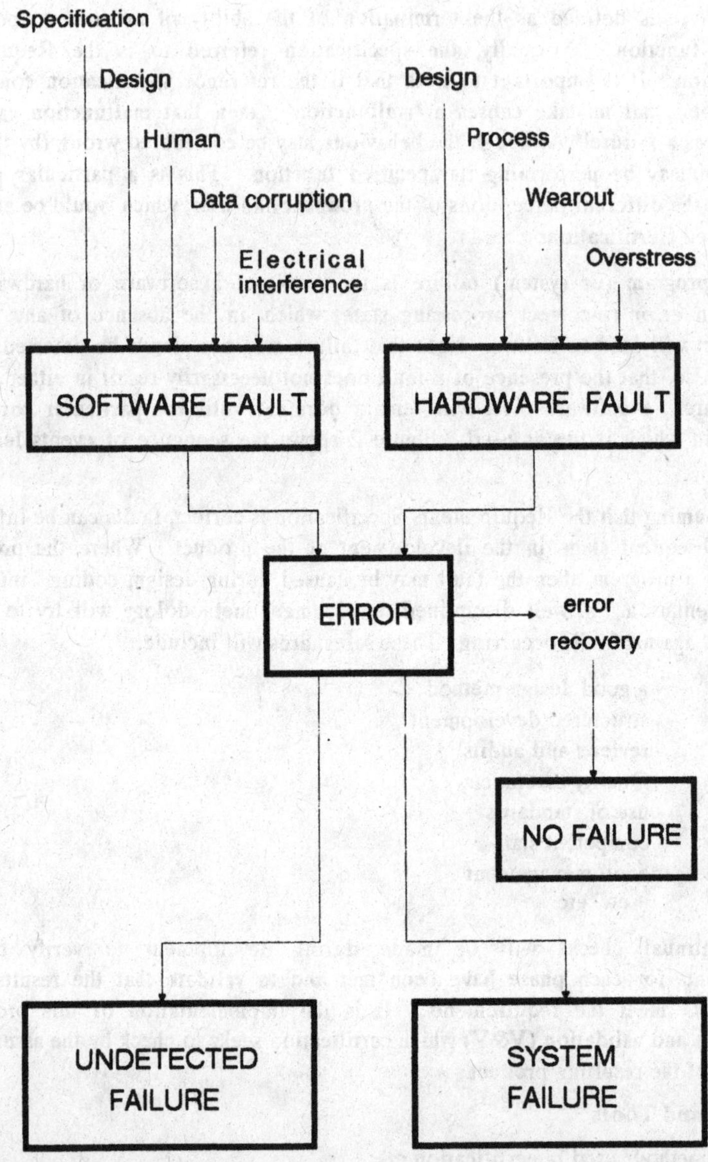

Figure 2. Sequence of Failure

the design, the code and aspects of the development process. For Extended Certification it will also be necessary to cover the requirements as well.

Design review and analysis should cover:

- analysis of the requirements for correctness, ambiguity and completeness. This may also involve safety analysis
- conformance of the design to the requirements
- adherence to standards
- conformance to the design method

Code review and test may include:

- code walkthroughs
- formal verification
- symbolic execution
- 'black box' and 'white box' testing
- static analysis
- dynamic analysis

There are aspects of the development process which might provide useful supportive evidence to the certifier. As has already been mentioned, process related attributes and metrics tell us little or nothing about the final product. But a properly organised and disciplined approach to developing a product will provide evidence from reviews, audits and tests. If this evidence can be properly authenticated (test results for instance), then it might be used to supplement the assurance work of the certification agency.

All the methods mentioned are supported by tools. These range from simple checklist techniques to complex static and dynamic analysers. The references cited above provide an insight to some of these.

A FRAMEWORK FOR SOFTWARE CERTIFICATION

Strategy

Software certification will not be an easy process to implement. The very nature of software, the circumstances of its use and the existing 'culture' of software development will demand a disciplined approach if the concept of certification is to be generally accepted.

Several fundamental principles must be followed in proposing a software certification process. These are:

- a need for evolution, not revolution, because of a
  - need to build on what is currently possible
  - need to recognise existing standards and codes of practice
  - need to harmonise different perceptions
  - need to take account of legal issues
  - need for tools and techniques not currently available

- a need to cater for a wide range of applications and risks
  - this would suggest a flexible, 'layered' approach with a range of possible certificates ranging from a simple certificate of conformance ('approved') to fully approved ('guaranteed')
- that the process should be economically viable
  - that is, that the cost of certification should not be greater than its economic and commercial advantages
- that for systems which are a combination of software and hardware, software certification should harmonise with hardware certification
- a need to recognise that there may need to be an acceptance that certain classes of software (eg those with extremely high reliability) cannot be fully certified
- a need to ensure that the reputation of a certificate cannot be compromised by some abuse or dilution of the system

Organisation & Control

Certification of software could be organised and controlled in a number of ways. It could cover some particular sector of software application, for instance, business, engineering, medicine, transportation etc. It might be organised some professional body for the benefit of its members as producers and users. A standards institute could possibly provide a national basis for certification and inter-governmental agreement could provide an international framework.

Figure 3 shows the outline for a certification scheme. A Certification Authority would be set up to regulate and administer the arrangements. It would also be responsible for awarding the Certificate to products which were recommended as suitable.

The primary reference for Certification must be a Certification Standard. This public document will provide details of the basis for certification, level of achievement and generally what must be done to secure a Certificate. The Standard will take account of any relevent legislation which might be applicable to software products and their use and will harmonise with other relevent software standards.

The Standard will need to be supplemented by authoritative Guides which will explain, in precise terms, exactly how the Certification Method will be applied, the attributes and characteristics that will be examined, the methods and tools to be used and the pass/fail criteria.

Certification will be undertaken by Authorised Certification Agencies. The Authorised Agencies will be responsible for assuring conformance of the Product that has been submitted for certification. All Agencies will use a uniform Certification Method which is laid down in the Standards and Guides regulated by the Certification Authority

The advantage of using a uniform Method of certification will be that the Certificate will be valid wherever the Certification Scheme is recognised, irrespective of

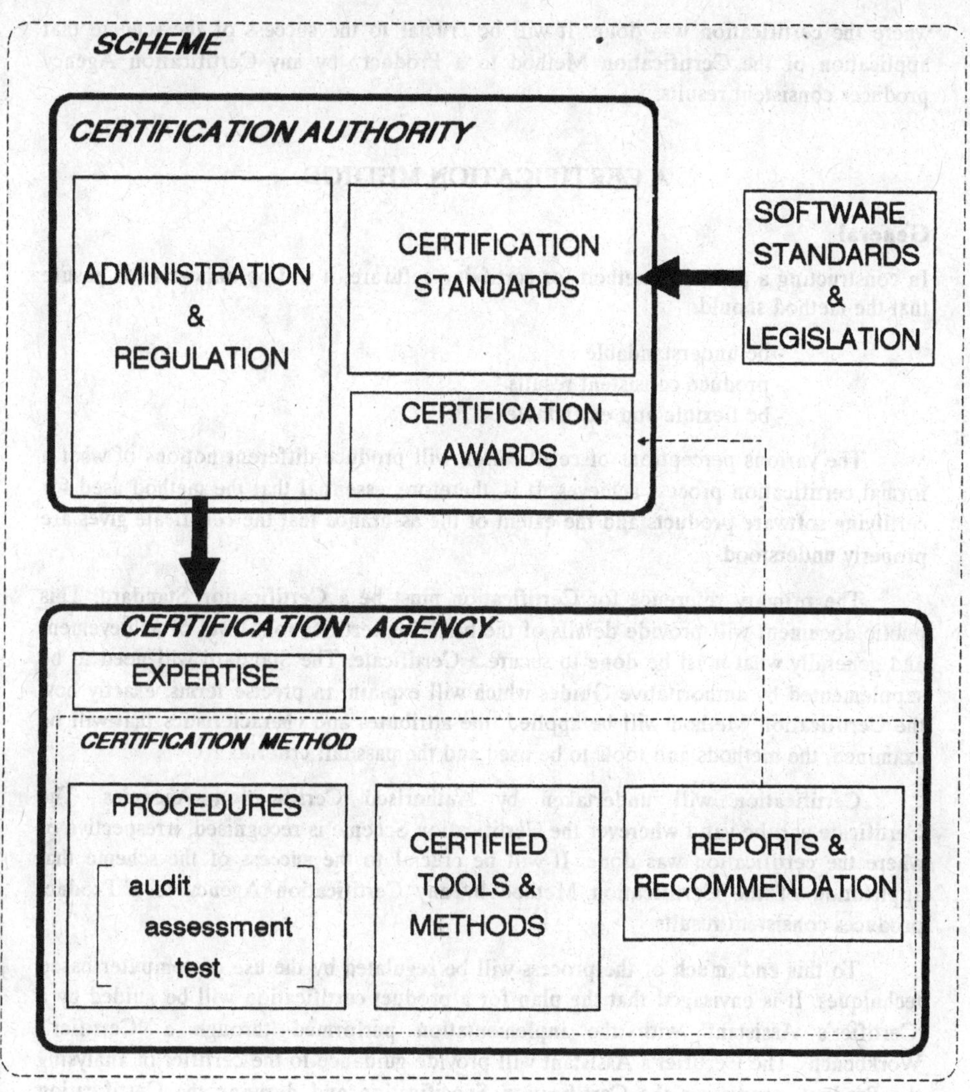

Figure 3. A Certification Scheme

where the certification was done. It will be crucial to the success of the scheme that application of the Certification Method to a Product by any Certification Agency produces consistent results.

A CERTIFICATION METHOD

General

In constructing a practical method for certifying software, it will be important to ensure that the method should:

- be understandable
- produce consistent results
- be flexible and extendable

The various perceptions of certification will produce different notions of what a formal certification process achieves. It is, therefore, essential that the method used for certifying software products and the extent of the assurance that the certificate gives are properly understood.

The primary reference for Certification must be a Certification Standard. This public document will provide details of the basis for certification, level of achievement and generally what must be done to secure a Certificate. The Standard will need to be supplemented by authoritative Guides which will explain, in precise terms, exactly how the Certification Method will be applied, the attributes and characteristics that will be examined, the methods and tools to be used and the pass/fail criteria.

Certification will undertaken by Authorised Certification Agencies. The Certificate will be valid wherever the Certification Scheme is recognised, irrespective of where the certification was done. It will be crucial to the success of the scheme that application of the Certification Method by any Certification Agency to a Product produces consistent results.

To this end, much of the process will be regulated by the use of computer based techniques. It is envisaged that the plan for a product certification will be guided by a 'Certifier's Assistant' with the inplementation performed through a 'Certifier's Workbench'. The Certifier's Assistant will provide guidance to the certifier in analysing the Product, producing the Certification Specification and deriving the Certification Plan. The Certifier's Workbench will provide the means of implementing tools and methods, encapsulated as a modular set of Certification Blocks.

Both the Certifier's Assistant and the Certifier's Workbench will include automated recording and documentation facilities which will provide a record of the certification and any necessary reports. The Assistant and Workbench programs will be common to all Certification Agencies to ensure uniformity.

Software is subject to frequent changes of methodology and application. New techniques and tools for certification will have to be adopted and incorporated without compromising the existing procedures. This will be possible since the Method has a modular design. Attributes and characteristics, together with the tools and methods required to assure their decomposed metrics, are arranged as linked modules which can be selected and arranged using the Certifier's Assistant to form a Certification Plan which can be implemented through the Certifier's Workbench. A brief description of the selection and application of Certification Blocks is given later.

Levels of certification

A key decision in setting up a software certification scheme will be the nature of the certificate which will be awarded. Should it be a single certificate or should the certificate be 'layered' with levels of attainment? This is an extremely difficult question to answer and, certainly, no attempt will be made to give an answer here.

A single certificate will certainly make for a simple scheme. It would be necessary to annotate each certificate awarded with the exact extent of the coverage of the assurance that had been performed; what attributes had been examined and what tests had been used. The great disadvantage would be that nobody bothers to read the 'small print' so there might be some doubt as to the true value of such a certificate. The face value of a common certificate would range from assurance of a computer game to assurance of a complex safety-critical system.

On the other hand, a layered approach would allow the award of certificates which were appropriate to, say, the risks involved in the use of the product. Thus, a computer game might be awarded a certificate at the lowest level while a safety-critical system would rate a certificate at the highest level. This would remove the need for any qualifications to be made on the certificate - certificates would be appropriate for the application or use of the product. The difficulty comes in deciding the number of levels and the boundaries to those levels. Too few levels will bring difficulties of a wide range of products falling into the same band (needing annotation like a single certificate); too many levels may create confusion.

Whatever the solution, it will have to be acceptable to everyone using or having an interest in a certification scheme. Fortunately the decision of one or many levels of certificate does not affect the discussion of a certification method which follows.

Stages of Certification

There are ten distinct stages in the certification of a software product. These are:

- submission of the product to the Certification Agency
- agreeing the Certification Requirement
- agreeing an initial Cost Estimate
- analysing the product
- producing a Certification Specification
- relating the Specification to tasks, techniques and tools
- producing a Certification Plan
- costing the Certification Plan

- implementing the Certification Plan
- producing a Certification Report

Each of these stages will be discussed in the sections that follow. Figure 4 shows a block diagram of the method.

Product submitted for Certification: When the producer decides that certification of a product is desirable (or necessary) a Product Package will be submitted to a Certification Agency for Certification. This Product Package will consist of at least the following Product Parts:

- a product specification
- the development plan or specification
- the program source code
- the program object code
- user instructions
- the development test plan and results

This minimum list of Product Parts is sufficient for undertaking a Basic Certification which will assure conformance between the specified and actual service. Basic Certification is not concerned with the correctness of the specification (is it the right product?) but only that the product does what the specification demands (is the product right?). Every Product Certificate will be annotated with the particular attributes and characteristics that have been uniquely assured for that product. It will be the responsibility of the user to ensure that the software product is suitable for any particular application.

However, there are some classes of software product, clearly designed for particular applications, where it is necessary to ensure that the software not only behaves reasonably, but also that its use carries no unacceptable risk; that is, it is fit for its intended purpose. In these cases it will be necessary to undertake Extended Certification. Extended Certification will require additional Product Parts such as a Product Requirements Specification, detailed technical documentation (eg design specifications, technical manuals, safety analyses etc), evidence of quality conformance, beta testing etc.

Agreeing the Certification Requirement: Since the Producer will, initially, be expected to bear the cost of certification, it will be necessary for the Certification Agency and the Producer to agree the attributes and characteristics which are to be assured. Also, whether Basic or Extended Certification is to be undertaken. The agreement about what must be done will be formalised as the Certification Requirement. This will provide a nominal list of Items (product attributes and characteristics) which must be assured, identify the sources of data and evidence to be used and the work to be done.

Agreeing the initial Cost Estimate: Once the Certification Requirement is agreed, an Initial Cost Estimate can be constructed from a knowledge of the list of

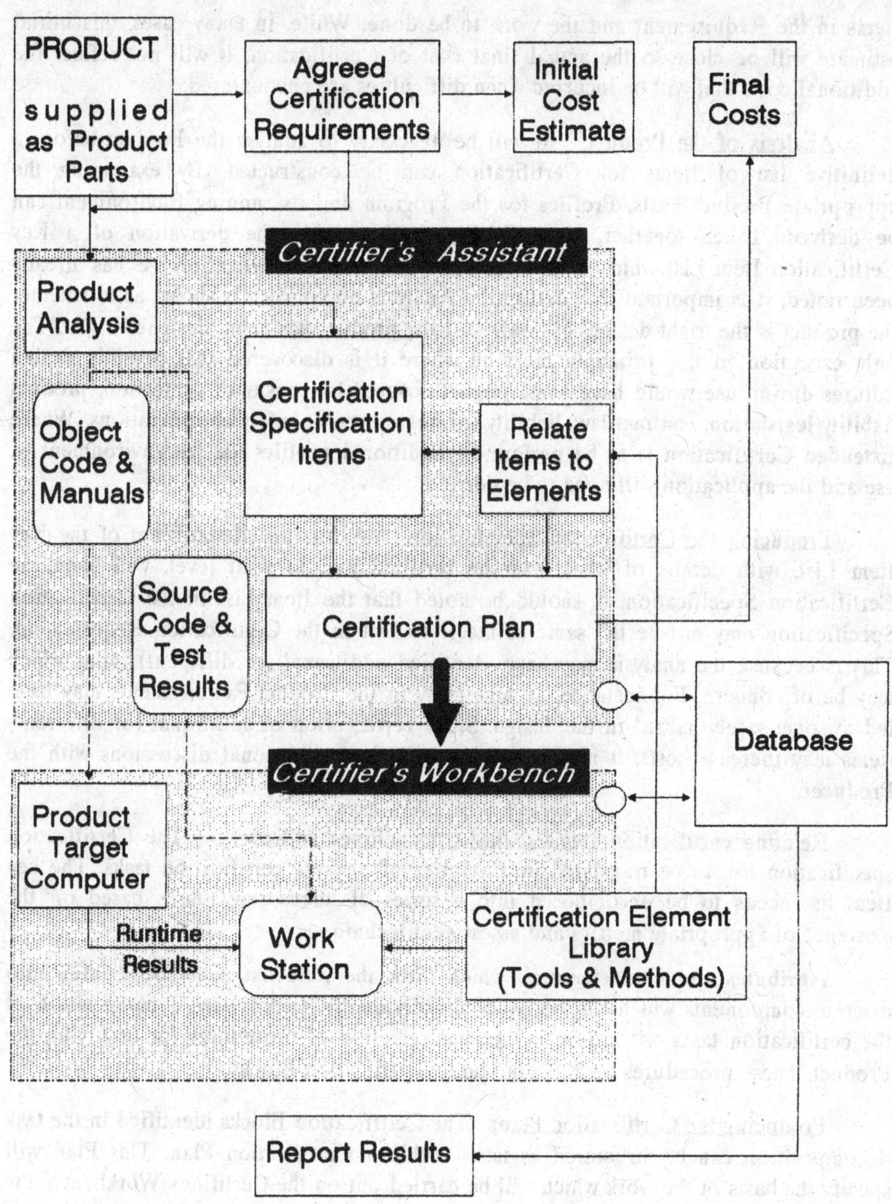

Figure 4. Certification Method

Items in the Requirement and the work to be done. While, in many cases, this initial estimate will be close to the actual final cost of Certification, it will not reflect the additional costs that will be incurred when difficulties are encountered.

Analysis of the Product: It will be necessary to analyse the Product before a definitive list of Items for Certification can be constructed. By examining the appropriate Product Parts, Profiles for the Program and its running Environment can be derived. Taken together, these Profiles will provide the derivation of a Key Certification Item List which will be the basis of a Basic Certification. As has already been noted, it is important that during the Analysis no concern is shown as to whether the product is the 'right design' but only that the product has been 'designed right'. The only exception to this principle must be where it is discovered that possible design failures during use would have some impact covered by consumer protection, product liability legislation, contract law, liability for negligence or safety considerations. Where Extended Certification is to be performed, additional profiles for the environment of use and the application will need to be derived.

Producing the Certification Specification: A formalised statement of the Key Item List, with details of what must be certified and to what level, will form the Certification Specification. It should be noted that the Item List in the Certification Specification may not be the same as the Item List in the Certification Requirement. This is because the analysis may have identified additional (or different) Items which may be of concern. For instance, an ambiguity in the Product Requirements may have led to some safety hazard in the design. Since certification of additional (or different) items may increase costs, it may be necessary to have additional discussions with the Producer.

Relating certification Items to tasks, techniques and tools: The Certification specification has to be translated into a series of discrete certification tasks. The key Item list needs to be decomposed into a series of 'elementary' tasks based on the existence of appropriate metrics and assessment techniques.

Attributes and characteristics, which form the item list, must be divided into discrete components which can be handled individually. In this way, decomposition of the certification tasks will allow an optimal selection of procedures for certifying the Product. These procedures form the modular Certification Blocks.

Producing the Certification Plan: The Certification Blocks identified in the task decomposition can be structured as tasks within a Certification Plan. This Plan will specify the basis of the work which will be carried out on the Certifier's Workbench, the Certification Blocks to be used and the goals together with pass/fail criteria. The modular arrangement of Blocks ensures that the choice of tools and techniques can be optimised to give maximum coverage with minimum cost.

Costing the Certification Plan: It will now be possible, given the definition of tasks, the individual Blocks being used and the cost of their use, to cost the certification of the Product.

Implementing the Certification Plan: The Certification Plan will be used as the basis of the Certification Implementation Procedures. The Plan will be constructed in such a way as to provide a clean and unambiguous interface with the Certifier's Workbench. The workbench acts as a platform for the tool and method elements (Blocks) which have been chosen to test, evaluate or assess the decomposed attributes and caaracteristics to be assured.

Anomalous results or problems may require some iteration of the previous stages, and further discussion with the Producer regarding total costs.

Reporting the results with recommendations: Finally, the results of the Certification must be reported to the appropriate authority responsible for awarding the Certificate. The main reporting function will be catered for by the built-in reporting feature of the Certifier's Assistant and the Certifier's Workbench.

There will be cases (particularly where attributes or characteristics have subjective measures) when it will be impossible to determine a precise pass/fail judgement. Some latitude may be necessary to allow submission of an overall recommendation to the authority. However, strict rules for adjudication of marginal decisions will need to be established to ensure that the final recommendation is repeatable.

Variations of method

Whilst the method described should be the norm, it may be necessary for practical or economic reasons, to adopt variations of the method in certain cases. Once again, strict regulation of any variation would be necessary to make sure that the scheme was not abused or diluted in any way. Three instances can be cited as examples.

First, at the simplest level of certification, it may be possible to introduce an element of supervised 'self-certification' by the producer. In this case, much of the work of the Certification Plan would be done by the producer under some form of supervision by the Certification Agency. The producer would need to have access to the appropriate methods and tools and be competent in their use. Supervision might be by direct physical presence of Agency staff or could, perhaps be by 'spot check' and audit of the work. Such a scheme could reduce the cost of certification and perhaps, more importantly to a producer, reduce the time taken to gain a certificate. The difficulty would be that this sort of arrangement might be more open to abuse by an unscrupulous producer, so would have to be policed very carefully.

The second example is the case of a safety-critical system, where it would be impossible to create a representative test environment for certification. Take, for instance, a plant safety system working in emergency mode. It would be impossible to create a genuine use environment without access to all the relevent components of the system. In this case, it may be necessary to perform part of the certification at the actual site of the system. It would be necessary for the certifiers to work closely with the producer during the late stages of development and commissioning of the plant.

The last example is that of a high quality but low cost package which was, initially, not expected to sell in large numbers. In this situation, the cost of certification would not be economic. To offset the lack of a certificate, the producer might guarantee users a high level of after-sale support. Now suppose the package was a great success and sold in large numbers with few significant faults being reported by users through the 'help line'. Provided the producer kept good records and could be trusted, it might be considered reasonable to have some mechanism where the product could be awarded a certificate on the basis of an audit of the product supported by the evidence of user's experience. After all, the cumulative 'test-time' built up by users could be considerable, far greater than would have been economic in regular certification testing.

These examples are typical of scenarios where alternative methods of certification may need to be considered. Variations to the regular certification method wold have to be regulated very carefully. Nevertheless, they might provide wider economic viability or solve particular technical difficulties in cases where the regular certification method could not be used or was too costly.

CONCLUSION

It is recognised that certification of software presents many difficulties. But against this, a recognised Certification Scheme would offer many benefits, especially to producers and users of software products.

Some determination would be necessary on the part of Industry Sectors, National authorities or the European Community to set up such a scheme. But, at least, the principle of a European scheme is being explored in the Esprit SCOPE Project which will produce a final report and draft Standard by the beginning of 1993.

Methods and tools are available already, which would allow Basic and Extended Certification of a wide range of software products. Whether the benefits which might be accrued would justify the cost of such certification is not certain. But it is to be hoped that in the future, when more advanced tools and techniques may be available, it will be possible to assure the more safety critical software-based applications to a much higher level than is currently achieved.

ACKNOWLEDGEMENT

Much of the source material used in this paper is derived from work done, by the author, for the Esprit SCOPE (Software CertificatiOn Programme in Europe) Project. Many thanks are due to all my SCOPE colleagues who have helped, by discussion , to clarify some of the ideas.

REFERENCES

1. CEN/Cenelec/CEPT/ITSTC, Certification of information technology products. M-IT-03.
2. Andersen, O. & Petersen, P. G., Handbook of Standards and Certification Requirements for Software. ECR-182, ElectronikCentralen, Venlighedsvej 4, DK-2970, Denmark.
3. National Computing Centre, Compiler Validation, Your questions answered. National Computing Centre Ltd., Oxford Road, Manchester, 1987.
4. Open Systems Interconnection, Methodology and framework for conformance testing. ISO/TC 97, ISO/IS 7498.
5. Wilson, R. & Lloyd, I., Report on the Legal Aspects of SCOPE. Esprit Project 2151 (SCOPE) - Project deliverable (to be published).
6. Boehm, B. W., Software Engineering Economics. Prentice-Hall, New York 1981
7. Boehm, B. W., A Spiral Model of software development and enhancement. Computer May 1988
8. Card, D. N., Mcgarry F. E., Page, G., et al., Measures and metrics for software development. SEL-83-002, Software Engineering Laboratory, Goddard Space Flight Center, Greenbelt, Maryland 20771, USA, March 1984.
9. Conte S. D., Dunsmore, H. E., Shen, V. Y., Software engineering models and metrics. Benjamin/Cummings Publishing Company Inc., 1986
10. Fenton N. E., Kaposi A. A., Metrics and software structure. Information and Software Technology, 29/60, 301-320, July/August 1987
11. Halstead, M. H., Elements of Software Science. Elsevier, 1977
12. Kitchenham, B. A., & McDermid, J. A., Software metrics and integrated project support environments. Software Engineering Journal, vol 1, no 1, January 1986, pp 58-64.
13. Kitchenham B. A., Software quality modelling, measurement and prediction; quality factors, quality criteria and quality metrics. REQUEST Report R1.6.4, July 1986, (published as 'Towards a Constructive Quality Model', Software Engineering Journal, July 1987, pp 105-113.
14. McCall J. A., Factors in software quality. General Electric nr 77C1502, June 1977
15. McCabe, T. J., A Complexity Measure. IEEE Trans. Software Eng., SE2, 308-320, June 1976.
16. Albrecht, A. J., Measuring application development productivity. Proc IBM Application Development Sympos., October 1979, pp 83-92
17. Littlewood, B., Forecasting software reliability. Lecture Notes in Computer Science, No 341, Springer-Verlag, Berlin, 1989.
18. Esprit Project P 2151, Software Certification Programme in Europe (SCOPE)
19. Ackermann, A. F., Fowler, P. J., Lewski, F. H., Software inspections; an effective verification process. IEEE Software, May 1989, pp 31-36.

20. Berry, D. M., Towards a formal basis for the Formal Development Method and the Ina-Jo Specification Language. IEEE Transactions on Software Engineering, vol 13, 1987.

21. Clarke, L. A., & Richardson, D. J., Symbolic evaluation; an aid to testing and verification. in Hausen, H. L. (ed) Software Validation, Horth Holland, 1984

22. Computer Research and Innovation Center, QUALIGRAPH - users guide. Computer Research and Innovation Center, Budapest.

23. Dahil, G., et al., Tools for standardised software safety assessment. HWR-211, May 1987, OECD Halden Reactor Project.

24. De Marco, T., Structured Analysis and system specification. Yourdon Press, 1979.

25. Department of Defense, Trusted computer system evaluation criteria (Orange Book) CSC-STD-001-83, August 1983.

26. Dunn, R. & Ullmann, Quality assurance for computer software. McGraw-Hill, 1982

27. Fagan, M. E., Advances in inspections. IEEE Trans. on Software Eng., July 1986, pp 744-751.

28. Howden, W. E., Functional program testing and analysis. McGraw-Hill Inc., New York, 1987.

29. Leelasena, L., QUALMS and CASSANDRA user manuals. CSSE, South Bank Polytechnic, London, 1989.

30. Miller, E. F. & Howden, W. E., (eds), Tutorial: Software testing and validation. IEEE EHO 138-8 1978.

31. Myers, G. I., The art of software testing. John Wiley & Sons, London, 1987.

32. Program Analysers, TESTBED Technical description. Program Analysers Ltd., 1989.

33. Petersen, P. G., Petri Nets. ACM Computing Surveys, vol 9, 1977.

34. Program Validation Ltd., SPADE brochure. Program Validation Ltd.

35. Rex, Thompson and Partners, MALPAS Executive Guide. Rex, Thompson and Partners Software Ltd., 1989

36. Reliability and Statistical Consultants Ltd., Software reliability modelling programs. Reliability and Statistical Consultants Ltd., 5 Jocelyn Rd., Richmond, Surrey, TW9 2TJ, UK.

37. Verilog, ASA technical brochure. Verilog, Toulouse, France, 1987.

38 Verilog, LOGISCOPE technical brochure. Verilog, Toulouse, France, 1989

39. Yourdon, E., Structured walkthroughs. Yourdon Inc., 1977.

40. SCOPE Project, Software Certification - State of the art. Report (to be published)

14

PRACTICAL BENEFITS OF GOAL-ORIENTED MEASUREMENT

H. DIETER ROMBACH
Department of Computer Science
and
Institute for Advanced Computer Studies
University of Maryland
College Park, Maryland 20742, USA

ABSTRACT

Software measurement is an essential component of mature software technology. It supports quality as well as project management. As far as quality management is concerned, measurement can help investigate software related phenomena and thus contribute to building better software product, process and quality models. As far as project management is concerned, measurement can help state software requirements unambiguously, assess their proper implementation throughout the software project, and achieve convincing product certification. The measurement goal of interest determines which metrics are appropriate. Over the years, several 'top-down' measurement approaches for deriving metrics from goals have been proposed. Examples include the QFD approach by Akao, the SQM approach by Murine based on prior work by Boehm and McCall, and the GQM approach by Basili. In this paper, the practical benefits of reliability measurement based on the GQM approach are discussed.

INTRODUCTION

The development of software must become a carefully planned, controlled, methodical and predictable enterprise. In order to achieve this objective software projects need to be performed according to a planning, execution and feedback oriented project model [1,4]. Sound planning includes the setting of project goals and their quantification based on models derived from past experience. Sound execution includes the capturing of the prescribed measurement data. Sound feedback includes checking for adherence to planned targets and replanning of the current project if necessary as well as packaging the experience gained from the current project for use in future projects.

According to such a project model a variety of software project goals exist, defined from a variety of perspectives, including the customer, the project personnel, and the corporation. For example, the customer may be interested in having a 'reliable' product delivered, the project personnel may be interested in producing the required reliable product on time and within budget, and the corporation may be interested in improving its ability to develop reliable products over time.

Measurement is an ideal mechanism for evaluating any software project goal. For example, 'reliability' needs to be defined in quantitative terms in order to communicate the requirements unambiguously between customer and project personnel and to allow the customer to certify the delivered product with regard to reliability. The project personnel needs to establish measurable milestones throughout the development process in order to assess the progress of the project with respect to reliability and take corrective actions if needed. The organization needs to be able to compare consecutive projects with respect to reliability.

One crucial planning issue is the identification of useful metrics. Several approaches have been proposed to identify useful metrics from goals in a 'top-down' manner: the QFD approach by Akao [9], the SQM approach by Murine [11] based on prior work by Boehm [7] and McCall [10], or the GQM approach by Basili [1,2,3,4,5,6].

This paper starts with a brief characterization and comparison of these 'top-down' measurement approaches. The emphasis of the remainder of the paper is on the GQM approach – the most comprehensive of these approaches in my opinion. The GQM approach supports the operational definition of measurement goals, their refinement into metrics, the explicit documentation of the refinement rationale, and the participation of all expected beneficiaries of measurement in the goal definition and metrics identification process. The definition of measurement goals and their refinement into metrics is guided by a set of templates and guidelines. These guidelines are applied to two example reliability goals. These examples are then used to illustrate some of the benefits of the GQM approach. GQM benefits include its general applicability to all kinds of measurement goals, as well as its support for identifying and tailoring of metrics, for interpreting collected data in context, for validating the usefulness of the selected metrics early on, for involving all interested parties in the measurement process, and for protecting sensitive data. The paper concludes with a description of future GQM-related research activities.

TOP-DOWN MEASUREMENT APPROACHES

In order for measurement to be successful, we need effective 'top-down' approaches which help derive metrics from goals and interpret metrics data in the context of goals. The identification of useful metrics needs to be based on models of the issues addressed in the goal of interest. For example, in order to derive metrics for a goal aimed at 'analyzing a source code component for the purpose of predicting its maintainability from a maintainer's perspective' one needs to understand the maintainer's models of maintainability (e.g., how many components get changed) and the source code component itself (i.e., structural aspects which may impact maintainability).

In this section, we provide a brief characterization of three existing top-down measurement approaches and compare them. Each measurement approach is characterized in terms of **scope of goals** (i.e., What types of development goals are supported?), its support for the **identification of metrics** (i.e., How are metrics identified for a given goal?), and the possible

scope of the approach (i.e., What can the approach be used for?). The scope of measurement goals is characterized in terms of what objects are measured (**objects**: products, processes, other quality models), why they are measured (**why**: understand, evaluate, manage, plan, predict, engineer, control, certify, motivate or improve); what aspect is measured (**focus**: cost, correctness, defects, changes, reliability, user friendliness), and who is interested in measurement (**who**: user, customer, manager, developer, corporation). This characterization scheme corresponds to the goal definition template presented later. The support for identifying metrics is characterized in terms of the actual **paradigm** for relating measurement goals and metrics and the **mechanism** for identifying metrics. The use of a measurement approach is either quality management or project management. Quality management may be limited to measuring just products or processes. Project management requires management of products **and** processes.

The QFD Approach

The Quality Function Deployment (QFD) approach was first proposed by Yoji Akao, Tamagawa University, Tokyo, Japan, in 1966. Its original purpose was to serve as a framework for dealing with quality at the planning stage of any manufacturing process. The basic idea is that customer and user needs determine which process and product aspects need to be planned, engineered and controlled throughout development. Since then, QFD has been adapted to the software domain [9].

Design Characteristics	Maintainability Characteristics of Final Product		
	Understandability	Modifiability	Ripple Effect
Coupling	high	low	high
Cohesion	average	average	low
Doc. Quality	average	high	low
Inf. Hiding	high	average	high

Figure 1. QFD Matrix Chart

QFD measurement goals are focused on all kinds of life–cycle products, aimed at planning, engineering and control, and focused on quality issues which are of importance to the user or customer. The basic idea is to relate **characteristics of the final product** to **characteristics of earlier products** (e.g., requirements, design, source code). For example, one might be interested in 'analyzing the design document for the purpose of predicting the maintainability of the final product'. The matrix chart in Figure 1 depicts a possible analysis result. It indicates which design characteristics are expected to impact which maintenance characteristics of the final product.

The QFD approach suggests to trace characteristics of the final product into related characteristics of products at earlier stages of development. However, no explicit support is provided for refining measurement goals into product characteristics or product characteristics into metrics.

One of the important differences between manufacturing and software development processes is that the latter vary from project to project [4]. This means that software development processes cannot be managed and controlled indirectly via products, but require direct attention. The limitation of the QFD approach to product issues suggests that it supports quality management but not software project management.

The SQM Approach

The Software Quality Metrics (SQM) approach has been proposed by Murine (METRICS Incorporated) [11]. It is based on prior work on quantifying software characteristics by Boehm et al. [7] and later by McCall et al. [10].

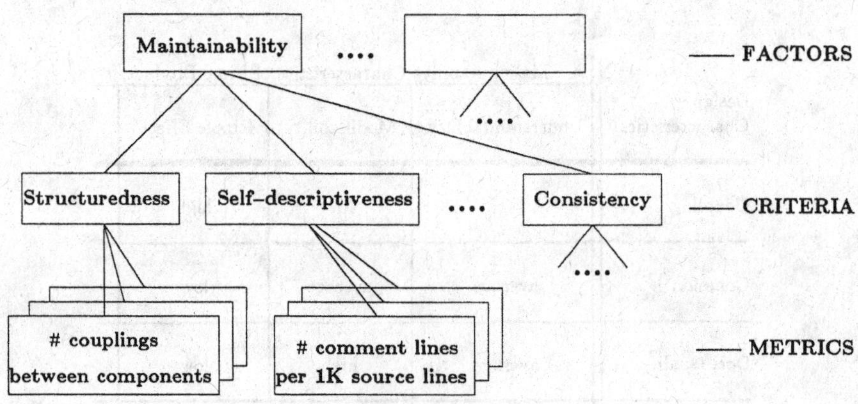

Figure 2. Factor/Criteria/Metrics Structure

SQM measurement goals are focused on the final product, aimed at assessment and certification, and focused on quality issues which are of importance to the user or customer. The basic idea is to derive software metrics from quality factors and criteria (see Figure 2). Each quality **factor** reflects the user oriented view of some product quality (e.g., maintainability). Factors are refined into a set of **criteria** which reflect software oriented characteristics which indicate quality (e.g., structuredness, self-descriptiveness, consistency). These criteria are in turn defined in terms of **metrics** (e.g., # couplings between components, # comment lines per 1K source lines).

The SQM approach supports the identification of metrics by providing a pre-defined factors/criteria/metrics graph from which the factors, criteria and metrics of interest can be chosen [7, 10]. A subset of such a pre-defined graph is depicted in Figure 2. No support is provided for modifying such a graph. It is assumed that all measurements can be performed based on a subset of the pre-defined factors, criteria and metrics.

The SQM approach seems useful for product quality management only. The exclusion of process metrics and even metrics of earlier life-cycle products makes the SQM approach unfit to support project management.

The GQM Approach
The Goal/Question/Metric (GQM) approach was first proposed by Victor Basili and Dave Weiss (University of Maryland) [6]. It was originally developed for evaluating defects for a set of projects in the NASA/SEL environment [5,6]. Later it was expanded and formalized to be used for all kinds of measurement goals [1,2,3,4].

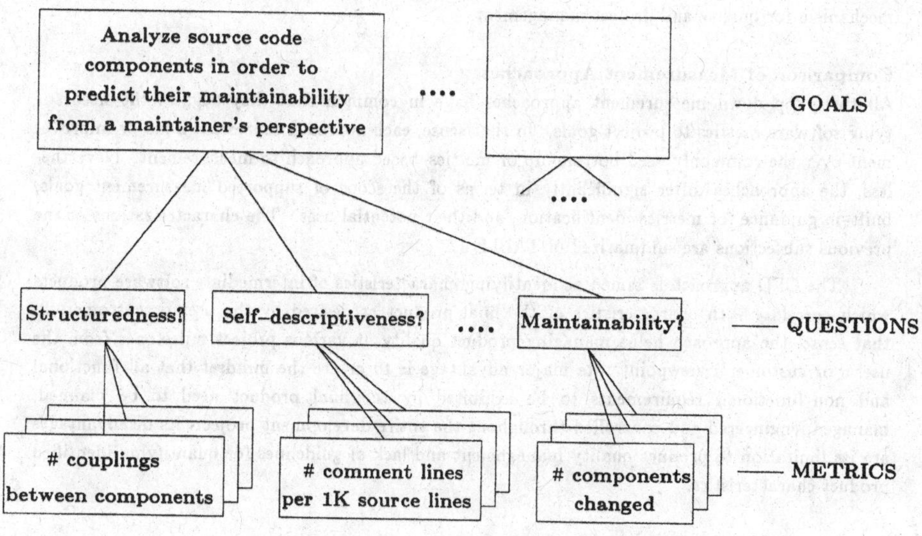

Figure 3. Example Goal/Question/Metrics Graph

GQM measurement goals may be focused on any type of software product or process, aimed at all kinds of purposes ranging from characterization and assessment to control and improvement, focused on any quality issues, and defined from the perspective of any person interested. The basic idea is to derive software metrics from measurement goals and questions (see Figure 3). Each measurement **goal** is defined in terms of objects (e.g., source code components), why (e.g., predict), focus (e.g., maintainability), and who (e.g., maintainer). Goals are refined into a set of

questions which collectively represent an operational definition of the goal at hand (e.g., what is the structure of the component?, how self-descriptive is the component?, how consistent is the component with its specification?). Each question defines a number of metrics (e.g., # couplings between components, # comment lines per 1K source lines, # components changed).

The GQM approach supports the identification of metrics for any type of measurement via a set of guidelines for how to formulate a goal comprehensibly, what types of questions to ask, and how to refine them into questions. There exists no pre-defined GQM graph; instead a customized GQM graph is instantiated for each measurement goal of interest according to these existing guidelines. This ability to create customized GQM graphs recognizes the fact that measurement goals need to be tailorable to the needs of changing project characteristics and goals. That does not mean that all GQM graphs are developed from scratch. How similar GQM graphs are across projects (i.e., how much of them can be reused) depends on how stable an organization we are looking at. If project goals and project characteristics change a lot it should be surprising if the corresponding measurement goals change to a similar degree. After all, measurement's main purpose is to 'visualize' certain aspects of these software projects.

The equal emphasis on product and process issues qualifies the GQM approach as a valuable mechanism for quality and project management.

Comparison of Measurement Approaches

All three top-down measurement approaches have in common that they suggest the need for tying software metrics to project goals. In that sense, each approach represents a major improvement over the commonly used bottom-up or metrics-based approach to measurement. Nevertheless, the approaches differ significantly in terms of the scope of supported measurement goals, built-in guidance for metrics identification, and their potential uses. The characterizations of the previous subsections are summarized in TABLE 1.

The QFD approach is aimed at identifying characteristics of intermediate software products which correlate with characteristics of the final product as desired by the user or customer. In that sense, the approach helps managing product quality at various project milestones from the user's or customer's viewpoint. Its major advantage is to create the mindset that all functional and non-functional requirements to be exhibited by the final product need to be planned, managed, engineered and controlled throughout the entire development project. Its disadvantages are its limitation to product quality management and lack of guidelines for quantifying identified product characteristics.

TABLE 1
Definition of Top–Down Measurement Approaches

Criteria	Measurement Approaches		
	QFD Approach	SQM Approach	GQM Approach
SCOPE OF GOALS:			
– Objects:	any product	final product	any process, product, model
– Purpose:	plan, engineer, control	assess, certify	characterize, evaluate, predict, motivate, plan, engineer, control, improve, ...
– Aspect:	any quality or productivity issue	any quality or productivity issue	any quality or productivity issue
– Viewpoint:	customer, user	customer, user	customer, user, developer, manager, corporation, ...
IDENTIFICATION OF METRICS:			
– Paradigm:	Trace user characteristics of final product into related product characteristics at various stages of development	Refine factors into criteria and metrics	Refine goals into questions and metrics
– Mechanism:	select/tailor	select	select/tailor
SCOPE OF THE APPROACH:			
– Use:	Quality Management	Quality Management	Quality and Project Management

The SQM approach is aimed at certifying certain qualities of the final product from the user's or customer's viewpoint. Its major advantage is that, as long as measurement needs are consistent with the implicit models underlying the pre–defined graph, the selection of factors, criteria and metrics is straightforward. This advantage becomes a disadvantage as soon as measurement needs are based on different models due to changing project characteristics and/or goals. Its disadvantages are its narrow focus on product issues only from a customer/user viewpoint, its lack of support for adding or changing elements of the pre–defined factors/criteria/metrics graph whenever needed, and its lack of any explicit rationale for the pre–defined breakdown.

The GQM approach is aimed at supporting any measurement goal. Its advantages are its general applicability and its support for defining goals and refining them into questions and metrics via a set of guidelines. There are no limitations regarding the objects to be measured, the purposes of measurement, the aspects to be measured, and the viewpoints of interest. It can be used for quality management of any process or product as well as project management. In that sense, the GQM approach is the most flexible and widely applicable of the three approaches. As far as defining metrics is concerned, SQM can be viewed as a special instantiation of the GQM approach. The reader is referred to [16] for a detailed comparison between the SQM and GQM approaches. The GQM guidelines help creating customized goal/question/metric graphs, establish tractable relations between goal, question and metric levels, and communicate the rationale for a given set of metrics. As the most comprehensive of the three approaches, there are no relative disadvantages.

THE GQM APPROACH

The process of setting goals and refining them into quantifiable questions is complex and requires experience. In order to support this process, a template for defining goals, and a set of guidelines for deriving questions and metrics have been developed [3]. These templates and guidelines reflect the experience from having applied the GQM paradigm in a variety of environments (e.g., NASA [6,14,15], Burroughs Corporation [13], etc.). It needs to be stressed that we do not claim that these templates and guidelines are complete; they will most likely change over time as our experience grows.

The following subsections introduce and illustrate the use of the template for defining goals, the guidelines for deriving product- and process-related questions, and the guidelines for deriving metrics.

Template for Goal Definition

Goals are defined according to the following template {3]:

- **Purpose**:

  Analyze some
  (*objects*: processes, products, other experience models, ...)
  for the purpose of
  (*why*: characterization, evaluation, prediction, motivation, engineering, control, certification, improvement, ...)

- **Perspective:**

  with respect to
  (*focus*: cost, correctness, defect removal, changes, reliability, user friendliness, maintainability, ...)
  from the point of view of the
  (*who*: user, customer, manager, developer, corporation, ...)

• **Environment:**

in the following context:

(*Environment factors*: problem, people, resources, processes, ...).

We distinguish between goals oriented towards products or processes. An example product goal created according to the above template is:

(G_1) Analyze the 'final product' for the purpose of 'certification' with respect to 'reliability' from the point of view of the 'customer' in the following context: 'NASA/SEL'.

An example process goal created according to the above framework is:

(G_2) Analyze the 'testing process' for the purpose of 'control' with respect to 'reliability' from the point of view of the 'developer' in the following context: 'NASA/SEL'.

Guidelines for Deriving Product–Related Questions

For each product under study there are three major subgoals that need to be addressed: (1) definition of the product, (2) definition of the quality perspectives of interest, and (3) feedback related to the quality perspectives of interest.

- **Definition of the product** includes questions related to logical and physical attributes (a quantitative characterization of the product in terms of physical attributes such as size, complexity, etc.), development cost (a quantitative characterization of the resources expended related to this product in terms of effort, computer time, etc.), development changes (a quantitative characterization of the errors, faults, failures, adaptations, and enhancements related to this product), and operational context (a quantitative characterization of the customer community using this product and their operational profiles).

- **Quality perspectives of interest** includes, for each quality perspective of interest (e.g., reliability, user friendliness), questions related to the major model(s) used (a quantitative specification of the quality perspective of interest), the validity of the model for the particular environment (an analysis of the appropriateness of the model for the particular project environment), the validity of the data collected (an analysis of the quality of data), and optionally, a substantiation of the model (use of an alternative model to help evaluate whether the results of the primary model are reasonable).

- **Feedback** includes questions related to improving the product relative to the quality perspective of interest (a quantitative characterization of the product quality, major problems regarding the quality perspective of interest, and suggestions for improvement during the ongoing project as well as during future projects).

Figure 4 depicts the derivation of thirteen example questions for goal G_1.

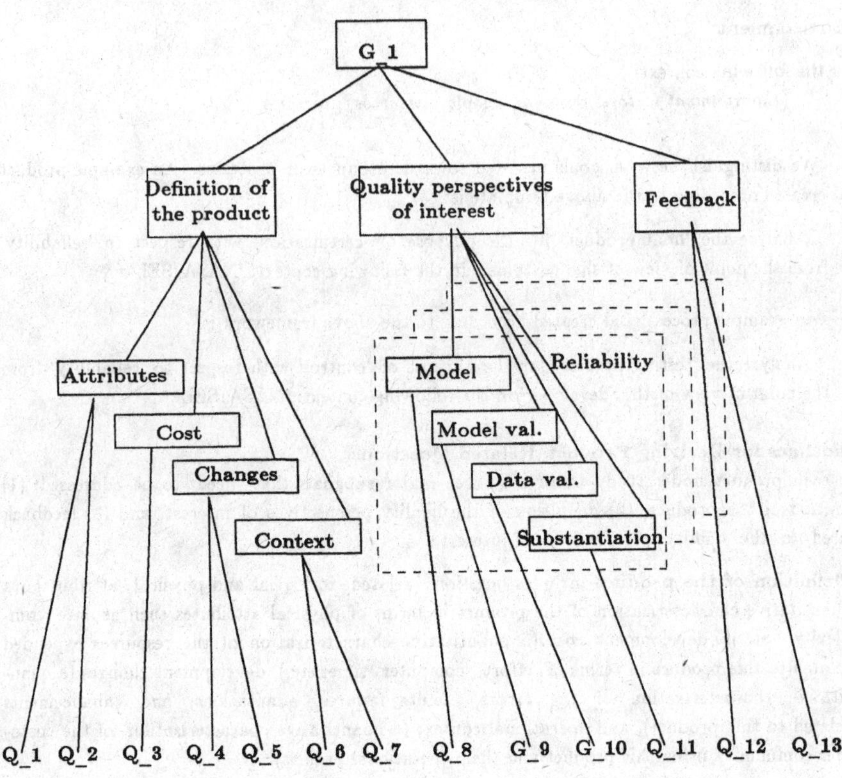

Figure 4. Example GQM graph for goal G_1

Definition of the product: Model of the final product in the NASA/SEL environment

Attributes: Logical/Physical attributes

* **Q_1**: What are application and solution domain of the final product?

Q_2: What is the complexity of the final product (with respect to cyclomatic complexity, data bindings, etc.)?

Cost: Development cost

Q_3: What is the effort used to develop the system (by phase, activity, personnel type, etc.)?

Changes: Development changes

Q_4: What is the number of failures in total and by type (e.g., failure detection time/phase, criticality, requirements affected, etc.)?

Q_5: What are the number of faults in total and by type (e.g., fault entry time/phase, fault detection time/phase, omission/commission, software aspect changed, components affected, etc.)?

Context: Operational context

* **Q_6**: What classes of customers are expected to use the system?

Q_7: What is the matrix of functional requirements vs. customer classes?

Quality perspectives of interest: Model of system reliability from the customer's perspective

Model: Major model: Critical Failure Rate

Q_8: What is the number of critical operational failures per month?

Model val.: Validity of the model for the project

Q_9: What is the number of critical failures found during operation?

Data val.: Validity of the data collected

Q_10: How valid is the failure and fault data?

Substantiation: Substantiation of the model(s)

Q_11: How satisfied are users with the operational system?

Feedback: Feedback

Q_12: Do existing reliability requirements truly reflect customer expectations?

Q_12: Which product characteristics affect reliability?

Guidelines for Deriving Process–Related Questions

For each process under study, there are three major subgoals that need to be addressed: (1) definition of the process, (2) definition of the quality perspectives of interest, and (3) feedback from using this process relative to the quality perspective(s) of interest.

- **Definition of the process** includes questions related to process conformance (a quantitative characterization of the process and an assessment of how well it is performed), and domain conformance (a quantitative characterization of the object to which the process is applied and an analysis of the process performer's knowledge concerning this object).
- **Quality perspectives of interest** follows a pattern similar to the corresponding product–oriented subgoal including, for each quality perspective of interest (e.g., reduction of

defects, cost effectiveness), questions related to the major model(s) used, the validity of the model for the particular environment, the validity of the data collected, the model effectiveness and the substantiation of the model).

- **Feedback** follows a pattern similar to the corresponding product-oriented subgoal.

Figure 5 depicts the derivation of twelve example questions for goal G_2.

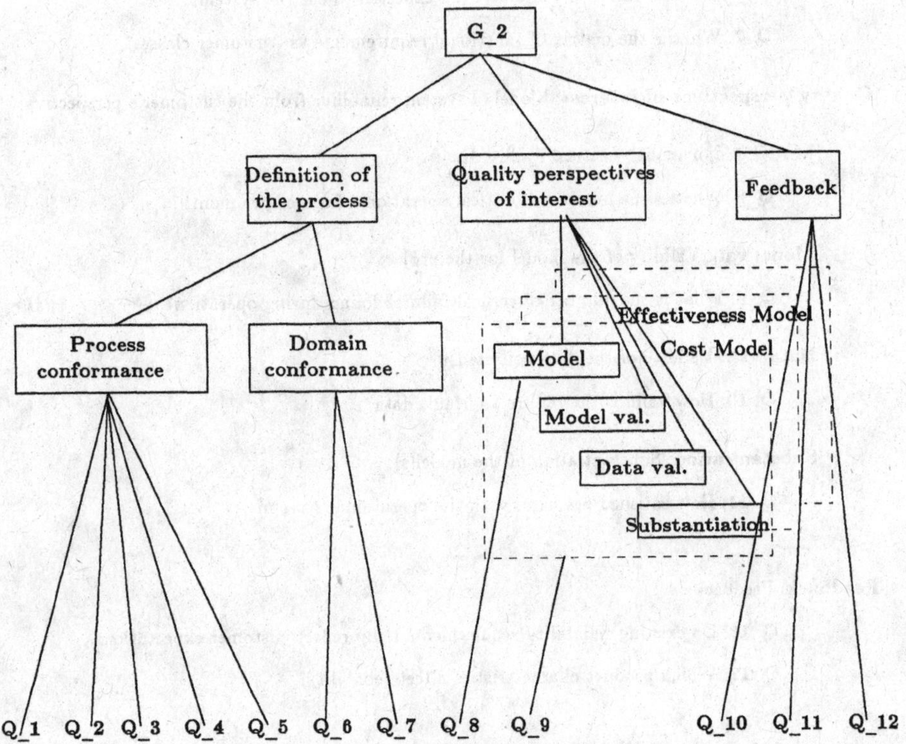

Figure 5. Example GQM graph for goal G_2

Definition of the process: process model

Process conformance: Process Conformance

* **Q_1**: What is the experience of the test team?

Q_2: How many requirements are there?

*** Q_3**: How important is each requirement from a customer perspective?

Q_4: What is the distribution of tests over requirements?

*** Q_5**: Is Q_4 consistent with Q_3?

Domain conformance: Domain Conformance

***Q_6**: How familiar is each tester with the domain?

*** Q_7**: How understandable are the requirements?

Quality perspectives of interest: Models of cost and effectiveness

Model: Major model(s) used

Cost:

Q_8: What is the cost of testing (in total, per phase)?

effectiveness:

Q_9: What is the number of critical failures discovered during system test, acceptance test and per month of operation?

Model val.: <similar to G_1>

Data val.: <similar to G_1>

Substantiation: <similar to G_1>

Feedback: Feedback

*** Q_10**: Does the overall testing methodology, the system test method or the acceptance test method need to be refined or modified?

Q_11: * Is different or more training needed in the testing method or technology?

Q_12: * Is different or more training needed in the application domain?

Guidelines for Deriving Metrics

The choice of metrics is determined by the quantifiable questions. The guidelines for questions acknowledge the need for generally more than one metric, for objective and subjective metrics, and for associating interpretations with metrics. The actual GQM graphs generated from these templates and guidelines will differ from project to project and organization to organization. This reflects their being tailored for the different needs in different projects and organizations. We use objective and subjective metrics. An objective metric is an absolute measure taken on a product or process. Examples include time for development, number of lines of code, and number of defects and changes. A subjective metric represents an estimate of extent or degree in the application of some technique or a classification or qualification of problem or experience. Examples include: the degree of use of a method or technique, and the experience of a programmer in the application. Subjective metrics are typically defined on a nominal scale. Depending on the type of each metric, we choose the appropriate mechanisms for data collection and validation. For each example question in the preceding examples we have indicated whether they suggest subjective metrics (marked with '*') or objective metrics (unmarked). As goals, questions and metrics provide for tractability of the (top-down) definitional quantification process, they also provide for the interpretation context (bottom-up). This integration of definition with interpretation allows for the interpretation process to be tailored to the specific needs of an environment.

BENEFITS OF THE GQM APPROACH

The GQM approach to measurement has a number of practical benefits: (1) general applicability, (2) support for identifying and tailoring metrics, (3) support for interpreting measurement data, (4) support for early validation of metrics, (5) support for involving all interested parties into the measurement process, and (6) support for protecting sensitive data.

General Applicability

Different software organizations exist at different levels of maturity. Correspondingly, their measurement goals are different. Organizations at low levels of maturity must be interested in creating initial models of the products they are producing, the processes they are employing, and the quality aspects of interest to their organization. The purpose of their measurement goals will be 'understanding'. Only when such initial models have been developed, can they be used to actively improve engineering and management practices, methods and tools within the organization. The GQM approach supports all these types of measurement goals. We have demonstrated the applicability of the GQM approach to two reliability goals. For further applications of the GQM approach, the reader is referred to examples in [3,13,14,15].

Identification and Tailoring of Metrics

The GQM approach recognizes the fact that all software projects are different [4]. As a result, it does not assume the existence of a set of pre-defined and generally applicable GQM graphs from which to select goals, questions and metrics unchanged. Instead, it assumes the creation of customized GQM graphs for each measurement goal. The degree to which existing GQM graphs can be reused to create a new goal depends on the similarities between the old and new measurement goals.

The need for tailoring requires traceability between the goal, question, and metric layers of each GQM graph. This traceability is not explicit in the current GQM guidelines. However, it exists implicitly. For example, the guidelines for product-related questions (Figure 4) suggest that the object mentioned in the goal definition (e.g., in G_1: the final product) needs to be further defined under the 'definition of the product' subgoal and that the qualities mentioned in the goal definition (G_1: reliability) need to be further defined under the 'quality perspectives of interest' subgoal. The same is true for deriving process–related questions. This implicit traceability between the object and focus mentioned in the goal definition and the questions listed under the respective subgoals can be utilized in order to tailor existing GQM graphs to changing project goals. Assume a measurement goal similar to G_1, except that the focus is 'maintainability' instead of 'reliability'. It should be easy to reuse the goal/question/metric structure depicted in Figure 4 unchanged, except for the 'quality perspectives of interest' subgoal. The 'reliability' related portion needs to be replaced by a 'maintenance' related one.

Interpretation of Measurement Data

Interpretation is the hardest part of measurement. Explicit GQM graphs provide the context for interpreting measurement data. The interpretation of data follows the respective GQM graph bottom–up. In the case of our partial GQM graph in Figure 6, each of the two questions is answered by interpreting the corresponding three metrics. In turn the answers to these two questions are interpreted in order to address subgoal 'quality perspectives of interest'. This interpretation process terminates with goal G_2.

Q_8: What is the cost of testing

M1: # staff_hours spent on system test

M2: # staff_hours spent on acceptance test

M3: # staff_hours spent per month of operation

Q_9: What is the number of critical failures discovered

M4: # critical failures discovered during system test

M5: # critical failures dicovered during acceptance test

M6; # critical failures discovered per month of operation

Figure 6. Metrics for Questions Q_8/Q_9 in Figure 5

Given the example data in TABLE 2, we could conclude that Project_1 is more reliable than Project_2 (e.g., 1 critical versus 5 critical failures). We also could observe that the better reliability of Project_1 has been achieved at higher cost (e.g., 750 versus 300 staff_hours during system and acceptance test). Whether the higher number of faults detected in Project_2 can be contributed to bad testing depends on answers to other questions. If, for example, process conformance was very good (i.e., questions Q_1 to Q_5 of goal G_2) and the requirements were badly understood (i.e., question Q_7 of goal G_2), it may suggest otherwise. Also, the lower testing cost per discovered fault in Project_2 could be caused by either a less complex application (i.e., question Q_1 of goal G_1) or more experienced test personnel (i.e., question Q_1 of goal G_2) than in Project_1.

TABLE 2
Hypothetical Project Data

Metrics	Projects	
	Project_1	Project_2
M_1	450	100
M_2	300	200
M_3	50	100
M_4	12	10
M_5	4	15
M_6	1	5

It is very important to package data interpretations together with the GQM graph used to derive them. The measurement and interpretation rationale encoded in the GQM graph makes it possible to judge the validity and generality of an interpretation. In practice, it frequently happens that data for computing one or more of the specified metrics cannot be collected. An interpretation derived from partial data can be assumed to be less valid than one derived from the complete set of data prescribed by the GQM graph. The generality of an interpretation (i.e., whether it can be used across projects or environments) depends on how similar the respective GQM graphs.

Early Validation of Metrics

Even without measurement, projects are being controlled and managed today. That means, people must have some implicit and possibly partial models of product, process and quality. In order to be acceptable, a set of metrics proposed to support a measurement goal of interest, needs to at least match the quality of existing intuitive human judgements. This can be checked by asking the people interested in measurement according to a certain GQM graph to interpret example sets of data – either hypothetical data or data from past projects – in the context of their GQM graph.

For example, assume that a GQM graph has been derived for goal G_2 which consists of only the two questions and six metrics in Figure 6. If this graph is valid it should be possible to make sense out of the data in TABLE 2. As discussed earlier, more information on the degree of process conformance and the understandability of the requirements is required to judge whether the higher number of faults detected in Project_2 can be contributed to bad testing. This is a typical situation where the attempt to use the GQM graph to interpret sample data would lead us to the inclusion of further metrics aimed at capturing the needed information.

Active Involvement of All Interested Parties

Frequently, externally defined sets of metrics are being imported unchanged to address an organization's measurement needs. Possible sources are the public literature, 'clever' consultants, other organizations, or standards. There exist two major problems with this approach. First, it is very likely that the organization's measurement goals are different from the ones the imported metrics were intended for. If one is lucky, the project personnel expected to collect data will eventually detect that discrepancy and, as a result, revolt or simply lose interest in measurement. If one is unlucky, data are being collected and misinterpreted. Second, it is hard to motivate project personnel to collect data if they haven't been actively involved in the measurement planning process from the very beginning. Lack of involvement results in lack of ownership, which in turn results in lack of motivation. Ownership can only be created by involving all project personnel that are expected to collect data in the measurement planning process.

The guidelines of the GQM approach provide an ideal tool for actively involving all interested parties from the very beginning. First, goals should be chosen which reflect the needs of the project personnel. Second, the viewpoint listed in each goal definition points to the type of personnel who need to be involved. For example, in the case of example goal G_1 user and customer representation is required. Third, the GQM guidelines represent a means for communicating the measurement plans to all interested parties and involving them in the review process. Typically, questions are identified through iterative brain-storming and review sessions. The GQM guidelines are used to structure brain-storming sessions and document the results for review. The traceable structure of a GQM graph allows the reviewers to validate whether their implicit understanding of the object of interest as well as their views of the quality perspectives of interest are represented properly. This aspect of the operational guidelines for goals and questions has proven to be most valuable in supporting organizations to set up initial measurement programs.

Protection of Sensitive Data

One frequently mentioned concern about measurement has to do with the fact that people as well as organizations hesitate to share data which is perceived as 'sensitive'. Measurement requires the collection of data at an individualized level (e.g., defects per staff_person). The project manager may only be interested in the accumulated defect numbers across the project in order to judge the effectiveness of the testing approach. However, the danger is to misuse the data for personnel evaluation. The hierarchical structure of GQM graphs can be overlaid with access control mechanisms reflecting the information needs of the people involved. In the context of a GQM graph, data protection is not so much a question of what data are being collected, but whether one enforces their agreed upon usage. The agreed upon usage is clearly specified in terms of questions and goals.

The GQM approach seems also fit to support data collection across organizations. As long as two organizations agree on a measurement plan (formulated as a GQM graph) and follow this plan, there is no need to exchange all low-level data. It seems, for example, perfectly appropriate, to decide that only data aggregated across projects can be exchanged without loss of confidentiality. Without underlying measurement rationale such aggregated data is useless. With an underlying measurement rationale – for example in the form of agreed upon GQM graphs – data can be compared at an aggregated level without compromising company-specific confidentiality requirements. In that sense, the GQM approach may be a useful tool not only to support measurement-based learning within, but also across organization entities (e.g., division, company).

FUTURE DIRECTIONS IN MEASUREMENT

Measurement is more than just an addition to current software development approaches. Instead, it provides the basis for introducing engineering discipline into software development. Engineering discipline requires that each software project consists of a planning and execution stage. Planning includes setting project goals in a measurable way, selecting the best suited development methods and tools based on available experience, and instrumenting these methods and tools so that the project goals can be monitored continuously. Execution includes collecting the prescribed data, interpreting them and feeding the results back to the ongoing project. Post-mortem, the project experience needs to be used to update current models of products, processes or qualities for future projects. Basili's quality improvement paradigm (QIP) is a promising basis for engineering-oriented software development [2]. The GQM approach is broad and flexible enough to support all measurement activities required in the context of software development according to the QIP.

In the context of the QIP, the GQM approach supports the operational definition of project goals during the planning phase, supports the analysis of measurement data and its feedback into the ongoing project, and allows the explicit capturing of measurement plans for reuse in future projects.

The TAME (Tailoring A Measurement Environment) project at the University of Maryland aims at developing technology to instantiate software development environments based on the QIP [4]. Current research activities in the TAME project are directed towards developing more formal GQM languages, schemas for experience bases containing an integrated set of product/process/quality models, and better automated support for all the activities required by the QIP [4]. Current activities in the MVP project, complementing the TAME efforts, are oriented towards designing and implementing a language for modeling software processes with a special emphasis on process measurement [12].

ACKNOWLEDGEMENTS

This work has been supported by NASA/GSFC contract NSG-5123.

REFERENCES

1. V. R. Basili, "Quantitative Evaluation of Software Engineering Methodology," Proceedings, 1st Pan Pacific Computer Conference, Melbourne, Australia, September 1985 [also available as: Technical Report CS-TR-1519, Department of Computer Science, University of Maryland, College Park, MD, July 1985].

2. V. R. Basili, "Software Development: A Paradigm for the Future", Proceedings, 13th Annual International Computer Software & Applications Conference, Orlando, FL, September 1989.

3. V. R. Basili, "Using Software Measurement to Learn and Improve," Proc. International Conference on Applications of Software Measurement, San Diego, November 12–15, 1990.

4. V. R. Basili and H. D. Rombach, The TAME Project: Towards Improvement–Oriented Software Environments," IEEE Transactions on Software Engineering, June 1988, pp. 758–773
[also available as: Technical Report CS–TR–1983/UMIACS–TR–88–8, Department of Computer Science/UMIACS, University of Maryland, College Park, MD, January 1988].

5. V. R. Basili and R. W. Selby, "Data Collection and Analysis in Research and Management," Proceedings, Amer. Statist. Ass. and Biomeasure Soc. Joint Statistical Meetings, Philadelphia, PA, August 1984.

6. V. R. Basili and D. M. Weiss, "A Methodology for Collecting valid Software Engineering Data, IEEE Transactions on Software Engineering, vol. SE–10, no. 3, November 1984, pp. 728–738.

7. B. W. Boehm, J. R. Brown and M. Lipow, "Quantitative Evaluation of Software Quality," Proc. of the 2nd International Conference on Software Engineering, 1976, pp. 592–605.

8. T. P. Bowen, G. B. Wigle and J. T. Tsai, "Specification of Software Quality Attributes," Technical Report, RADC–TR–85–37, Rome Air Development Center, Griffiss Air Force Base, NY 13441–5700, February 1985.

9. M. Kogure and Y. Akao, "Quality Function Deployment and CWQC in Japan," Quality Progress, October 1983, pp. 25–29.

10. J. A. McCall, P. K. Richards, G. F. Walters, "Factors in Software Quality," RADC TR–77–369, 1977.

11. G. E. Murine, "Applying Software Quality Metrics in the Requirements Analysis Phase of a Distributive System," Proceedings, Minnowbrook Workshop, Blue Mountain Lake, New York, 1980.

12. H. D. Rombach, "MVP: An Approach to Descriptive Process Modeling", Proceedings, Software Process Seminar, Milano, Italy, October 1990.

13. H. D. Rombach and V. R. Basili, "Quantitative Assessment of Maintenance: An Industrial Case Study," Proceedings IEEE Conference on Software Maintenance, Austin, Texas, September 1987, pp. 134–143.

14. H. D. Rombach and B. T. Ulery, "Improving Software Maintenance through Measurement," Proceedings of the IEEE, vol. 77, no. 4, April 1989, pp. 581–595 (invited paper).

15. H. D. Rombach, B. T. Ulery and J. Valett, "Measurement based Improvement of Maintenance in the SEL," Proc. 14th Annual Software Engineering Workshop, NASA/Goddard Space Flight Center, Greenbelt, MD 20771, November 1989.

16. T. Sunazuka and V. R. Basili, "Integrating Automated Support for a Software Management Cycle into the TAME System," Technical Report, Dept. of Computer Science and Umiacs (CS–TR–2289 and UMIACS–TR–89–75), University of Maryland, College Park, MD, USA, July 1989.